Lecture Notes in Computer Science 10702

Commenced Publication in 1973
Founding and Former Series Editors:
Gerhard Goos, Juris Hartmanis, and Jan van Leeuwen

More information about this series at http://www.springer.com/series/7408

Francesco Calimeri · Kevin Hamlen
Nicola Leone (Eds.)

Practical Aspects of Declarative Languages

20th International Symposium, PADL 2018
Los Angeles, CA, USA, January 8–9, 2018
Proceedings

 Springer

Editors
Francesco Calimeri ⓘ
Department of Mathematics and Computer
  Science
University of Calabria
Rende
Italy

Nicola Leone
Department of Mathematics and Computer
  Science
University of Calabria
Rende
Italy

Kevin Hamlen
Computer Science Department
University of Texas at Dallas
Richardson, TX
USA

ISSN 0302-9743   ISSN 1611-3349   (electronic)
Lecture Notes in Computer Science
ISBN 978-3-319-73304-3   ISBN 978-3-319-73305-0   (eBook)
https://doi.org/10.1007/978-3-319-73305-0

Library of Congress Control Number: 2017962893

LNCS Sublibrary: SL2 – Programming and Software Engineering

Printed on acid-free paper

This Springer imprint is published by Springer Nature
The registered company is Springer International Publishing AG
The registered company address is: Gewerbestrasse 11, 6330 Cham, Switzerland

Preface

This volume contains the papers presented at the 20th Symposium on Practical Aspects of Declarative Languages (PADL 2018), held during January 8–9, 2018, in Los Angeles, USA. The symposium was co-located with the 45th ACM SIGPLAN Symposium on Principles of Programming Languages (POPL 2018).

PADL is a forum for scientists and practitioners that gathers original works focusing on declarative languages relying on sound theoretical bases; in particular, it fosters novel applications and implementation techniques for all forms of declarative formalisms, including, but not limited to, logic, constraint, and functional languages.

Thanks to the work of several neighbor communities, solid theoretical results coupled with robust and efficient implementations made the application of declarative languages successful in many different real-world situations, such as artificial intelligence, the Semantic Web, database management, active networks, software engineering, decision support systems, and more.

Further developments in theory and implementation have recently opened up new application areas; at the same time, applications of declarative languages to novel problems raise numerous interesting research questions and issues. Examples include scalability, language extensions, and proper means for application deployment, and tools for development and interoperability with different formalisms and technologies. We observe that applications and attention to practical challenges drive the progress in the theory and implementation of efficient and reliable systems supporting declarative languages, and, at the same time, steer attention to timely challenges while benefiting from this progress as well.

Originally established as a workshop (PADL 1999 in San Antonio, Texas), the PADL series developed into a regular annual symposium; previous editions took place in San Antonio, Texas (1999), Boston, Massachusetts (2000), Las Vegas, Nevada (2001), Portland, Oregon (2002), New Orleans, Louisiana (2003), Dallas, Texas (2004), Long Beach, California (2005), Charleston, South Carolina (2006), Nice, France (2007), San Francisco, California (2008), Savannah, Georgia (2009), Madrid, Spain (2010), Austin, Texas (2012), Rome, Italy (2013), and San Diego, California (2014), Portland, Oregon (2015), St. Petersburg, Florida (2016), and Paris, France (2017).

This year, the Program Committee received 23 submissions. Each submission was reviewed by three Program Committee members, and 13 papers were accepted, based only on the merit of each submission and regardless of scheduling or space constraints.

The program also included two invited talks:

- Carlo Zaniolo, "Declarative Algorithms on Big Data: A Logic-Based Solution"
- Todd Millstein, "'Safe' Languages Require Sequential Consistency"

Two out of the 13 accepted papers were nominated for the Best Paper Award, via a secret ballot among the Program Committee members:

- Francesco Calimeri, Davide Fuscà, Simona Perri, Jessica Zangari, "Optimizing Answer Set Computation via Heuristic-Based Decomposition" (Most Practical Paper Award)
- Sandra Dylus, Jan Christiansen, Finn Teegen, "Probabilistic Functional Logic Programming" (Best Student Paper Award)

Springer sponsored 250 Euro for each of these awards. The authors were encouraged to submit the long versions of their work for the rapid publication track to the journal of *Theory and Practice of Logic Programming*.

We would like to express thanks to the Association of Logic Programming (ALP) and the Association for Computing Machinery (ACM) for their continuous support of the symposium, and Springer for the longstanding, successful cooperation with the PADL series. We are very grateful to the 31 members of the PADL 2018 Program Committee and external reviewers for their invaluable work and for the precious help in selecting the two best papers. The chairs of POPL 2018 were also of great help in steering the organizational details of the event.

We are happy to note that the conference was successfully managed with the help of EasyChair.

November 2017

Francesco Calimeri
Nicola Leone
Kevin Hamlen

Organization

Program Committee

Erika Abraham	RWTH Aachen University, Germany
Marcello Balduccini	Saint Joseph's University, USA
Lars Bergstrom	Mozilla Research
Edwin Brady	University of St. Andrews, UK
Francesco Calimeri	University of Calabria, Italy
Mats Carlsson	SICS, Sweden
Manuel Carro	Universidad Politécnica de Madrid, Spain
James Cheney	The University of Edinburgh, UK
Stefania Costantini	University of L'Aquila, Italy
Karl Crary	Carnegie Mellon University, USA
Esra Erdem	Sabanci University, Turkey
Wolfgang Faber	University of Huddersfield, UK
Marco Gavanelli	University of Ferrara, Italy
Martin Gebser	University of Potsdam, Germany
Jurriaan Hage	Utrecht University, The Netherlands
Kevin Hamlen (Chair)	University of Texas at Dallas, USA
Daan Leijen	Microsoft
Nicola Leone (Chair)	University of Calabria, Italy
Geoffrey Mainland	Drexel University, USA
Marco Maratea	University of Genoa, Italy
Paulo Oliva	Queen Mary University of London, UK
Enrico Pontelli	New Mexico State University, USA
Ricardo Rocha	University of Porto, Portugal
Grigore Rosu	University of Illinois at Urbana-Champaign, USA
Konstantin Schekotihin	Alpen-Adria Universität Klagenfurt, Austria
Peter Schüller	Marmara University, Turkey
Meera Sridhar	University of North Carolina at Charlotte, USA
Paul Tarau	University of North Texas, USA
David Van Horn	University of Maryland, USA
Daniel Winograd-Cort	University of Maryland, USA
Stefan Woltran	Vienna University of Technology, Austria
Neng-Fa Zhou	CUNY Brooklyn College and Graduate Center, USA
Lukasz Ziarek	SUNY Buffalo, USA

Publicity Chair

Marco Manna   University of Calabria, Italy

Additional Reviewers

Leblanc, Emily
Morak, Michael
Obermeier, Philipp

Abstracts of Invited Talks

Declarative Algorithms on Big Data: A Logic-Based Solution

Carlo Zaniolo

Computer Science Department, University of California at Los Angeles

Abstract. The ability of combining declarative specifications with efficient implementations is critical to achieve portability and scalability via parallelization of Big Data applications. We will describe the recent progress made toward these objectives at UCLA, progress which is confirming the great potential that logic-based languages can have in this role over a wide range of applications. Indeed our Bigdatalog system on Apache Spark outperforms GraphX on graph applications[1] and has achieved portability[2] over multiple platforms[3]. These high levels of performance, portability and scalability have been obtained while preserving a totally declarative stable-model semantics for recursive Datalog programs that use aggregates in recursion[4] when these programs satisfy a condition called pre-mappability[5]. We show that textbook polynomial-time algorithms can be tersely expressed using such programs, and provide simple conditions that allow users to verify that pre-mappability holds for their programs—thus allowing them to assure that efficiently-computable unique stable models exist for their declarative algorithms. Finally, we will discuss applications of these advances to other systems, and overview the design and implementation of an SQL DBMS prototype that supports similar advances[6].

[1] Alexander Shkapsky, Mohan Yang, Matteo Interlandi, Hsuan Chiu, Tyson Condie, Carlo Zaniolo: Big Data Analytics with Datalog Queries on Spark. SIGMOD Conference 2016: 1135–1149.

[2] Mohan Yang, Alexander Shkapsky, Carlo Zaniolo: Scaling up the performance of more powerful Datalog systems on multicore machines, The VLDB Journal 1–20, December 2016.

[3] Alexander Shkapsky, Mohan Yang, Carlo Zaniolo: Optimizing recursive queries with monotonic aggregates in DeALS. ICDE 2015: 867–878.

[4] Mirjana Mazuran, Edoardo Serra, Carlo Zaniolo: A declarative extension of Horn clauses, and its significance for Datalog and its applications. TPLP 13(4–5): 609–623 (2013).

[5] Carlo Zaniolo, Mohan Yang, Matteo Interlandi, Ariyam Das, Alexander Shkapsky, Tyson Condie: Fixpoint Semantics and Optimization of Recursive Datalog Programs with Aggregates, ICLP 2017.

[6] Jiaqi Gu, Ling Ding, Ariyam Das, Tyson Condie, Carlo Zaniolo: RamSQL: SQL with Recursion and Aggregate Mapping, UCLA Technical Report, November 2017.

"Safe" Languages Require Sequential Consistency

Todd Millstein

Computer Science Department, University of California at Los Angeles

Abstract. Almost all languages today are memory safe, thereby providing simple and strong guarantees to all programs. Yet the concurrency semantics of these "safe" languages causes similar problems as arise in memory-unsafe languages: small program errors can expose implementation details, violate fundamental language abstractions, and compromise program safety. Perhaps surprisingly, this is the case not only for imperative languages like Java and C++ but also for functional languages that support shared-memory concurrency. In this talk Ill overview the state of concurrency semantics as it exists today and argue that "safe" languages (and particularly declarative ones) must support the simple interleaving semantics of threads known as sequential consistency (SC). Along the way Ill debunk a few persistent myths about SC and argue that it is a practical choice for many languages today.

Contents

Functional Programming

Probabilistic Functional Logic Programming

Sandra Dylus[1(✉)] , Jan Christiansen[2] , and Finn Teegen[1]

[1] University of Kiel, Kiel, Germany
{sad,fte}@informatik.uni-kiel.de
[2] Flensburg University of Applied Sciences, Flensburg, Germany
jan.christiansen@hs-flensburg.de

Abstract. This paper presents *PFLP*, a library for probabilistic programming in the functional logic programming language Curry. It demonstrates how the concepts of a functional logic programming language support the implementation of a library for probabilistic programming. In fact, the paradigms of functional logic and probabilistic programming are closely connected. That is, we can apply techniques from one area to the other and vice versa. We will see that an implementation based on the concepts of functional logic programming can have benefits with respect to performance compared to a standard list-based implementation.

1 Introduction

The probabilistic programming paradigm allows the succinct definition of probabilistic processes and other applications based on probability distributions, for example, Bayesian inference as used in machine learning. The idea of probabilistic programming has been quite successful. There are a variety of probabilistic programming languages supporting all kinds of programming paradigms. For example, the programming languages Church [12] and Anglican [21] are based on the functional programming language Scheme, ProbLog [9] is an extension of the logic programming language Prolog, and Probabilistic C [17] is based on the imperative language C. Besides full-blown languages there are also embedded domain specific languages that implement probabilistic programming as a library. For example, FACTORIE [16] is a library for the hybrid programming language Scala and Erwig and Kollmansberger [10] present a library for the functional programming language Haskell. We recommend the survey by Gordon et al. [13] about the current state of probabilistic programming for further information.

This paper presents *PFLP*, a library providing a domain specific language for probabilistic programming in the functional logic programming language Curry [2]. PFLP makes heavy use of functional logic programming concepts and shows that this paradigm is well-suited for implementing a library for probabilistic programming. In fact, there is a close connection between probabilistic programming and functional logic programming. For example, non-deterministic choice and probabilistic choice are similar concepts. Furthermore, the concept of call-time choice as known from functional logic programming coincides with

© Springer International Publishing AG 2018
F. Calimeri et al. (Eds.): PADL 2018, LNCS 10702, pp. 3–19, 2018.
https://doi.org/10.1007/978-3-319-73305-0_1

(stochastic) memoization [8] in the area of probabilistic programming. We are not the first to observe this close connection between functional logic programming and probabilistic programming. For example, Fischer et al. [11] present a library for modeling functional logic programs in the functional language Haskell. As they state, by extending their approach to weighted non-determinism we can model a probabilistic programming language.

Besides a lightweight implementation of a library for probabilistic programming in a functional logic programming language, this paper makes the following contributions.

- We investigate the interplay of probabilistic programming with the features of a functional logic programming language. For example, we show how call-time choice and non-determinism interplay with probabilistic choice.
- We discuss how we utilize functional logic features to improve the implementation of probabilistic combinators.
- On one hand, we will see that an implementation of probability distributions using non-determinism in combination with non-strict probabilistic combinators can be more efficient than an implementation using lists.
- On the other hand, we illustrate that the combination of non-determinism and non-strictness with respect to distributions has to be handled with care. More precisely, it is important to enforce a certain degree of strictness in order to guarantee correct results.
- Finally, this paper is supposed to foster the exchange between the community of probabilistic programming and of functional logic programming. That is, while the connection exists for a long time, there has not been much exchange between the communities. We would like to take this paper as a starting point to bring these paradigms closer together. Thus, this paper introduces the concepts of both, the functional logic and probabilistic programming, paradigms.

Last but not least, we also want to state a non-contribution. We do not plan to compete against full-blown probabilistic languages or mature libraries for probabilistic programming. Nevertheless, we think that this library is a great showcase for languages with built-in non-determinism, because the functional logic approach can be superior to the functional approach using lists.

2   The Basics

In this section we discuss the core of the PFLP library[1]. The implementation is based on a Haskell library for probabilistic programming presented by Erwig and Kollmansberger [10]. We will not present the whole *PFLP* library, but only core functions. The paper at hand is a literate Curry file. We use the Curry compiler KiCS2[2] by Braßel et al. [5] for all code examples.

---

[1] We provide the code for the library at https://github.com/finnteegen/pflp.
[2] We use version 0.6.0 of KiCS2 and the source is found at https://www-ps. informatik.uni-kiel.de/kics2/.

2.1 Modeling Distributions

One key ingredient of probabilistic programming is the definition of distributions. A distribution consists of pairs of elementary events and their probability. We model probabilities as *Float* and distributions as a combination of an elementary event and the corresponding probability.

> **type** *Probability* = *Float*
> **data** *Dist a* = *Dist a Probability*

In a functional language like Haskell, the canonical way to define distributions uses lists. Here, we use Curry's built-in non-determinism as an alternative for lists to model distributions with more than one event-probability pair. As an example, we define a fair coin, where *True* represents heads and *False* represents tails, as follows.[3]

> *coin* :: *Dist Bool*
> *coin* = *Dist True* $\frac{1}{2}$? *Dist False* $\frac{1}{2}$

In Curry the (?)-operator non-deterministically chooses between two given arguments. Non-determinism is not reflected in the type system, that is, a non-deterministic choice has type $a \to a \to a$. Such non-deterministic computations introduced by (?) describe two individual computation branches; one for the left argument und one for the right argument of (?). Printing an expression in the REPL[4] evaluates the non-deterministic computations, thus, yields one result for each branch as shown in the following examples.

> λ> *coin*　　　　　　　　　　λ> 1 ? 2
> *Dist True* 0.5　　　　　　　　　1
> *Dist False* 0.5　　　　　　　　 2

It is cumbersome to define distributions explicitly as in the case of *coin*. Hence, we define helper functions for constructing distributions. Given a list of events and probabilities, *enum* creates a distribution by folding these pairs non-deterministically with a helper function *member*.[5]

> *member* :: [a] $\to$ a
> *member* = *foldr* (?) *failed*
> *enum* :: [a] $\to$ [Probability] $\to$ Dist a
> *enum vs ps* = *member* (*zipWith Dist vs ps*)

In Curry the constant *failed* is a silent failure that behaves as neutral element with respect to (?). That is, the expression *True* ? *failed* has the same semantics as *True*. Hence, the function *member* takes a list and yields a non-deterministic choice of all elements of the list.

---

[3] Here and in the following we write probabilities as fractions for readability.
[4] We visualize the interactions with the REPL using λ> as prompt.
[5] We shorten the implementation of *enum* for presentation purposes; actually, *enum* only allows valid distributions, e.g., that the given probabilities add up to 1.0.

As a short-cut, we define a function that yields a *uniform* distribution given a list of events as well as a function *certainly*, which yields a distribution with a single event of probability one.

$$uniform :: [a] \rightarrow Dist\ a$$
$$uniform\ xs = \textbf{let}\ len = length\ xs\ \textbf{in}\ enum\ xs\ (repeat\ \tfrac{1}{len})$$
$$certainly :: a \rightarrow Dist\ a$$
$$certainly\ x = Dist\ x\ 1.0$$

The function *repeat* yields a list that contains the given value infinitely often. Because of Curry's laziness, it is sufficient if one of the arguments of *enum* is a finite list because *zipWith* stops when one of its arguments is empty.

We can refactor the definition of *coin* using *uniform* as follows.

$$coin :: Dist\ Bool$$
$$coin = uniform\ [True, False]$$

In general, the library hides the constructor *Dist*, that is, the user has to define distributions by using the combinators provided by the library.

The library provides additional functions to combine and manipulate distributions. In order to work with dependent distributions, the operator ($\ggg\!\!=$) applies a function that yields a distribution to each event of a given distribution and multiplies the corresponding probabilities.[6]

$$(\ggg\!\!=) :: Dist\ a \rightarrow (a \rightarrow Dist\ b) \rightarrow Dist\ b$$
$$d \ggg\!\!= f = \textbf{let}\ Dist\ x\ p = d$$
$$Dist\ y\ q = f\ x$$
$$\textbf{in}\ Dist\ y\ (p *. q)$$

The implementation via **let**-bindings seems a bit tedious, however, it is important that we define ($\ggg\!\!=$) as it is. The canonical implementation performs pattern matching on the first argument but uses a **let**-binding for the result of f. That is, it is strict in the first argument but non-strict in the application of f, the second argument. We discuss the implementation in more detail later. For now, it is sufficient to note that ($\ggg\!\!=$) yields a partial *Dist*-constructor without evaluating any of its arguments. In contrast, a definition using pattern matching or a case expression needs to evaluate its argument first, thus, is more strict.

Intuitively, we have to apply the function f to each event of the distribution d and combine the resulting distributions into a single distribution. In a Haskell implementation, we would use a list comprehension to define this function. In the Curry implementation, we model distributions as non-deterministic computations, thus, the above rule describes the behavior of the function for an arbitrary pair of the first distribution and an arbitrary pair of the second distribution, that is, the result of f.

---

[6] Due to the lack of overloading in Curry, operations on *Float* have a (floating) point suffix, e.g. (*.), whereas operations on *Int* use the common operation names.

For independent distributions we provide the function *joinWith* that combines two distributions with respect to a given function. We implement *joinWith* by means of ($\ggg$).

$joinWith :: (a \rightarrow b \rightarrow c) \rightarrow Dist\ a \rightarrow Dist\ b \rightarrow Dist\ c$
$joinWith\ f\ d1\ d2 = d1 \ggg \lambda x \rightarrow d2 \ggg \lambda y \rightarrow certainly\ (f\ x\ y)$

In a monadic setting this function is sometimes called *liftM2*. Here, we use the same nomenclature as Erwig and Kollmansberger [10].

As an example of combining multiple distinct distributions, we define a function that flips a coin *n* times.

$flipCoin :: Int \rightarrow Dist\ [Bool]$
$flipCoin\ n\ |\ n \equiv 0 \quad\quad = certainly\ []$
$\quad\quad\quad\quad |\ otherwise = joinWith\ (:)\ coin\ (flipCoin\ (n-1))$

When we run the example of flipping two coins in the REPL of KiCS2, we get four events.

$\lambda> flipCoin\ 2$
$Dist\ [True, True]\ 0.25$
$Dist\ [True, False]\ 0.25$
$Dist\ [False, True]\ 0.25$
$Dist\ [False, False]\ 0.25$

In the example above, *coin* is a non-deterministic operation, namely, $coin = Dist\ True\ \frac{1}{2}\ ?\ Dist\ False\ \frac{1}{2}$. Applying *joinWith* to *coin* and *coin* combines all possible results of two coin tosses.

2.2 Querying Distributions

With a handful of building blocks to define distributions available, we now want to calculate total probabilities, thus, perform queries on our distributions. We provide an operator $(??) :: (a \rightarrow Bool) \rightarrow Dist\ a \rightarrow Probability$ to extract the probability of a distribution with respect to a given predicate. The operator filters events that satisfy the given predicate and computes the total probability of the remaining elementary events. It is straightforward to implement this kind of filter function on distributions in Curry.

$filterDist :: (a \rightarrow Bool) \rightarrow Dist\ a \rightarrow Dist\ a$
$filterDist\ p\ d@(Dist\ x\ \_)\ |\ p\ x = d$

The implementation of *filterDist* is a partial identity on the event-probability pairs. Every event that satisfies the predicate is part of the resulting distribution. The function fails for event-predicate pairs that do not satisfy the predicate. The definition is equivalent to the following version using an **if-then-else**-expression.

$filterDist'\ p\ d@(Dist\ x\ \_) = \textbf{if}\ p\ x\ \textbf{then}\ d\ \textbf{else}\ failed$

Computing the total probability, i.e., summing up all remaining probabilities, is a more advanced task in the functional logic approach. Remember that we represent a distribution by chaining all event-probability pairs with (?), thus, constructing non-deterministic computations. These non-deterministic computations introduce individual branches of computations that cannot interact with each other. In order to compute the total probability of a distribution, we have to merge these distinct branches. Such a merge is possible by the encapsulation of non-deterministic computations. Similar to the *findall* construct of the logic language Prolog, in Curry we encapsulate a non-deterministic computation by using a primitive called *allValues*[7]. The function *allValues* operates on a polymorphic—and potentially non-deterministic—value and yields a multi-set of all non-deterministic values.

$$allValues :: a \rightarrow \{a\}$$

In order to work with encapsulated values, Curry provides the following two functions to fold and map the resulting multi-set.

$$foldValues :: (a \rightarrow a \rightarrow a) \rightarrow a \rightarrow \{a\} \rightarrow a$$
$$mapValues :: (a \rightarrow b) \rightarrow \{a\} \rightarrow \{b\}$$

We do not discuss the implementation details behind *allValues* here. It is sufficient to know that, as a library developer, we can employ this powerful function to encapsulate non-deterministic values and use these values in further computations. However, due to intransparent behavior in combination with sharing as discussed by Braßel et al. [4], a user of the library should not use *allValues* at all. In a nutshell, inner-most and outer-most evaluation strategies may cause different results when combining sharing and encapsulation.

With this encapsulation mechanism at hand, we can define the extraction operator (??) as follows.

$$prob :: Dist\ a \rightarrow Probability$$
$$prob\ (Dist\ \_\ p) = p$$
$$(??) :: (a \rightarrow Bool) \rightarrow Dist\ a \rightarrow Probability$$
$$(??)\ p = foldValues\ (+.)\ 0.0 \circ allValues \circ prob \circ filterDist\ p$$

First we filter the elementary events by some predicate and project to the probabilities only. Afterwards we encapsulate the remaining probabilities and sum them up. As an example for the use of (??), we may flip four coins and calculate the probability of at least two heads—that is, *True*.

$$\lambda > ((\geqslant 2) \circ length \circ filter\ id)\ ??\ flipCoin\ 4$$
$$0.6875$$

---

[7] We use an abstract view of the result of an encapsulation to emphasize that the order of encapsulated results does not matter. In practice, we can, for example, use the function *allValues* :: $a \rightarrow [a]$ defined in the library *Findall*.

3   The Details

Up to now, we have discussed a simple library for probabilistic programming that uses non-determinism to represent distributions. In this chapter we will see that we can highly benefit from Curry-like non-determinism with respect to performance when we compare PFLP's implementation with a list-based implementation. More precisely, when we query a distribution with a predicate that does not evaluate its argument completely, we can possibly prune large parts of the search space. Before we discuss the details of the combination of non-strictness and non-determinism, we discuss aspects of sharing non-deterministic choices. At last, we discuss details about the implementation of ($\ggg$) and why PFLP does not allow non-deterministic events within distributions.

3.1   Call-Time Choice vs. Run-Time Choice

By default Curry uses call-time choice, that is, variables denote single deterministic choices. When we bind a variable to a non-deterministic computation, one value is chosen and all occurrences of the variable denote the same deterministic choice. Often call-time choice is what you are looking for. For example, the definition of *filterDist* makes use of call-time choice.

$filterDist :: (a \rightarrow Bool) \rightarrow Dist\ a \rightarrow Dist\ a$
$filterDist\ p\ d@(Dist\ x\ \_) \mid p\ x = d$

The variable d on the right-hand side denotes a single deterministic choice, namely, the one that satisfies the predicate and not the non-deterministic computation that was initially passed to *filterDist*.

Almost as often run-time choice is what you are looking for and call-time choice gets in your way; probabilistic programming is no exception. For example, let us reconsider flipping a coin n times. We parametrize the function *flipCoin* over the given distribution and define the following generalized function.

$replicateDist :: Int \rightarrow Dist\ a \rightarrow Dist\ [a]$
$replicateDist\ n\ d \mid n \equiv 0 \quad\quad = certainly\ []$
$\qquad\qquad\qquad \mid otherwise = joinWith\ (:)\ d\ (replicateDist\ (n-1)\ d)$

When we use this function to flip a coin twice, the result is not what we intended.

$\lambda> replicateDist\ 2\ coin$
$Dist\ [True, True]\ 0.25$
$Dist\ [False, False]\ 0.25$

Because *replicateDist* shares the variable d, we only perform a choice once and replicate deterministic choices. In contrast, top-level nullary functions like *coin* are evaluated every time, thus, exhibit run-time choice, which is the reason why the previously shown *flipCoin* behaves properly.

In order to implement *replicateDist* correctly, we have to enforce run-time choice. We introduce the following type synonym and function to model and work with values with run-time choice behavior.

type $RT\ a = ()\ \to\ a$
$pick :: RT\ a \to a$
$pick\ rt = rt\ ()$

We can now use the type RT to hide the non-determinism on the right-hand side of a function arrow. This way, *pick* explicitly triggers the evaluation of *rt*, performing a new choice for every element of the result list.

$replicateDist :: Int \to RT\ (Dist\ a) \to Dist\ [a]$
$replicateDist\ n\ rt\ |\ n \equiv 0 \quad\ = certainly\ []$
$\qquad\qquad\qquad\quad |\ otherwise = joinWith\ (:)\ (pick\ rt)\ (replicateDist\ (n-1)\ rt)$

In order to use *replicateDist* with *coin*, we have to construct a value of type $RT\ (Dist\ Bool)$. However, we cannot provide a function to construct a value of type RT that behaves as intended. Such a function would share a deterministic choice and non-deterministically yield two functions, instead of one function that yields a non-deterministic computation. The only way to construct a value of type RT is to explicitly use a lambda abstraction.

$\lambda >\ replicateDist\ 2\ (\lambda() \to coin)$
$Dist\ [True, True]\ 0.25$
$Dist\ [True, False]\ 0.25$
$Dist\ [False, True]\ 0.25$
$Dist\ [False, False]\ 0.25$

Instead of relying on call-time choice as default behavior, we could model *Dist* as a function and make run-time choice the default in PFLP. In this case, to get call-time choice we would have to use a special construct provided by the library—as it is the case in many probabilistic programming libraries, e.g., *mem* in Church. We have decided to go with the current modeling based on call-time-choice, because the alternative would work against the spirit of the Curry programming language.

There is a long history of discussions about the pros and cons of call-time choice and run-time choice. It is common knowledge in probabilistic programming [8] that, in order to model stochastic automata or probabilistic grammars, memoization—that is, call-time choice—has to be avoided. Similarly, Antoy [1] observes that you need run-time choice to elegantly model regular expressions in the context of functional logic programming languages. Then again, probabilistic languages need a concept like memoization in order to use a single value drawn from a distribution multiple times. If we flip a coin and have more than one dependency on its result in the remaining program, the result of that flip is not supposed to change between one occurrence and the other.

3.2   Combination of Non-strictness and Non-determinism

This section illustrates the benefits from the combination of non-strictness and non-determinism with respect to performance. More precisely, in a setting that uses Curry-like non-determinism, non-strictness can prevent non-determinism from being "spawned". Let us consider calculating the probability for throwing only sixes when throwing n dice. First we define a uniform die as follows.

> **data** $Side = One \mid Two \mid Three \mid Four \mid Five \mid Six$
> $die :: Dist\ Side$
> $die = uniform\ [\,One, Two, Three, Four, Five, Six\,]$

We define the following query by means of the combinators introduced so far. The function all simply checks that all elements of a list satisfy a given predicate; it is defined by means of the boolean conjunction ($\wedge$).

> $allSix :: Int \rightarrow Probability$
> $allSix\ n = all\ (\equiv Six)\ ??\ replicateDist\ n\ (\lambda() \rightarrow die)$

The following table compares running times[8] of this query for different numbers of dice. The row labeled "Curry ND" lists the running times for an implementation that uses the operator ($\ggg$). The row "Curry List" shows the numbers for a list-based implementation in Curry, which is a literal translation of the library by Erwig and Kollmansberger [10]. The row labeled "Curry ND!" uses an operator ($\ggg$!) instead, which we will discuss shortly. Finally, we compare our implementation to the original list-based implementation, which the row labeled "Haskell List" refers to. The table states the running times in milliseconds of a compiled executable for each benchmark as a mean of three runs. Cells marked with "–" take more than a minute.

# of dice	5	6	7	8	9	10	100	200	300
Curry ND	<1	<1	<1	<1	<1	<1	48	231	547
Curry List	2	13	72	419	2554	15 394	–	–	–
Curry ND!	52	409	2568	16 382	–	–	–	–	–
Haskell List	1	5	30	210	1415	6538	–	–	–

Obviously, the example above is a little contrived. While the query is exponential in both list versions, it is linear in the non-deterministic setting[9].

---

[8] All benchmarks were executed on a Linux machine with an Intel Core i7-6500U (2.50 GHz) and 8 GiB RAM running Fedora 25. We used the Glasgow Haskell Compiler (version 8.0.2, option -02) and set the search strategy in KiCS2 to depth-first.

[9] Non-determinism causes significant overhead for KiCS2, thus, "Curry ND" does not show linear development, but we measured a linear running time using PAKCS [14].

In order to illustrate the behavior of the example above, we consider the following application for an arbitrary distribution *dist* of type *Dist* [*Side*].

$$\textit{filterDist} \; (\textit{all} \; (\equiv \textit{Six})) \; (\textit{joinWith} \; (:) \; (\textit{Dist One} \; \tfrac{1}{6}) \; \textit{dist})$$

This application yields an empty distribution without evaluating the distribution *dist*. The clou here is that *joinWith* yields a *Dist* constructor without inspecting its arguments. When we demand the event of the resulting *Dist*, *joinWith* has to evaluate only its first argument to see that the predicate *all* (≡ *Six*) yields *False*. The evaluation of the expression fails without inspecting the second argument of *joinWith*. Figure 1 illustrates the evaluation in more detail.

In case of the example *allSix*, all non-deterministic branches that contain a value different from *Six* fail fast due to the non-strictness. Thus, the number of evaluation steps is linear in the number of rolled dice. Note that a similar behavior is *not* possible in a list-based implementation that implements (⋙=) with *concatMap*. In such an implementation, we have to traverse the entire distribution before we can evaluate the predicate *all* (≡ *Six*). The consequence is that the running times of "Haskell List" cannot compete with "Curry ND" when the number of dice increases.

We can only benefit from the combination of non-strictness and non-determinism if we define (⋙=) with care. Let us take a look at a strict variant of (⋙=) and discuss its consequences.

$\textit{filterDist} \; (\textit{all} \; (\equiv \textit{Six})) \; (\textit{joinWith} \; (:) \; (\textit{Dist One} \; \tfrac{1}{6}) \; \textit{dist})$
≡   { Def. of *joinWith* }
$\textit{filterDist} \; (\textit{all} \; (\equiv \textit{Six}))$
          $(\textit{Dist One} \; \tfrac{1}{6} \ggg \lambda x \rightarrow \textit{dist} \ggg \lambda xs \rightarrow \textit{certainly} \; (x : xs))$
≡   { Def. of (⋙=) (twice) }
$\textit{filterDist} \; (\textit{all} \; (\equiv \textit{Six}))$
          (**let** $\textit{Dist } x \; p = \textit{Dist One} \; \tfrac{1}{6}; \textit{Dist } xs \; q = \textit{dist}; \textit{Dist } ys \; r = \textit{certainly} \; (x : xs)$
          in $\textit{Dist } ys \; (p \ast . (q \ast . r))$)
≡   { Def. of *filterDist* }
let $\textit{Dist } x \; p = \textit{Dist One} \; \tfrac{1}{6}; \textit{Dist } xs \; q = \textit{dist}; \textit{Dist } ys \; r = \textit{certainly} \; (x : xs)$
in if $\textit{all} \; (\equiv \textit{Six}) \; ys$ **then** $\textit{Dist } ys \; (p \ast . (q \ast . r))$ **else** *failed*
≡   { Def. of *certainly* }
let $\textit{Dist } x \; p = \textit{Dist One} \; \tfrac{1}{6}; \textit{Dist } xs \; q = \textit{dist}$
in if $\textit{all} \; (\equiv \textit{Six}) \; (x : xs)$ **then** $\textit{Dist} \; (x : xs) \; (p \ast . (q \ast . 1.0))$ **else** *failed*
≡   { Def. of *all* }
let $\textit{Dist } x \; p = \textit{Dist One} \; \tfrac{1}{6}; \textit{Dist } xs \; q = \textit{dist}$
in if $x \equiv \textit{Six} \wedge \textit{all} \; (\equiv \textit{Six}) \; xs$ **then** $\textit{Dist} \; (x : xs) \; (p \ast . (q \ast . 1.0))$ **else** *failed*
≡   { Def. of (≡) and (∧) }
let $\textit{Dist } x \; p = \textit{Dist One} \; \tfrac{1}{6}; \textit{Dist } xs \; q = d$
in if $\textit{False}$ **then** $\textit{Dist} \; (x : xs) \; (p \ast . (q \ast . 1.0))$ **else** *failed*
≡   { Def. of **if** − **then** − **else** }
failed

Fig. 1. Simplified evaluation illustrating non-strict non-determinism

$$(\ggg\!!) :: Dist\ a \rightarrow (a \rightarrow Dist\ b) \rightarrow Dist\ b$$
$$Dist\ x\ p \ggg\!!\ f = \textbf{case}\ f\ x\ \textbf{of}\ Dist\ y\ q \rightarrow Dist\ y\ (p *. q)$$

This implementation is strict in its first argument as well as in the result of the function application. When we use $(\ggg\!!)$ to implement the *allSix* example, we lose the benefit of Curry-like non-determinism. The row labeled "Curry ND!" shows the running times when using $(\ggg\!!)$ instead of $(\ggg\!)$. As $(\ggg\!!)$ is strict, the function *joinWith* has to evaluate both its arguments to yield a result.

Intuitively, we expect similar running times for "Curry ND!" and "Curry List". However, this is not the case. "Curry ND!" heavily relies on non-deterministic computations, which causes significant overhead for KiCS2. We do not investigate these differences here but propose it as a direction for future research.

Obviously, turning an exponential problem into a linear one is like getting only sixes when throwing dice. In most cases we are not that lucky. For example, consider the following query for throwing n dice that are either five or six.

$$allFiveOrSix :: Int \rightarrow Probability$$
$$allFiveOrSix\ n = all\ (\lambda s \rightarrow s \equiv Five \vee s \equiv Six)\ ??\ replicateDist\ n\ (\lambda() \rightarrow die)$$

We again list running times for different numbers of dice for this query.

# of dice	5	6	7	8	9	10
Curry ND	4	7	15	34	76	163
Curry List	2	13	84	489	2869	16 989
Curry ND!	49	382	2483	15 562	–	–
Haskell List	2	5	31	219	1423	6670

As we can see from the running times, this query is exponential in all implementations. Nevertheless, the running time of the non-strict, non-deterministic implementation is much better because we only have to consider two sides—six and five—while we have to consider all sides in the list implementations and the non-deterministic, strict implementation. That is, while the basis of the complexity is two in the case of the non-deterministic, non-strict implementation, it is six in all the other cases. Again, we get an overhead of a factor around 25 in the case of the strict non-determinism compared to the list implementation.

3.3   Definition of the Bind Operator

In this section we discuss our design choices concerning the implementation of the bind operator. We illustrate that we have to be careful about non-strictness, because we do not want to lose non-deterministic results. Most importantly, the final implementation ensures that users cannot misuse the library if they stick to one simple rule.

First, we revisit the definition of ($\ggg$) introduced in Sect. 2.

$$(\ggg) :: Dist\ a \to (a \to Dist\ b) \to Dist\ b$$
$$d \ggg f = \textbf{let } Dist\ x\ p = d$$
$$Dist\ y\ q = f\ x$$
$$\textbf{in } Dist\ y\ (p *. q)$$

We can observe two facts about this definition. First, the definition yields a *Dist*-constructor without matching any argument. Second, if neither the event nor the probability of the final distribution is evaluated, the application of the function *f* is not evaluated as well.

We can observe these properties with some exemplary usages of ($\ggg$). As a reference, we see that pattern matching the *Dist*-constructor of a *coin* triggers the non-determinism and yields two results.

$\lambda> (\lambda(Dist\ \_\ \_) \to True)\ coin$
True
True

In contrast, distributions resulting from an application of ($\ggg$) behave differently. This time, pattern matching on the *Dist*-constructor does not trigger any non-determinism.

$\lambda> (\lambda(Dist\ \_\ \_) \to True)\ (certainly\ () \ggg \lambda\_ \to coin)$
True
$\lambda> (\lambda(Dist\ \_\ \_) \to True)\ (coin \ggg certainly)$
True

We observe that the last two examples yield a single result, because the ($\ggg$)-operator changes the position of the non-determinism. That is, the non-determinism does not reside at the same level as the *Dist*-constructor, but in the arguments of *Dist*. Therefore, we have to be sure to trigger all non-determinism when we compute probabilities. Not evaluating non-determinism might lead to false results when we sum up probabilities. Hence, non-strictness is a crucial property for positive pruning effects, but has to be used carefully.

Consider the following example usage of ($\ggg$), which is simply an inlined version of *joinWith* applied to the boolean conjunction ($\wedge$).

$\lambda> (\lambda(Dist\ x\ \_) \to x)\ (coin \ggg \lambda x \to coin \ggg \lambda y \to certainly\ (x \wedge y))$
False
True
False

We lose one expected result from the distribution, because ($\wedge$) is non-strict in its second argument in case the first argument is *False*. When the first *coin* evaluates to *False*, ($\ggg$) ignores the second coin and yields *False* straightaway. In this case, the non-determinism of the second *coin* is not triggered and we get only three instead of four results. The non-strictness of ($\wedge$) has no consequences when using ($\ggg=!$), because the operator evaluates both arguments and, thus, triggers the non-determinism.

As we have seen above, when using the non-strict operator ($\wedge$), one of the results gets lost. However, when we sum up probabilities, we do not want events to get lost. For example, when we compute the total probability of a distribution, the result should always be 1.0. However, the query above has only three results and every event has a probability of 0.25, resulting in a total probability of 0.75.

Here is the good news. While events can get lost when passing non-strict functions to ($\ggg=$), probabilities never get lost. For example, consider the following application.

$\lambda> (\lambda(Dist \_ p) \to p) (coin \ggg= \lambda x \to coin \ggg= \lambda y \to certainly\ (x \wedge y))$
0.25
0.25
0.25
0.25

Since multiplication is strict, if we demand the resulting probability, the operator ($\ggg=$) has to evaluate the $Dist$-constructor and its probability. That is, no values get lost if we evaluate the resulting probability. Fortunately, the query operation (??) calculates the total probability of the filtered distributions, thus, evaluates the probability as the following example shows.

$\lambda> not\ ??\ (coin \ggg= \lambda x \to coin \ggg= \lambda y \to certainly\ (x \wedge y))$
0.75

We calculate the probability of the event $False$ and while there where only two $False$ events, the total probability is still 0.75, i.e., three times 0.25.

All in all, in order to benefit from non-strictness, all operations have to use the right amount of strictness, not too much and not too little. For this reason PFLP does not provide the $Dist$-constructor nor the corresponding projection functions to the user. With this restriction, the library guarantees that no relevant probabilities get lost.

3.4   Non-deterministic Events

We assume that all events passed to library functions are deterministic, thus, do not support non-deterministic events within distributions. In order to illustrate why, we consider an example that breaks this rule here.

Curry provides free variables, that is, expressions that non-deterministically evaluate to every possible value of its type. When we revisit the definition of a die, we might be tempted to use a free variable instead of explicitly enumerating all values of type $Side$. For example, consider the following definition of a die.

$die2 :: Dist\ Side$
$die2 = Dist\ unknown\ \frac{1}{6}$

We just use a free variable—the constant *unknown*—and calculate the probability of each event ourselves. The free variable non-deterministically yields all constructors of type *Side*. Now, let us consider the following query.

$\lambda>$ *const True ?? die2*
0.16666667

The result of this query is $\frac{1}{6}$ and not 1.0 as expected. This example illustrates that probabilities can get lost if we do not use the right amount of strictness. The definition of (??) first projects to the probability of *die2* and throws away all non-determinism. Therefore, we lose probabilities we would like to sum up.

As a consequence for PFLP, non-deterministic events within a distribution are not allowed. If users of the library stick to this rule, it is not possible to misuse the operations and lose non-deterministic results due to non-strictness.

4   Related and Future Work

The approach of this paper is based on the work by Erwig and Kollmansberger [10], who introduce a Haskell library that represents distributions as lists of event-probability pairs. Their library also provides a simple sampling mechanism to perform inference on distributions. Inference algorithms come into play because common examples in probabilistic programming have an exponential growth and it is not feasible to compute the whole distribution. Similarly, Ścibior et al. [19] present a more efficient implementation using a DSL in Haskell. They represent distributions as a free monad and inference algorithms as an interpretation of the monadic structure. Thanks to this interpretation, the approach is competitive to full-blown probabilistic programming languages with respect to performance. PFLP provides functions to sample from distributions as well. However, in this work we focus on modeling distributions and do not discuss any sampling mechanism. In particular, as future work we plan to investigate whether we can benefit from the improved performance as presented here in the case of sampling. Furthermore, a more detailed investigation of the performance of non-determinism in comparison to a list model is a topic for another paper.

The benefit with respect to the combination of non-strictness and non-determinism is similar to the benefit of property-based testing using Curry-like non-determinism in Haskell [18] and Curry [6]. In property-based testing, sometimes we want to generate test cases that satisfy a precondition. With Curry-like non-determinism the precondition can prune the search space early, while a list-based implementation has to generate all test cases and filter them afterwards. Both applications, probabilistic programming and property-based testing, are examples, where built-in non-determinism outperforms list-based approaches as introduced by Wadler [20]. In comparison to property-based testing, here, we observe that we can even add a kind of monadic layer on top of the non-determinism that computes additional information and still preserve the demand driven behavior. However, the additional information has to be evaluated strictly—as it is the case for probabilities, otherwise we might lose non-deterministic results.

There are other more elaborated approaches to implement a library for probabilistic programming. For example, Kiselyov and Shan [15] extend their library for probabilistic programming in OCAML with a construct for lazy evaluation to achieve similar positive effects. However, they use lazy evaluation for a concrete application based on importance sampling. Due to the combination of non-strictness and non-determinism, we can efficiently calculate the total probability of the resulting distribution without utilizing sampling.

As future work, we see a high potential for performance improvements for the Curry compiler KiCS2. PFLP serves as a starting point for further studies of functional logic features in practical applications. For example, we would expect the running times of the strict implementation based on non-determinism to be approximately as efficient as a list-based implementation. However, as the numbers in Sect. 3 show, the list approach is considerably faster.

The library's design does not support the use of non-determinism in events or probabilities of a distribution. In case of deeper non-determinism, we have to be careful to trigger all non-determinism when querying a distribution as shown in Sect. 3. Hence, the extension of the library with an interface using non-determinism on the user's side is an idea worth studying.

Last but not least, we see an opportunity to apply ideas and solutions of the functional logic paradigm in probabilistic programming. For instance, Christiansen et al. [7] investigate free theorems for functional logic programs. As their work considers non-determinism and sharing, adapting it to probabilistic programming should be easy. As another example, Braßel [3] presents a debugger for Curry that works well with non-determinism. Hence, it should be easy to reuse these ideas in the setting of probabilistic programming as well.

5   Conclusion

We have implemented a simple library for probabilistic programming in a functional logic programming language, namely Curry. Such a library proves to be a good fit for a functional logic language, because both paradigms share similar features. While other libraries need to reimplement features specific to probabilistic programming, we solely rely on core features of functional logic languages.

The key idea of the library is to use non-determinism to model distributions. We discussed design choices as well as corresponding disadvantages and advantages of this approach. In the end, the library uses non-strict probabilistic combinators in order to avoid spawning unnecessary non-deterministic computations and, thus, benefit in terms of performance due to early pruning. However, we have observed that the combination of non-strictness and non-deterministic needs to be taken with a pinch of salt. Using combinators that are too strict leads to a loss of the aforementioned performance benefit.

Acknowledgements. We are thankful for fruitful discussions with Michael Hanus as well as suggestions of Jan Bracker and the anonymous reviewers to improve the readability of this paper.

References

1. Antoy, S.: Evaluation strategies for functional logic programming. J. Symbolic Comput. **40**(1), 875–903 (2005)
2. Antoy, S., Hanus, M.: Functional logic programming. Commun. ACM **53**(4), 74–85 (2010)
3. Braßel, B.: A technique to build debugging tools for lazy functional logic languages. Electron. Notes Theoret. Comput. Sci. **246**, 39–53 (2009)
4. Braßel, B., Hanus, M., Huch, F.: Encapsulating non-determinism in functional logic computations. J. Funct. Logic Program. **2004** (2004)
5. Braßel, B., Hanus, M., Peemöller, B., Reck, F.: KiCS2: a new compiler from Curry to Haskell. In: Kuchen, H. (ed.) WFLP 2011. LNCS, vol. 6816, pp. 1–18. Springer, Heidelberg (2011). https://doi.org/10.1007/978-3-642-22531-4_1
6. Christiansen, J., Fischer, S.: EasyCheck - test data for free. In: Proceedings of the International Symposium on Functional and Logic Programming (2008)
7. Christiansen, J., Seidel, D., Voigtländer, J.: Free theorems for functional logic programs. In: Proceedigns of the Workshop on Programming Languages Meets Program Verification (2010)
8. De Raedt, L., Kimmig, A.: Probabilistic Programming Concepts. arXiv:1312.4328 (preprint) (2013)
9. De Raedt, L., Kimmig, A., Toivonen, H.: ProbLog: a probabilistic prolog and its application in link discovery. In: Proceedings of the International Joint Conference on Artifical Intelligence (2007)
10. Erwig, M., Kollmansberger, S.: Functional pearls: probabilistic functional programming in Haskell. J. Funct. Program. **16**(1), 21–34 (2006)
11. Fischer, S., Kiselyov, O., Shan, C.: Purely functional lazy non-deterministic programming. In: Proceedings of the International Conference on Functional Programming (2009)
12. Goodman, N.D., Mansinghka, V.K., Roy, D.M., Bonawitz, K., Tenenbaum, J.B.: Church: A Language for Generative Models. CoRR (2012)
13. Gordon, A.D., Henzinger, T.A., Nori, A.V., Rajamani, S.K.: Probabilistic programming. In: Proceedings of the on Future of Software Engineering (2014)
14. Hanus, M. (ed.): PAKCS: The Portland Aachen Kiel Curry System (2017). http://www.informatik.uni-kiel.de/pakcs/
15. Kiselyov, O., Shan, C.: Embedded probabilistic programming. In: Taha, W.M. (ed.) DSL 2009. LNCS, vol. 5658, pp. 360–384. Springer, Heidelberg (2009). https://doi.org/10.1007/978-3-642-03034-5_17
16. McCallum, A., Schultz, K., Singh, S.: FACTORIE: probabilistic programming via imperatively defined factor graphs. In: Proceedings of International Conference on Neural Information Processing Systems (2009)
17. Paige, B., Wood, F.: A compilation target for probabilistic programming languages. In: Proceedings of the International Conference on Machine Learning (2014)
18. Runciman, C., Naylor, M., Lindblad, F.: SmallCheck and Lazy SmallCheck: automatic exhaustive testing for small values. In: Proceedings of the Symposium on Haskell (2008)
19. Ścibior, A., Ghahramani, Z., Gordon, A.D.: Practical probabilistic programming with monads. In: Proceedings of the Symposium on Haskell (2015)

20. Wadler, P.: How to replace failure by a list of successes. In: Proceedings of the Conference on Functional Programming Languages and Computer Architecture (1985)
21. Wood, F., Meent, J.W., Mansinghka, V.: A new approach to probabilistic programming inference. In: Artificial Intelligence and Statistics (2014)

Rewriting High-Level Spreadsheet Structures into Higher-Order Functional Programs

Florian Biermann[1]([✉])[iD], Wensheng Dou[2][iD], and Peter Sestoft[1][iD]

[1] Computer Science Department, IT University of Copenhagen,
Copenhagen, Denmark
{fbie,sestoft}@itu.dk
[2] State Key Laboratory of Computer Science,
Institute of Software, Chinese Academy of Sciences, Beijing, China
wsdou@otcaix.iscas.ac.cn

Abstract. Spreadsheets are used heavily in industry and academia. Often, spreadsheet models are developed for years and their complexity grows vastly beyond what the paradigm was originally conceived for. Such complexity often comes at the cost of recalculation performance. However, spreadsheet models usually have some high-level structure that can be used to improve performance by performing independent computation in parallel. In this paper, we devise rules for rewriting high-level spreadsheet structure in the form of so-called cell arrays into higher-order functional programs that can be easily parallelized on multicore processors. We implement our rule set for the experimental Funcalc spreadsheet engine which already implements parallelizable higher-order array functions as well as user-defined higher-order functions. Benchmarks show that our rewriting approach improves recalculation performance for spreadsheets that are dominated by cell arrays.

1 Introduction

Spreadsheets are abundant in research and industry and used heavily by professionals who are not educated as programmers. Spreadsheets often become highly complex over time. Not only is it hard to maintain an understanding of the underlying model, but this complexity can also lead to slow recalculation of the entire spreadsheet. For large and complex spreadsheet models, recalculation performance may be critical.

Dou et al. [6] report that 69% of all spreadsheets with formulas in the Enron [10] and EUSES [8] spreadsheet corpora contain *cell arrays*. A cell array is a rectangular block of copy equivalent formulas [15], like the cell areas B2:F6 and B8:F12 in Fig. 2. Such a cell array is created when the spreadsheet user writes a formula, typically with a carefully crafted mix of absolute and relative references, and copies it to a rectangular cell range.

F. Biermann—Supported by the Sino-Danish Center for Education and Research.

W. Dou—Supported by the National Natural Science Foundation of China (61702490) and Beijing Natural Science Foundation (4164104).

F. Calimeri et al. (Eds.): PADL 2018, LNCS 10702, pp. 20–35, 2018.
https://doi.org/10.1007/978-3-319-73305-0_2

Spreadsheets are first-order purely functional programs [2]. In purely functional programs, all values are immutable. Immutability guarantees data-race freedom and therefore allows for easy parallelization and hence a speedup of disjoint computations. If we can detect formula cells on a spreadsheet that do not depend on each other, we can safely compute these in parallel.

In functional languages, disjoint computations on values of an array can be expressed explicitly by means of higher-order functions. For instance, the higher-order function *map* explicitly applies a pure function to each element of an array individually. Hence, *map* can easily be parallelized.

In this paper, we design a source-to-source rewriting semantics for converting cell array computations into parallel higher-order functional programs to improve recalculation performance. We do this by correlating cell array structure with higher-order array functions.

Our rewriting semantics uses a common feature of spreadsheet software, called *array formulas*. An array formula must evaluate to an array of the same size and shape as the spreadsheet cell range that contains the formula. The array is then unpacked and its scalar values are placed directly in the cells according to their position in the array, such that the containing array disappears.

We target the experimental spreadsheet engine Funcalc [17]. Funcalc provides higher-order functions on immutable two-dimensional arrays, which correspond to cell ranges, as well as efficient sheet-defined higher-order functions. For our purpose, we extend Funcalc with additional functions on arrays.

To our knowledge, there is no literature on exploiting parallelism in cell arrays to improve recalculation performance. Some researchers have investigated whole-sheet graph parallelism on spreadsheets [19–21]. Prior work on high-level spreadsheet array structure has either focused on making the user aware of high-level models [11,15,16]; on correcting errors in cell formulas by analyzing the structure around given cells [3,4,6,12]; or on synthesizing templates from spreadsheets to allow for reuse of the high-level structure [1,13].

With our rewriting semantics, Funcalc can exploit implicit parallelism in spreadsheets dominated by large or computation-heavy cell arrays. We compare the performance of our approach on two idealized and six synthetic spreadsheets as well as twelve real-world spreadsheets from the EUSES [8] corpus. Our results show that we can indeed improve spreadsheet recalculation by parallelizing cell array computations. However, our results also show that the achievable speedup is limited by the sequential dependencies of the spreadsheet models.

2   From Cell Arrays to Higher-Order Functions

Our idea is based on the observation that the references in cell arrays often form a pattern that corresponds to one of two higher-order functions on 2D arrays [20,21]. We define our variants of these two functions with variadic arity k to make them as general as possible.

The first function is commonly known as *map*. It takes as arguments a k-ary function f and k arrays x_1 through x_k of n rows and m columns each. We say they are of shape $n \times m$. We require at least one argument array, i.e. $k \geq 1$. The result of the function is a new $n \times m$ array containing the results of applying f to the k elements of the input arrays at the same index:

$$\texttt{MAP}(f, x_1, \ldots, x_k) = X, \text{ where } X[i,j] = f(x_1[i,j], \ldots, x_k[i,j])$$

The other function is commonly known as *scan* or *generalized prefix sum*. We use a variant on 2D arrays that computes a wavefront prefix sum for arbitrary functions. It takes a $(k+3)$-ary function f, a $n \times 1$ single-column array γ, a scalar value δ and a $1 \times m$ single-row array ρ as well as, again, k arrays $x_1, \ldots, x_k$ of shape $n \times m$. Its result is a new $n \times m$ array $\texttt{PREFIX}(f, \gamma, \delta, \rho, x_1, \ldots, x_k) = X$, where:

$$X[1,1] = f(\gamma[1], \qquad \delta, \qquad \rho[1], \qquad x_1[1,1], \ldots, x_k[1,1]) \quad (1)$$
$$X[1,j] = f(X[1,j-1], \rho[j-1], \qquad \rho[j], \qquad x_1[1,j], \ldots, x_k[1,j]) \quad (2)$$
$$X[i,1] = f(\gamma[i], \qquad \gamma[i-1], \qquad X[j-1,1], x_1[i,1], \ldots, x_k[i,1]) \quad (3)$$
$$X[i,j] = f(X[i-1,j], X[i-1,j-1], X[i,j-1], x_1[i,j], \ldots, x_k[i,j]) \quad (4)$$

Here we allow $k = 0$, meaning only the input arrays γ and ρ as well as the scalar δ are required. We use the values from γ, ρ and δ as if they were positioned around the upper and left fringes of the original arrays $x_1 \ldots x_k$, see also Fig. 6. Equation (1) defines the first element of X at $(i,j) = (1,1)$, on which all other values of X depend. Since no values precede it, we must refer to values from γ, δ and ρ instead. Equation (2) defines the first row and hence refers to ρ; Eq. (3) defines the first column and therefore refers to γ. Finally, Eq. (4) is the general case for all remaining index pairs (i,j).

2.1   A Formal Spreadsheet Language

For presentation purposes, we use a simplified formal spreadsheet language, λ-calc, as shown in Fig. 1. The e form includes lambda expressions of arbitrary arity and with named parameters. All expressions must be closed. Users are only allowed to enter expressions in u, which is a subset of e without anonymous functions and variables. References r to cells and to cell ranges are shown in the R1C1 format, but translated to the "usual" A1 format in examples. For instance, the absolute reference R6C2 in R1C1 format would in A1 format be $B\$6, referring to column 2, row 6. Row-absolute column-relative reference R6C[2] in R1C1 format would in A1 format be G\$6 if the reference appeared anywhere in column E — that being column 5 and so the reference would be to column $5 + 2 = 7$, which is column G. See also function *lookup*[] in Sect. 3.1.

   Function $\phi \in r \to e$ maps a cell address r to the formula $e = \phi(r)$ in that cell. When $r_1 : r_2$ is a cell array of copy equivalent formulas, we write $\phi(r_1 : r_2)$ for the common formula (see Sect. 3.1).

2.2   Example: DNA Sequence Alignment

We illustrate the rewriting of cell arrays with the spreadsheet shown in Fig. 2. It computes the optimal local alignment of two DNA sequences using the standard

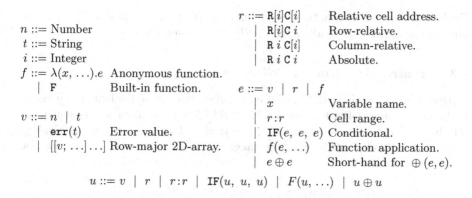

$$n ::= \text{Number}$$
$$t ::= \text{String}$$
$$i ::= \text{Integer}$$
$$f ::= \lambda(x, \ldots).e \quad \text{Anonymous function.}$$
$$\mid \quad F \qquad\qquad \text{Built-in function.}$$

$$v ::= n \mid t$$
$$\mid \quad \text{err}(t) \qquad \text{Error value.}$$
$$\mid \quad [[v; \ldots]\ldots] \quad \text{Row-major 2D-array.}$$

$$r ::= \text{R}[i]\text{C}[i] \qquad \text{Relative cell address.}$$
$$\mid \quad \text{R}[i]\text{C}\, i \qquad \text{Row-relative.}$$
$$\mid \quad \text{R}\, i\, \text{C}[i] \qquad \text{Column-relative.}$$
$$\mid \quad \text{R}\, i\, \text{C}\, i \qquad \text{Absolute.}$$

$$e ::= v \mid r \mid f$$
$$\mid \quad x \qquad\qquad \text{Variable name.}$$
$$\mid \quad r:r \qquad\qquad \text{Cell range.}$$
$$\mid \quad \text{IF}(e,\, e,\, e) \quad \text{Conditional.}$$
$$\mid \quad f(e, \ldots) \qquad \text{Function application.}$$
$$\mid \quad e \oplus e \qquad\quad \text{Short-hand for } \oplus (e,e).$$

$$u ::= v \mid r \mid r:r \mid \text{IF}(u,\, u,\, u) \mid F(u, \ldots) \mid u \oplus u$$

Fig. 1. The λ-calc syntax with variables and lambda expressions. Form u is a subset of e and contains "user expressions", i.e. expressions that a user is allowed to write.

	A	B	C	D	E	F
1		A	G	C	T	A
2	T	= IF($A2 = B$1, 3, −3)	...	...	...	= IF($A2 = F$1, 3, −3)
3	G	...	...	...	...	...
4	T	...	...	...	...	...
5	T	...	...	...	...	...
6	T	= IF($A6 = B$1, 3, −3)	...	...	...	= IF($A6 = F$1, 3, −3)
7	0	0	0	0	0	0
8	0	= MAX(A7 + B2, A8 − 2, B7 − 2, 0)	...	...	...	= MAX(E7 + F2, E8 − 2, F7 − 2, 0)
9	0	...	...	...	...	...
10	0	...	...	...	...	...
11	0	...	...	...	...	...
12	0	= MAX(A12 + B6, A11 − 2, B11 − 2, 0)	...	...	...	= MAX(E12 + F6, E11 − 2, F11 − 2, 0)

Fig. 2. A spreadsheet to compute a best local DNA sequence alignment. One DNA sequence is in cells B1:F1, the other in cells A2:A6. Cells B2:F6 defines a substitution matrix. Cells B8:F12 compute the scoring matrix. Ellipses denote repeated formulas. Cell areas with light gray background have the same formula.

algorithm, based on dynamic programming (Smith-Waterman [18]). A substitution matrix s is defined in cell range B2:F6 (upper gray cell area), and the scoring matrix H in cell range B8:F12 (lower gray cell area). The substitution matrix assigns score $+3$ to identical nucleotides (DNA "letters") and score -3 to distinct nucleotides.

The scoring matrix (B8:F12) computes the best score $H(i, j)$ for any alignment between the i-length prefix of one sequence with the j-length prefix of the other. This can be defined recursively as:

$$H(i,j) = \max(H(i-1, j-1) + s(i,j), H(i-1, j) - 2, H(i, j-1) - 2, 0)$$

By backtracking through the scoring matrix H from its maximal entry, one obtains the optimal local alignment of the two sequences.

2.3   Intuitive Rewriting of Cell Arrays

First consider the range B2:F6, whose formulas are copy equivalent [15]: it could be filled by copying the formula in B2 to B2:F6 with automatic adjustment of relative row and column references. (The B8:F12 formulas are copy equivalent also). In R1C1 reference format, the range B2:F6 (upper gray cell area) can be written as:

$$\phi(\texttt{R2C2:R6C6}) \ := \ \texttt{IF(R[0]C1 = R1C[0], 3, -3)}$$

The row- and column-relative structure of the two references builds a cross-product of the column and the row containing the input sequences. While it is straightforward to build such an ad-hoc cell structure, this has two disadvantages. First, this implementation does not generalize to sequences with more than five elements. Second, and more important to us, the formula itself does not capture the structure of the computation. This structure is implicit in the cell references and only emerges from the context — the entire spreadsheet and the formula's location in it — in which it is computed.

Ideally, we would like to retain high-level information about the computation that we want to perform inside the expression, and also find the most general way to express it. Our intuition as functional programmers is to rewrite the formulas as a 2D MAP over repeated row and column values:

$$\phi(\texttt{R2C2:R6C6}) \ := \ \{\texttt{MAP } (\lambda(\texttt{x, y}).\texttt{IF(x = y, 3, -3))},$$
$$\texttt{HREP(COLS(R1C2:R1C6), R2C1:R6C1)},$$
$$\texttt{VREP(ROWS(R2C1:R6C1), R1C2:R1C6))}\}$$

The curly braces around the expression denote an *array formula*: a formula that evaluates to an array and whose values are unpacked into the individual cells of the cell array R2C2:R6C6 (B2:F6), as described in Sect. 1.

Now, this expression may look convoluted at first sight, especially to someone without a functional programming background. But indeed, it does exactly what the entire cell array B2:F6 did by replicating the formula:

– HREP(n, x) creates a new two-dimensional array of size $n \times$ COLS(x) by repeating x exactly n times.
– VREP(m, x) creates a new two-dimensional array of size ROWS$(x) \times m$; it works exactly like HREP but in the vertical direction.
– MAP(f, x_1, x_2) combines x_1 and x_2 pointwise by applying f.

Concretely, the new expression extends the one-dimensional ranges B1:F1 and A2:A6 into two matrices of size 5×5 and combines them pointwise using the function originally written in each cell.

What have we gained from this transformation? First, we have found a generalized expression of the algorithm that was originally distributed over a number of cells, and we can use it to write a more general version of the algorithm.

Second, and more importantly, we now have an expression which describes the structure of the computation independently from its context. This is useful, as we have recovered some high-level information that we can exploit to improve performance: there is no dependency between the individual points in this combination of two matrices, or two-dimensional arrays. Hence, it is now straightforward to parallelize the computation of the result matrix.

2.4 Different Kinds of Cell Arrays

Now consider the cell array B8:F12 (lower gray cell area), which contains the following formula in R1C1 format:

$$\phi(\texttt{R8C2:R12C6}) := \texttt{MAX}(\texttt{R}[-1]\texttt{C}[-1] + \texttt{R}[1]\texttt{C}[-6], \texttt{R}[0]\texttt{C}[-1] - 2, \texttt{R}[-1]\texttt{C}[0] - 2, 0)$$

We cannot use MAP to rewrite this cell array. There is a *sequential dependency* between the cells of the cell array because the cell E10 (R10C5) depends on E9 (R9C5), D10 (R10C4) and D9 (R9C4). These cells are inside the cell array itself. We therefore call this kind of cell array *transitive*, as opposed to *intransitive* cell arrays, which can be rewritten by using MAP, as in Sect. 2.3. Hence, we need to target the second higher-order function on arrays, namely PREFIX:

$$\phi(\texttt{R8C2:R12C6}) := \{\texttt{PREFIX}\ (\lambda(x, y, z, w).\texttt{MAX}(y + w, x - 2, z - 2, 0),$$
$$\texttt{R8C1:R12C1},$$
$$\texttt{R7C1},$$
$$\texttt{R8C1:R8C6},$$
$$\texttt{R2C2:R6C6})\}$$

Rewriting transitive cell arrays requires a bit more work: a transitive cell array could be written in either orientation (e.g. starting at the bottom right instead at the top left); and cell references in the expression might not occur in the same order as required by the semantics of PREFIX for the argument function, as we can see in our rewritten expression above. Hence, we must order the variable names correctly.

In the remainder of this paper, we formally define these properties of cell arrays and show how to rewrite them using a straightforward rewriting semantics.

3 Rewriting Cell Arrays

The overall idea of rewriting cell arrays, is to (1) rewrite the cell array's expression by systematically replacing non-absolute cell references with fresh variable names, consistently using the same variable name for multiple occurrences of the same cell reference; (2) use the fresh variable names as arguments to an anonymous function whose body is the rewritten expression; (3) infer an input range for each replaced cell reference by looking it up at the upper left and lower right cell addresses of the array that we are rewriting; and (4) create a new expression in which we pass the anonymous function as an argument to a higher-order array function, together with the inferred input cell ranges.

For brevity, we gloss over rotated and mirrored cases of transitive cell references. Hence, we assume that all transitive references are of the form $R[-1]C[0]$, $R[-1]C[-1]$ or $R[0]C[-1]$, referring to the previous row, same column; previous row, previous column; or same row, previous column. It is straightforward to implement rules for rotated and mirrored cases via array reversal in either dimension, or both.

3.1 Cell Arrays and Transitive and Intransitive Cell References

The formal definition of intransitive and transitive cell references extends set-notation to operate on cells and cell ranges. To state that a cell reference r is inside a cell array $r_1 : r_2$, we simply write $r \in r_1 : r_2$. A *cell array* is a cell range $r_1 : r_2$ satisfying $\forall r_i, r_j \in r_1 : r_2.\ \phi(r_i) = \phi(r_j)$, i.e. all cells of the cell range are copy equivalent [15].

Relative cell references (first argument) are converted into absolute cell references by adding the row- and column-offset to their own location in the sheet (second argument), as defined by the function *lookup*:

$$
\begin{aligned}
lookup[\![R[i_{r1}]C[i_{c1}], R\ i_{r2}\ C\ i_{c2}\ ]\!] &= R\ (i_{r1} + i_{r2})\ C\ (i_{c1} + i_{c2}) \\
lookup[\![R\ i_{r1}\ C[i_{c1}], R\ i_{r2}\ C\ i_{c2}\ ]\!] &= R\ i_{r1}\ C\ (i_{c1} + i_{c2}) \\
lookup[\![R[i_{r1}]C\ i_{c1}\ , R\ i_{r2}\ C\ i_{c2}\ ]\!] &= R\ (i_{r1} + i_{r2})\ C\ i_{c1} \\
lookup[\![R\ i_{r1}\ C\ i_{c1}\ , \_]\!] &= R\ i_{r1}\ C\ i_{c1}
\end{aligned}
$$

A cell reference is intransitive if it never refers back into the cell array, no matter the location of the containing cell. We formulate this as follows:

$$\{ lookup[\![r, r_0]\!] \mid r_0 \in r_1 : r_2 \} \cap r_1 : r_2 = \emptyset \Rightarrow r \text{ is intransitive in } r_1 : r_2.$$

Conversely, we can define transitive cell references by inverting the equation:

$$\{ lookup[\![r, r_0]\!] \mid r_0 \in r_1 : r_2 \} \cap r_1 : r_2 \neq \emptyset \Rightarrow r \text{ is transitive in } r_1 : r_2.$$

Absolute references $RiCi$ are neither transitive nor intransitive and we treat them like constants during rewriting.

3.2 Rewriting Semantics

We use reducible expressions and a reduction relation to formalize the rewriting process. The $\rightsquigarrow$ relation in Fig. 4 defines rewriting cell arrays from plain spreadsheet formulas to higher-order functional programs in λ-calc. More precisely, the relation $\rightsquigarrow$ rewrites an expression u to an expression l without relative references; see Fig. 3.

$$l ::= v \mid x \mid l \oplus l \mid \texttt{IF}(l,\, l,\, l) \mid F(l, \ldots) \mid RiCi:RiCi \mid RiCi$$
$$\mathcal{L} ::= \circ \mid \mathcal{L} \oplus u \mid l \oplus \mathcal{L} \mid F(l, \ldots, \mathcal{L}, u, \ldots)$$
$$\mid \texttt{IF}(\mathcal{L},\, u,\, u) \mid \texttt{IF}(l,\, \mathcal{L},\, u) \mid \texttt{IF}(l,\, l,\, \mathcal{L})$$
$$\Gamma ::= \texttt{more}(\underbrace{[(r,\, x)\ldots];}_{\text{Transitive}} \underbrace{[(r,\, x)\ldots];}_{\text{Intransitive}} \phi(r:r) := \mathcal{L}) \mid \texttt{done}(\phi(r:r) := \{e\})$$

Fig. 3. Rewriting context and transformation language for λ-calc. The form l is a subset of e, with only absolute cell references.

The form Γ describes a rewriting in progress. It is either **more** with transitive cell references and their substitutions, intransitive cell references and their substitutions, a cell range, and the expression that it contains; or it is **done** with a cell range and its rewritten expression. We use $(r^T,\, x^T)$ to denote a substitution pair of a transitive cell reference and $(r^I,\, x^I)$ to denote a substitution pair of an intransitive cell reference.

In plain English, the rules in Fig. 4 perform the following operations:

- Rule EXIST-I replaces a cell reference r with an already existing variable x from the list of intransitive substitutions.
- Rule EXIST-T replaces a cell reference r with an already existing variable x from the list of transitive substitutions.
- Rule SUBST-I replaces an intransitive cell reference r with a fresh variable x and stores the substitution (r, x) in the list of intransitive substitutions.
- Rule SUBST-T replaces a transitive cell reference r with a fresh variable x and stores the substitution (r, x) in the list of transitive substitutions.
- Rule SYNTH-MAP takes a rewritten expression l and wraps it in a λ-expression whose variables are the variable names from the intransitive substitutions. It places the resulting function as first argument to a call to MAP; the remaining arguments are the substituted cell references, converted to cell ranges by performing a lookup from r_{ul} and r_{lr} for each of them and extended to match the cell array's size. The result is an expression that can be plugged into an array formula.
- Rule SYNTH-PFX takes a rewritten expression l and wraps it in a λ-expression whose first three parameters are the variable names from the list of "sorted" transitive substitutions. The remaining parameters are taken from the intransitive substitutions, as in rule SYNTH-MAP. The rule constructs the initial row- and column-array by combining the result of the lookup of the first and last transitive reference on r_{ul} and the row, or column, of r_{lr}. The transitive cell references are converted as in rule SYNTH-MAP. The result is an expression that can be plugged into an array formula.

Both rule SYNTH-MAP and SYNTH-PFX make use of the meta-function *extd*, short for "extend". It returns an expression that, if necessary, replicates the intransitive input arrays to match the cell array $r_1:r_2$ being rewritten:

$$extd[\![r_1^I\!:\!r_2^I,\ r_1\!:\!r_2]\!] = \mathtt{VREP}(n, r_1^I\!:\!r_2^I) \qquad \text{where } n = rows[\![r_1\!:\!r_2]\!],$$
$$rows[\![r_1^I\!:\!r_2^I]\!] = 1$$

$$extd[\![r_1^I\!:\!r_2^I,\ r_1\!:\!r_2]\!] = \mathtt{HREP}(m, r_1^I\!:\!r_2^I) \qquad \text{where } m = columns[\![r_1\!:\!r_2]\!],$$
$$columns[\![r_1^I\!:\!r_2^I]\!] = 1$$

$$extd[\![r_1^I\!:\!r_2^I,\ r_1\!:\!r_2]\!] = r_1^I\!:\!r_2^I \qquad \text{otherwise.}$$

Finally, rule SYNTH-PFX uses the meta-functions *fill* and *sort*. We require that there are three transitive substitutions in the order R[0]C[−1], R[−1]C[−1] and R[−1]C[0]. Therefore, *fill* generates placeholder substitutions for each not

$$\mathtt{more}([(r^T,x^T)\ldots]; [(r_1^I,x_1^I)\ldots(r,x)(r_2^I,x_2^I)\ldots]; \phi(r_{ul}\!:\!r_{lr}) := \mathcal{L}[r]) \rightsquigarrow \qquad \text{[EXIST-I]}$$
$$\mathtt{more}([(r^T,x^T)\ldots]; [(r_1^I,x_1^I)\ldots(r,x)(r_2^I,x_2^I)\ldots]; \phi(r_{ul}\!:\!r_{lr}) := \mathcal{L}[x])$$

$$\mathtt{more}([(r_1^T,x_1^T)\ldots(r,x)(r_2^T,x_2^T)\ldots]; [(r^I,x^I)\ldots]; \phi(r_{ul}\!:\!r_{lr}) := \mathcal{L}[r]) \rightsquigarrow \qquad \text{[EXIST-T]}$$
$$\mathtt{more}([(r_1^T,x_1^T)\ldots(r,x)(r_2^T,x_2^T)\ldots]; [(r^I,x^I)\ldots]; \phi(r_{ul}\!:\!r_{lr}) := \mathcal{L}[x])$$

$$\mathtt{more}([(r^T,x^T)\ldots]; [(r^I,x^I)\ldots]; \phi(r_{ul}\!:\!r_{lr}) := \mathcal{L}[r]) \rightsquigarrow \qquad \text{[SUBST-I]}$$
$$\mathtt{more}([(r^T,x^T)\ldots]; [(r^I,x^I)\ldots(r,x)]; \phi(r_{ul}\!:\!r_{lr}) := \mathcal{L}[x])$$
$$\textbf{where } r \text{ is intransitive in } r_{ul}\!:\!r_{lr}$$
$$x \text{ fresh}$$

$$\mathtt{more}([(r^T,x^T)\ldots]; [(r^I,x^I)\ldots]; \phi(r_{ul}\!:\!r_{lr}) := \mathcal{L}[r]) \rightsquigarrow \qquad \text{[SUBST-T]}$$
$$\mathtt{more}([(r^T,x^T)\ldots(r,x)]; [(r^I,x^I)\ldots]; \phi(r_{ul}\!:\!r_{lr}) := \mathcal{L}[x])$$
$$\textbf{where } r \text{ is transitive in } r_{ul}\!:\!r_{lr}$$
$$x \text{ fresh}$$

$$\mathtt{more}([]; [(r^I,x^I)\ldots]; \phi(r_{ul}\!:\!r_{lr}) := l) \rightsquigarrow \qquad \text{[SYNTH-MAP]}$$
$$\mathtt{done}(\phi(r_{ul}\!:\!r_{lr}) := \{\mathtt{MAP}(\lambda(x^I,\ldots).l, r_{ul}^{I+}\!:\!r_{lr}^{I+}, \ldots)\})$$
$$\textbf{where } [(r^I,x^I)\ldots] \text{ is non-empty}$$
$$r_{ul}^I\ldots = lookup[\![r^I, r_{ul}]\!]\ldots$$
$$r_{lr}^I\ldots = lookup[\![r^I, r_{rl}]\!]\ldots$$
$$r_{ul}^{I+}\!:\!r_{lr}^{I+}\ldots = extd[\![r_{ul}^I\!:\!r_{lr}^I,\ r_{ul}\!:\!r_{lr}]\!]\ldots$$

$$\mathtt{more}([(r^T,x^T)\ldots]; [(r^I,x^I)\ldots]; \phi(r_{ul}\!:\!r_{lr}) := l) \rightsquigarrow \qquad \text{[SYNTH-PFX]}$$
$$\mathtt{done}(\phi(r_{ul}\!:\!r_{lr}) := \{\mathtt{PREFIX}(\lambda(x_1^T,x_2^T,x_3^T,x^I,\ldots).l,$$
$$r_{c0}\!:\!r_{c1},\ r_d,\ r_{r0}\!:\!r_{r1},\ r_{ul}^{I+}\!:\!r_{lr}^{I+}, \ldots)\})$$
$$\textbf{where } [(r^T,x^T)\ldots] \text{ is non-empty}$$
$$r_{ul}^I\ldots = lookup[\![r^I, r_{ul}]\!]\ldots$$
$$r_{lr}^I\ldots = lookup[\![r^I, r_{rl}]\!]\ldots$$
$$r_{ul}^{I+}\!:\!r_{lr}^{I+}\ldots = extd[\![r_{ul}^I\!:\!r_{lr}^I,\ r_{ul}\!:\!r_{lr}]\!]\ldots$$
$$(r_1^T,x_1^T),(r_2^T,x_2^T),(r_3^T,x_3^T) = sort[\![fill[\![[(r^T,x^T)\ldots]]\!]]\!]$$
$$r_d = lookup[\![r_2^T, r_{ul}]\!]$$
$$r_{c0} = lookup[\![r_1^T, r_{ul}]\!]$$
$$r_{r0} = lookup[\![r_3^T, r_{ul}]\!]$$
$$r_{c1} = \mathtt{R}(row[\![r_{lr}]\!])\mathtt{C}(column[\![r_{c0}]\!])$$
$$r_{r1} = \mathtt{R}(row[\![r_{r0}]\!])\mathtt{C}(column[\![r_{lr}]\!])$$

Fig. 4. The $\rightsquigarrow$ relation for rewriting cell array formulas into λ-calc. The rules are explained in detail in Sect. 3.2.

encountered transitive reference; *sort* sorts the three substitutions after their respective references, as described above.

3.3 Preemptive Cycle Detection

Rewriting cell arrays to array formulas changes the dependency structure of the spreadsheet: where before a cell of the cell array may only have depended on a single cell the of input range, it now depends on the entire range. The rewritten cell has become part of an unpacked array, whose formula explicitly references the aforementioned range. It is easy to come up with an example that would lead to the creation of cyclic dependencies if rewritten. We require two or more cell arrays that refer to cells of each other. Rewriting the contrived spreadsheet shown in Fig. 5 leads to the creation of cyclic dependencies.

	A	B
1	=B1	1
2	=B2	=A1+B1
3	=B3	=A2+B2

$\leadsto$

	A	B
1	={MAP(λ(x).x,B1:B3)}	1
2	={MAP(λ(x).x,B1:B3)}	={PREFIX(λ(x,y,z).x+y,A2:A3,A1,B1:B1)}
3	={MAP(λ(x).x,B1:B3)}	={PREFIX(λ(x,y,z).x+y,A2:A3,A1,B1:B1)}

Fig. 5. A spreadsheet (top) whose rewritten variant (bottom) contains cyclic dependencies. The cell arrays A1:A3 and B1:B3 are not copy equivalent. Rewriting both results in an explicit cyclic dependency between the array formulas: ϕ(A1:A3) refers to B1:B3 and ϕ(B2:B3) refers to A2:A3.

To avoid this, we perform a preemptive detection of cyclic references. We walk the reference graph from each intransitive cell reference and each cell from the initial row and column, and check that we never arrive at a cell that is part of the cell array. We use a depth-first search without repetition to detect possible cyclic references. If we detect one, we do not rewrite the cell array.

3.4 Correctness

We do not currently have a formal proof of correctness for our rewriting semantics. However, the slightly informal semantics in Sect. 2 for MAP and PREFIX are carefully chosen to capture the semantics of the original cell array structure, so we believe that our rewriting semantics are correct. The proof would require a formal semantics for spreadsheet recalculation and functions on arrays, which is beyond the scope of this paper.

With a formal semantics, we believe that one can show that rewritten cell arrays are observationally equivalent to the original formulas for cell arrays with and without transitive cell references and hence prove that the rewriting semantics is correct. More formally, if

$$\texttt{more}([]; []; \phi(r_1\!:\!r_2) := u) \rightsquigarrow \texttt{done}(\phi(r_1\!:\!r_2) := \{e\})$$

and $\phi(r_1 : r_2) := u$ evaluates to v, then we want to prove that $\phi(r_1 : r_2) := \{e\}$ also evaluates to v.

4   Implementation

We have implemented the rewriting semantics from Sect. 3 in Funcalc [17], a prototype spreadsheet engine with efficient sheet-defined functions. The formula language in Funcalc is higher-order. We use a modified variant of Funcalc, where bulk operations on arrays are executed in parallel.

Instead of writing our own detection of cell arrays, we piggyback on Funcalc's algorithm for rebuilding the support graph [17, Sect. 4.2.9], which runs in linear time in the number of cells in the cell array.

4.1   Parallelization Strategies

Since Funcalc runs on the .Net platform, we use the parallelization mechanisms from the Task Parallel Library [14]. We can parallelize MAP by iterating over either rows or columns in a parallel for-loop. Parallelizing the PREFIX function is slightly more complicated.

Recall from Sect. 2 that, in order to compute the value at $X[i,j]$ we must already have computed $X[i, j-1]$, $X[i-1, j]$ and $X[i-1, j-1]$. Hence, there exists a sequential dependency between the computations.

Figure 6 illustrates the order in which PREFIX processes parts of the argument array. Even though both q_2 and q_3 depend on q_1, there is no sequential dependency between q_2 and q_3. We can therefore compute the prefix of q_2 and q_3 in parallel. When both are computed, we can proceed to compute q_4. We use this parallelization scheme recursively on each sub-array and stop recursing as soon as either a minimum size is reached or if we have spawned as many parallel tasks as there are processors.

4.2   Handling Over-Generalization

We can describe relative references in terms of their *stride*:

$$stride[\![\text{R}[i_1]\text{C}[i_2]]\!] = \max(|i_1|, |i_2|)$$

In real-world spreadsheets, it may happen that a transitive reference has a stride larger than one, but the PREFIX function and its variants do not generalize to

Fig. 6. Wave front scheme of the `PREFIX` function. We process from the top left to the bottom right of the 2D array, as indicated by the red arrows. The quadrants q_2 and q_3 depend on q_1, while q_4 depends on all of these, as indicated by the blue arrows. Values γ, δ and ρ are initial values at the fringes, as described in Sect. 2

such references. Hence, we cannot directly rewrite cell arrays with transitive cell references of a stride larger than one.

Strides larger than one seem to be artifacts of the generality of the support graph rebuilding algorithm (see Sect. 4). Our key observation here is that one can turn transitive cell references into intransitive cell references by splitting up the cell array into two sub-arrays. Consider the cell array R5C1:R15C5 whose expression contains the transitive cell reference R[−5]C[0]. We can split it up into the two sub-arrays R5C1:R10C5 and R11C1:R15C5, in both of which the reference R[−5]C[0] is intransitive.

We call the rewriting algorithm recursively on each of the sub-arrays until we either end up with a cell array that has transitive cell references with stride at most one, or until there is only a single cell left, in which case we abort.

5   Performance Evaluation

To demonstrate the feasibility of our technique, we have conducted performance benchmarks on synthetic and real-world spreadsheets. To avoid the overhead of excess parallelism, we impose a minimum of 64 cells per cell array on the rewriting algorithm, such that smaller cell arrays will not be rewritten. Times for rewriting are not included in the measurements, since we consider this a one-time operation. For comparison, we also benchmark performance for naively launching a parallel task per cell.

Our benchmarks are the average of 100 full recalculations of the entire spreadsheet. Full recalculation is easier to control during automatic benchmarks, but does not reflect how rewriting cell arrays may affect the dependency structure of spreadsheets negatively for efficient minimal recalculation.

Funcalc runs on the .Net platform. To trigger JIT compilation, we run three warm-up iterations which we do not count prior to benchmarking. Our test machines are an Intel i7-6500U with four cores at 2.5 GHz and 32 GB of RAM, 64 bit Windows 7 and .Net Framework 4.7, as well as an Intel Xeon E5-2680 v3 with 48 cores at 2.5 GHz and 32 GB of RAM, 64 bit Windows 10 and .Net Framework 4.6.2. We only use 32 cores on the Xeon.

5.1 Spreadsheet Selection

We use two contrived, idealized spreadsheets to measure the isolated effect of rewriting transitive and intransitive cell arrays. Both contain one cell array of size 100×100. The first one contains an intransitive cell array that applies the sinus function on each input cell. The second one computes a cell array's prefix sum using transitive cell references and then calls the sinus function on the result of each cell.

Furthermore, we have chosen three spreadsheets from Filby's [7] book from the EUSES corpus [8], as well as three Funcalc-related spreadsheets for synthetic benchmarks. All of these sheets contain large cell arrays.

Finally, we use real-world spreadsheets from the EUSES spreadsheet corpus [8]. We have selected twelve spreadsheets with relatively large and relatively many cell arrays. Selection criteria were (1) applicability of our rewriting technique and (2) effort required to make the spreadsheets compatible with Funcalc. Funcalc syntax differs from Excel in a number of ways, which requires modifications to the sheets. Additionally, we have implemented some Excel and VBA functions as sheet-defined functions[1].

5.2 Results

Table 1 shows speedup after rewriting idealized spreadsheets with only intransitive or only transitive cell references. On the i7, we achieve good parallel speedup for intransitive cell arrays; on the Xeon, parallelism doesn't scale. The very large speedup for transitive cell arrays is likely due to (1) using a more specialized machinery to refer to values in other cells; and (2) that Funcalc compiles the functions we synthesize to byte-code, which alleviates the overhead of interpreting the expression in each cell, as during Funcalc's "standard" recalculation.

Table 1. Average speedup and standard deviation for 100 recalculations of idealized spreadsheets that only consist of either an intransitive or transitive cell array of size 100×100. Speedup is relative to sequential recalculation on the same machine; higher is better.

	Intel i7	Intel Xeon
Intransitive	2.77 ± 0.317	3.14 ± 0.059
Transitive	11.26 ± 0.881	10.3 ± 0.655

Figure 7 shows the speedup after rewriting the more realistic spreadsheets. On the i7, we achieve good speedups for synthetic spreadsheets. Running on the Xeon with eight times as many cores does not improve performance. On both machines,

---

[1] The Funcalc compatible spreadsheets from the EUSES corpus are available at https://github.com/popular-parallel-programming/funcalc-euses/.

the average speedup for real-world spreadsheets is lower than we would expect, given the numbers from Table 1. We have two explanations for this.

First, the achievable speedup is bound by Amdahl's law [9, Sect. 1.5]. If a spreadsheet contains 4500 cells with formulas and a single intransitive cell array of size 500, then the maximum speedup factor we can expect to see on 32 cores is roughly 1.26. This holds for both synthetic and real-world spreadsheets. Unless rewriteable cell arrays either dominate the spreadsheet, as in `financial.xml` and `PLANCK.xml`, or contain very costly computations, as in `testsdf.xml`, the overall performance will still be determined by the sequential computations.

Secondly, real-world spreadsheets have undergone continuous development and are often cluttered with small experiments. Their design is often less stream-lined towards a single large computation than that of synthetic spreadsheets. Even if there are lots of disjoint computations, our technique is unable to exploit these unless they are structured in an array-like fashion.

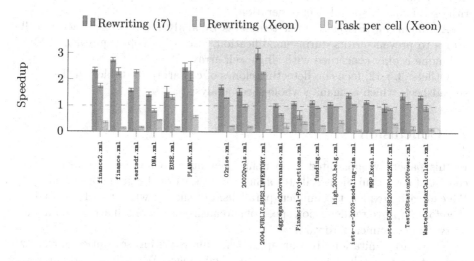

Fig. 7. Average benchmark results over 100 runs for synthetic (left part) and real-world (right part on gray background) spreadsheets. Values are speedup factors over sequential performance on the same machine; higher is better. Error bars indicate the standard deviation.

6   Alternative Usages and Related Work

Neither parallel recalculation of spreadsheets nor high-level structure analysis are new ideas. To our knowledge, however, no prior work has combined both in a practical application of functional programming.

Wack [19] focused on a dataflow approach to whole-spreadsheet paralleliza-tion, in contrast to our idea that harnesses local array parallelism. Yoder and Cohn [20,21] investigate spreadsheets from a theoretical point of view, also with data flow parallelism in mind. They observe that high-level array programming intuitively maps to spreadsheets [21]; this is the core of our technique.

Much research on high-level spreadsheet structures focuses on user understanding; either by highlighting areas with equal or similar formulas [15], whose definition is highly related to cell arrays, or by drawing dataflow diagrams [11] to illustrate relations between sheets and cell arrays. Our rewriting technique could be adapted to give such a high-level overview over operations on cell arrays by displaying the synthesized function.

Rewriting of cell arrays is related to template synthesis from spreadsheets. Isakowitz et al. [13] describe a method to synthesize either a model from a spreadsheet or instantiate a spreadsheet from a model. The notable difference to our work is that they generate a whole-sheet model. Furthermore, they use an external language to describe the model, whereas we perform source-to-source rewriting. Generating local high-level abstractions, as opposed to whole-sheet models, could be useful for expert spreadsheet developers when devising algorithms, similar to spreadsheet generation.

Abraham and Erwig [1] infer templates by analyzing references across cell arrays to prevent errors during modification, also using copy equivalence. Our technique is only concerned with single cell arrays.

Others [3, 5, 12] focus on detecting clones of cell arrays or tables on the same spreadsheet, which is again a whole-sheet analysis.

7   Conclusion

In this paper, we presented a rewriting semantics to rewrite cell arrays that consist of copy equivalent cells to higher-order functional expressions on arrays. We can easily exploit the implicit parallelism of these rewritten cell arrays and therefore improve recalculation speed of spreadsheets where cell arrays dominate on typical consumer hardware.

There are limitations to our approach. Our rewriting semantics currently does not support cell arrays that reference cell ranges. We believe that this will be easy to add. We have furthermore not yet presented a formal proof that our rewriting semantics preserves the semantics of the cell array's expression.

Naively rewriting all detectable cell arrays can introduce cyclic references and hence change the semantics of the original spreadsheet. Detecting these before rewriting comes at the cost of an additional walk of the dependency graph. Moreover, the parallel speedup we can achieve is limited by the ratio of parallelizable cell arrays to inherently sequential dependencies in the spreadsheet.

Our experimental results show that only spreadsheets consisting of large cell arrays achieve good speedups on consumer hardware. This suggests that our rewriting approach should not be automatic but instead a manual tool for expert spreadsheet developers, and also that it makes sense to investigate how our technique can be combined with other parallelization techniques, for instance data flow parallelism.

References

1. Abraham, R., Erwig, M.: Inferring templates from spreadsheets. In: ICSE 2006
2. Casimir, R.J.: Real programmers don't use spreadsheets. ACM SIGPLAN Not. Homepage Arch. **27**(6), 10–16 (1992)
3. Cheung, S.C., Chen, W., Liu, Y., Xu, C.: CUSTODES: automatic spreadsheet cell clustering and smell detection using strong and weak features. In: ICSE 2016
4. Dou, W., Cheung, S.C., Wei, J.: Is spreadsheet ambiguity harmful? Detecting and repairing spreadsheet smells due to ambiguous computation. In: ICSE 2014
5. Dou, W., Cheung, S.C., Gao, C., Xu, C., Xu, L., Wei, J.: Detecting table clones and smells in spreadsheets. In: FSE 2016
6. Dou, W., Xu, C., Cheung, S.C., Wei, J.: CACheck: detecting and repairing cell arrays in spreadsheets. IEEE Trans. Softw. Eng. **43**(3), 226–251 (2016)
7. Filby, G. (ed.): Spreadsheets in Science and Engineering. Springer, New York (1998). https://doi.org/10.1007/978-3-642-80249-2
8. Fisher, M., Rothermel, G.: The EUSES spreadsheet corpus: a shared resource for supporting experimentation with spreadsheet dependability mechanisms. In: WEUSE I
9. Herlihy, M., Shavit, N.: The Art of Multiprocessor Programming. Elsevier/Morgan Kaufmann, Amsterdam (2008). ISBN 9780123705914
10. Hermans, F., Murphy-Hill, E.: Enron's spreadsheets and related emails: a dataset and analysis. In: ICSE 2015
11. Hermans, F., Pinzger, M., van Deursen, A.: Supporting professional spreadsheet users by generating leveled dataflow diagrams. In: ICSE 2011
12. Hermans, F., Sedee, B., Pinzger, M., van Deursen, A.: Data clone detection and visualization in spreadsheets. In: ICSE 2013
13. Isakowitz, T., Schocken, S., Lucas, H.C.: Toward a logical/physical theory of spreadsheet modeling. ACM Trans. Inf. Syst. **13**(1), 1–37 (1995)
14. Leijen, D., Schulte, W., Burckhardt, S.: The design of a task parallel library. In: OOPSLA 2009
15. Mittermeir, R., Clermont, M.: Finding high-level structures in spreadsheet programs. In: WCRE 2002
16. Sajaniemi, J.: Modeling spreadsheet audit: a rigorous approach to automatic visualization. J. Vis. Lang. Comput. **11**(1), 49–82 (2000)
17. Sestoft, P.: Spreadsheet Implementation Technology: Basics and Extensions. The MIT Press, Cambridge (2014). ISBN 0262526646
18. Smith, T.F., Waterman, M.S.: Identification of common molecular subsequences. J. Mol. Biol. **147**(1), 195–197 (1981)
19. Wack, A.P.: Partitioning dependency graphs for concurrent execution: a parallel spreadsheet on a realistically modeled message passing environment. Ph.D. thesis, Newark, DE, USA (1996)
20. Yoder, A., Cohn, D.L.: Observations on spreadsheet languages, intension and dataflow. Technical report
21. Yoder, A.G., Cohn, D.L.: Domain-specific and general-purpose aspects of spreadsheet language. In: DSL 1997

SNÅRKL: Somewhat Practical, Pretty Much Declarative Verifiable Computing in Haskell

Gordon Stewart$^{(\boxtimes)}$ ⓘ, Samuel Merten ⓘ, and Logan Leland ⓘ

Ohio University, Athens, OH, USA
{gstewart,sm137907,ll734713}@ohio.edu

Abstract. Verifiable computing (VC) uses cryptography to delegate computation to untrusted workers. But in most VC schemes, the delegated program must first be *arithmetized* – expressed as a circuit with multiplication and addition over a finite field. Previous work has compiled subsets of languages like C, LLVM, and bespoke assembly to arithmetic circuits. In this paper, we report on a new DSL for VC, called SNÅRKL ("Snorkel"), that supports encodings of language features familiar from functional programming such as products, case analysis, and inductive datatypes. We demonstrate that simple constraint-minimization techniques are an effective means of optimizing the resulting encodings, and therefore of generating small circuits.

1 Introduction

It is now possible, using today's cryptographic techniques and systems, to execute a computation remotely – on an untrusted computer such as an AWS virtual machine – while verifying locally without re-execution that the computation was done correctly. Due to recent advances in the systems and theory behind this kind of *verifiable computing* (VC), it is occasionally even practical to delegate a computation in this way: depending on the system and computation, the total latency to arithmetize a program (as an arithmetic circuit or set of arithmetic constraints), set up shared parameters like cryptographic keys, remotely execute the computation, and locally verify the result is now just a few orders of magnitude higher than the time it would have taken to execute the computation locally (cf. [16, Sect. 5]).

These performance results have not been easily won, however. Since about 2007,[1] cryptographers have worked to refine the underlying cryptographic and complexity-theoretic techniques – probabilistically checkable proofs [1,2], interactive proofs [13], efficient arguments systems [6]. Most systems now use variants of the protocol and representation published by Gennaro, Gentry, Parno, and Raykova (GGPR) in 2013 [11]. At the same time, researchers in practical cryptography have applied tools from the systems and compilers literatures to build verifiable computing platforms that are approaching practicality [4,8,21].

---

[1] See Walfish and Blumberg ACM survey [22] for a summary of the recent history.

F. Calimeri et al. (Eds.): PADL 2018, LNCS 10702, pp. 36–52, 2018.
https://doi.org/10.1007/978-3-319-73305-0_3

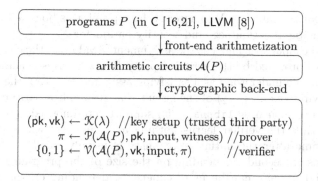

Fig. 1. Architecture of verifiable computing (VC) systems

The architectures of the most recent systems follow a common pattern (Fig. 1). At the top of the VC pipeline, a compiler translates the high-level representation of a program – in a language like C or LLVM – to an equivalent representation either as an arithmetic circuit or as a set of constraints that encodes the behavior of an arithmetic circuit. Only terminating programs can be arithmetized in this way.[2] For example, Fig. 2 gives an arithmetic circuit respresentation of the expression out = if b then x else y. The variables

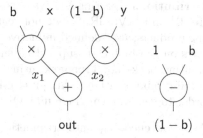

Fig. 2. An arithmetic circuit implementing (out = if b then x else y). The variable b ranges over $\{0,1\}$, a constraint that must be encoded separately.

b, x, and y are input "wires" to the circuit. The italicized variables x_1 and x_2 are internal wires that must be instantiated by the proving party. The gates perform field operations such as multiplication and addition.

In the second phase, a cryptographic backend computes from the circuit representation three subroutines:

- a key generator $\mathcal{K}$ which establishes proving and verification keys to be used by the prover (remote) and verifier (local);
- a prover $\mathcal{P}$ which solves for witness values and constructs a succinct cryptographic proof π that the computation was executed correctly; and
- a verifier $\mathcal{V}$ which checks that the proof is valid.

The system is complete when $\mathcal{V}$ never rejects proofs generated by $\mathcal{P}$. The system is secure when, for adversarial but computationally bounded provers $\mathcal{P}'$, the

---

[2] BCGTV [3] approximates potentially nonterminating programs by first translating to assembly (for the bespoke TINYRAM architecture), then "executing" a bounded number of steps of the program by arithmetizing the transition relation of the underlying instruction set architecture (ISA).

probability that $\mathcal{P}'$ convinces $\mathcal{V}$ to accept a false proof π' is bounded by $\mathsf{negl}(\lambda)$, for some negligible function negl and security parameter λ.

In Fig. 1, the input to $\mathcal{P}$ and $\mathcal{V}$ is the assignment of values to the computation's input variables provided by the verifying party. The witness is generated by the prover, and can be understood as a satisfying assignment – given the inputs – of the internal wires (e.g., x_1, x_2) of the circuit that results from arithmetizing P. Some VC systems, such as `libsnark` [5], support zero-knowledge computation in the sense that the verifier learns nothing about witness when verifying π. Verification time after the initial setup phase is usually small – on the order of milliseconds to seconds, depending on the size of the program input. Key-generation and proving can be more expensive, depending on the number of circuit variables and constraints; `libsnark` reports times in the tens of minutes for large circuits.

Contributions. Existing VC systems support imperative source languages like C [16,21] and LLVM IR [8] but not features found in functional languages like sums, products, user-defined inductive datatypes and case analysis. This paper reports on the first DSL supporting such features that compiles to a verifiable computing back-end, `libsnark`, using tools that apply systematic and general constraint-minimization techniques to the arithmetic encodings of such programs in order to generate small circuits. Our primary contributions are threefold:

- We show encodings into arithmetic constraints of language features familiar from type theory and functional programming: sums and products, inductive datatypes, and case-analysis (Sect. 3). As far as the authors are aware, no other VC tool has direct encodings for these features.
- We demonstrate that straightforward constraint minimization, when applied systematically to the arithmetic encodings of such programs, is a viable method of generating and of solving small circuits. Small circuits lead to concomitant low key-generation and proving times (Sect. 5).
- We implement everything described in the paper as a prototype Haskell DSL, called SNÅRKL ("Snorkel"), that is open source and freely available.[3]

Organization. In Sect. 2 we introduce the fundamentals of SNÅRKL by example. Section 3 presents the compilation toolchain, and gives arithmetic encodings of language features like sums, products, inductive datatypes, and case-analysis. Section 4 is devoted to SNÅRKL's constraint-minimization algorithm. We report in Sect. 5 on preliminary measurements of SHA3 KECCAK-f and other microbenchmarks and, in Sect. 6, put SNÅRKL in its broader research context.

Zero-Knowledge Proof. SNÅRKL's verifiable computing backend, `libsnark`, supports the construction of zero-knowledge proofs (the π's of Fig. 1), in which the verifier $\mathcal{V}$ learns only the validity of the witness, not the witness itself. While we do not stress zero-knowledge proof in the remainder of the paper, we point out here that SNÅRKL is entirely compatible with zero knowledge as implemented in

---

[3] https://github.com/gstew5/snarkl.

Listing 2.1. Syntax of SNÅRKL's typed expression language TExp

```
1   data TExp :: Ty → * → * where
2     TEVar :: TVar ty → TExp ty a
3     TEVal :: Val ty a → TExp ty a
4     TEUnop :: Typeable ty1 ⇒ TUnop ty1 ty → TExp ty1 a → TExp ty a
5     TEBinop :: (Typeable ty1, Typeable ty2) ⇒
6       TOp ty1 ty2 ty → TExp ty1 a → TExp ty2 a → TExp ty a
7     TEIf :: TExp 'TBool a → TExp ty a → TExp ty a → TExp ty a
8     TEAssert :: Typeable ty ⇒ TExp ty a → TExp ty a → TExp 'TUnit a
9     TESeq :: TExp 'TUnit a → TExp ty2 a → TExp ty2 a
10    TEBot :: Typeable ty ⇒ TExp ty a
11  data Ty where
12    TField :: Ty
13    TBool :: Ty
14    TArr :: Ty → Ty
15    TProd :: Ty → Ty → Ty
16    TSum :: Ty → Ty → Ty
17    TMu :: TFunct → Ty
18    TUnit :: Ty deriving Typeable
19  data TFunct where
20    TFConst :: Ty → TFunct
21    TFId :: TFunct
22    TFProd :: TFunct → TFunct → TFunct
23    TFSum :: TFunct → TFunct → TFunct
24    TFComp :: TFunct → TFunct → TFunct deriving Typeable
```

libsnark: whether π can be made zero knowledge depends on the cryptographic backend (libsnark), not the compiler that arithmetizes programs (SNÅRKL).

2 SNÅRKL by Example

SNÅRKL programs are embedded in Haskell through the use of GHC's [12] RebindableSyntax and DataKinds language extensions. RebindableSyntax co-opts Haskell's do-notation for sequencing SNÅRKL commands. DataKinds is used to embed SNÅRKL's type system into Haskell. As an example, consider the following snippet of SNÅRKL code.

```
1   arr_ex :: TExp 'TField Rational → Comp 'TField
2   arr_ex x = do
3     a ← arr 2
4     forall [0..1] (λ i → set (a,i) x)
5     y ← get (a,0)
6     z ← get (a,1)
7     return $ y + z
```

Line 3 uses the arr keyword to allocate an array of size 2, bound in the remainder of the function body to variable a. In line 4, SNÅRKL's forall combinator, of type

$$[b] \rightarrow (b \rightarrow Comp\ 'TUnit) \rightarrow Comp\ 'TUnit$$

initializes a. The function set in the body of the lambda is the standard array update, with complement get satisfying the usual McCarthy laws. Lines 5 and 6 read twice from a, at indices 0 and 1.

In the type of arr_ex, TExp t r is the type of expressions in SNÅRKL's typed intermediate language, with t ranging over SNÅRKL types and the metavariable r a Haskell type. Comp is SNÅRKL's compilation monad (about which we say more in Sect. 3). Higher-level SNÅRKL code is built using combinators that operate over and return TExps, in the style of an embedded DSL. The full syntax of the TExp expression language is given in Listing 2.1. In what follows, we discuss the relevant points.

SNÅRKL's *type system* is embedded into Haskell using the GADT [23] TExp. TExp is parameterized by a SNÅRKL type t, of (data-)kind Ty, and a Haskell type r (of kind $*$). The type system is mostly standard. TField is the type of field elements in the underlying field, typically **Rational**. In expression types TExp t r, we often omit the r to save space in listings. In each such case, r is specialized to **Rational**. The constructor TEBot provides an escape hatch (used to compile sums and bounded recursion, Sect. 3). There are no constructors for the complex types in Ty (TProd, TSum, etc.). Values of these types are built using higher-level Haskell combinators.

To support user-defined inductive types, the recursive-type constructor TMu quantifies over a user-defined type functor TFunct. In the signatures of SNÅRKL's (iso-recursive) roll and unroll combinators, we use a Haskell type family Rep

```
type family Rep (f :: TFunct) (x :: Ty) :: Ty
type instance Rep ('TFConst ty) x = ty
type instance Rep 'TFId x = x
type instance Rep ('TFProd f g) x = 'TProd (Rep f x) (Rep g x) ...
```

to encode the semantics of these functors. The signatures of roll and unroll are:

```
unroll :: ... ⇒ TExp ('TMu f) → Comp (Rep f ('TMu f))
roll :: ... ⇒ TExp (Rep f ('TMu f)) → Comp ('TMu f)
```

Elided in ... are Typeable-instance constraints for type Rep f ('TMu f) and the promoted[4] type f. These constraints, which appear elsewhere in Listing 2.1,

---

[4] The effect of GHC's DataKinds extension is to implicitly promote datatypes like TFunct to kinds, and constructors of user-defined datatypes (TFConst, TFId, etc.) to type constructors. Type constructors that have been promoted in this way are marked by an initial apostrophe, as in 'TFId.

facilitate reflective programming on TExps. For example, it is possible to write a function var_is_bool with type Typeable ty ⇒ TVar ty → **Bool** that determines statically whether a given program variable x is boolean.

More interesting programs are also encodable. Consider the following code, which implements the type of untyped lambda-calculus terms.

type TTerm = 'TMu TF
type TF = 'TFSum ('TFConst 'TField) ('TFSum 'TFId ('TFProd 'TFId 'TFId))

In math, the functor TF is $F(\tau) = \mathsf{TField} + \tau + \tau \times \tau$. A lambda term (in DeBruijn-style) is either a field element (type TField) encoding a DeBruijn index, an abstraction with body of type μF, or an application (a pair of lambda terms $\mu F \times \mu F$). The constructor for application is:

```
1  app :: TExp TTerm → TExp TTerm → Comp TTerm
2  app t1 t2 = do
3    t ← pair t1 t2
4    t' ← inr t
5    v ← inr t'
6    roll v
```

Assuming t1 and t2 are lambda terms (SNÅRKL expressions of type TTerm), pair t1 t2 constructs an expression t of type 'TProd TTerm TTerm (line 3). Lines 4 and 5 inject t to an expression v of type 'TField + (TTerm + (TTerm × TTerm)). In line 6, we roll v as an expression of type 'TMuTF = TTerm.

3   Compiling to R1CS

Encoding a small functional language into Haskell is all well and good. But how do we go about compiling to arithmetic circuits? Fig. 3 provides an overview of the general strategy. The target language, Rank-1 Constraint Systems (R1CS),

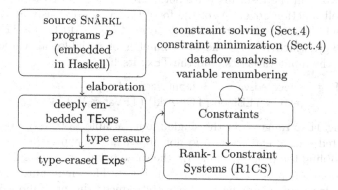

Fig. 3. The SNÅRKL compiler

SNÅRKL Code (from Sect.2)	Step-by-Step Elaboration to TExp
1 arr_ex2 :: Comp 'TField	// **let** elaboration environment $\rho_0 = \emptyset$ **in**
2 arr_ex2 = **do**	
3 x ← fresh_input	// freshvar x_0; mark x_0 as input; **let** x = TEVar x_0 **in**
4 a ← arr 2	// freshloc l_0; freshvars a_0, a_1; **let** a = l_0 **in**
5	// **let** $\rho_1 = \rho_0[(a, 0) \mapsto a_0][(a, 1) \mapsto a_1]$ **in**
6 set (a,0) x	// **let** $\rho_2 = \rho_1[(a, 0) \mapsto x]$ **in**
7 set (a,1) x	// **let** $\rho_3 = \rho_2[(a, 1) \mapsto x]$ **in**
8 y ← get (a,0)	// **let** y = $\rho_3[(a, 0)]$ **in**
9 z ← get (a,1)	// **let** z = $\rho_3[(a, 1)]$ **in**
10 **return** $ y + z	// TEBinop (TOp Add) y z

Fig. 4. SNÅRKL to TExp

is `libsnark`'s input specification. At the top of the compiler stack, we elaborate SNÅRKL programs P to the deeply embedded TExp language of Sect. 2. Then we erase types, which facilitates later phases, by compiling TExps to a similar but untyped language Exp. Exps are compiled to a language of CONSTRAINTS designed for easy optimization. It is at this CONSTRAINTS level that we run most optimizations, including constraint minimization (Sect. 4) and dataflow analysis. The minimizer doubles as a constraint solver for generating witness values (given inputs) to assign to the internal "wires" in the circuit representation of a computation (the witness of Fig. 1).

3.1 Elaboration

Elaboration uses a code-generation state monad Comp that incorporates gensym for fresh names and a compile-time symbol table that maps "objects" in the source language (values of nonscalar types such as arrays, products, sums) to associated constraint variables. As an example, consider the array code we presented in Sect. 2, re-listed and slightly modified in the first column of Fig. 4.

The main difference is at line 3 where the variable x is now a program input (an "input wire" in the resulting arithmetic circuit) as opposed to a parameter of the Haskell function arr_ex. Also, the forall that was previously at line 4 has been unrolled. This function arr_ex2 is elaborated by SNÅRKL to a TExp package (TExpPkg), which records the total number of variables allocated during elaboration, the input variables, and the TExp itself:

$$\text{TExpPkg \{ allocated\_vars = 3, input\_vars = } \{x_0\},$$
$$\text{texp = TEBinop (TOp Add) (TEVar } x_0\text{) (TEVar } x_0\text{) \}}$$

The resulting TExp ranges over the single input variable x_0 (the two other variables allocated during elaboration do not appear). The expression returns the result of doubling the input variable x_0, the same behavior as arr_ex2.

The elaboration process is explained in Fig. 4. The environment $\rho : \text{loc} \times \text{int} \to \text{var} + \text{loc}$ maps symbolic locations (introduced during elaboration) and integer offsets to SNÅRKL program variables and other symbolic locations. The declaration x ← fresh_input on line 3 allocates a new variable TEVar x_0 bound to x in the remainder of the function. In line 4, we "allocate" an array (of field elements) of size 2. At elaboration, the effect of this command is to:

- generate a fresh symbolic location l_0, the base of the array a;
- generate two fresh variables a_0 and a_1, the array's initial contents;
- update the elaboration environment ρ to map (a, 0) to a_0 and (a, 1) to a_1.

The array updates of lines 6 and 7 overwrite ρ to map both (a, 0) and (a, 1) to the input variable x. The array gets of lines 8 and 9 look up the bindings associated with a at offsets 0 and 1. The Haskell metavariables a, x, y, and z are used only during elaboration, and are distinct from the object-language variables x_0, a_0, and a_1, which may appear in the generated TExp. The location l_0 is drawn from a distinct namespace and does not appear in the elaborated expression.

3.2 Products, Sums, Recursion

Products can be elaborated as if they were heterogeneous two-dimensional arrays. For example, the code fragment **do** { p ← pair 1.0 2.0; fst_pair p } that builds a pair and projects its first element elaborates to

TESeq (TEAssert (TEVar p_0) (TEVal 1.0))
  (TESeq (TEAssert (TEVar p_1 (TEVal 2.0))) (TEVar p_0)).

Here p_0 and p_1 are variables that stand for the first and second projections of the pair. Behind the scenes, a location p = l_0 was allocated such that $\rho[(p, 0)]$ maps to p_0 and $\rho[(p, 1)]$ maps to p_1. TEAssert (TEVarp_0) (TEVal 1.0) – asserting that the variable p_0 equals 1.0 – ensures that p_0 is resolved, in the eventual rank-1 constraint system, to the value 1.0.

Compiling sums is trickier. Since the target execution model is arithmetic circuits (specifically, their generalization as the arithmetic constraint language R1CS), we cannot – when implementing case-analysis – just "jump" to the code for the left or right of a match on an expression like

  e : TExp ('TSum 'TBool TField) **Rational**.

Whether e was built with inl or inr may depend on an input variable of the compiled circuit, as in:

  do { b ← fresh_input; x ← inl false; y ← inr 0.0; z ← **if** b **then** x **else** y;
    case_sum z (λ b_0 → ...) (λ n_0 → ...) }

SNÅRKL's solution is to elaborate both branches of the case_sum and combine the results, dependent on the value of the input b (not known at compile-time). To avoid large blowups in the size of the generated code, the compiler performs constant propagation to eliminate spurious branches whenever possible. When a conditional cannot be determined statically, the compiler *zips* (Fig. 5) the branches to the leaves of the syntax tree to ensure that expressions of compound type (TSum, TProd, etc.) are represented by location expressions at elaboration time – an invariant that facilitates the compilation of eliminators such as fst_pair.

Internally, sums are represented as pairs (b, (e1, e2)) where b is a boolean expression indicating left or right, e1 is the left-hand expression of the sum (if one exists) and e2 the right-hand (if one exists). In the constructors inl and inr, the uninstantiated branch (right for inl, left for inr) is populated by the expression TEBot, which may assume any type. The elaborator implements a simple static analysis to track both TEBots and boolean expressions with known values.

Modulo such optimizations, case_sum is implemented:

$$\boxed{\vdash^b_\tau \; e1 \bowtie e2 = e12}$$

$$\frac{}{\vdash^b_{\text{TUnit}} e1 \bowtie e2 = \text{TEVal VUnit}} \; \text{zipUnit} \qquad \frac{\tau \in \{\text{TField}, \text{TBool}\}}{\vdash^b_\tau e1 \bowtie e2 = \text{TEIf b e1 e2}} \; \text{zipBase}$$

$$\frac{\vdash^b_{\tau_1} (\text{fst\_pair } e1) \bowtie (\text{fst\_pair } e2) = p1 \qquad \vdash^b_{\tau_2} (\text{snd\_pair } e1) \bowtie (\text{snd\_pair } e2) = p2}{\vdash^b_{\text{TProd } \tau_1 \; \tau_2} e1 \bowtie e2 = \text{pair p1 p2}} \; \text{zipProd}$$

$$\frac{\vdash^b_{\text{TProd TBool (TProd } \tau_1 \; \tau_2)} (\text{rep\_sum } e1) \bowtie (\text{rep\_sum } e2) = p}{\vdash^b_{\text{TSum } \tau_1 \; \tau_2} e1 \bowtie e2 = \text{unrep\_sum p}} \; \text{zipSum}$$

$$\frac{\vdash^b_{\text{Rep f (TMu f)}} (\text{unroll } e1) \bowtie (\text{unroll } e2) = r}{\vdash^b_{\text{TMu f}} e1 \bowtie e2 = \text{roll r}} \; \text{zipRec}$$

Fig. 5. Type-directed zipping

```
case_sum :: forall τ₁ τ₂ τ. ... ⇒
  (TExp τ₁→ Comp τ)→ (TExp τ₂ → Comp τ)→ TExp ('TSum τ₁ τ₂)→ Comp τ
case_sum f1 f2 e =
  do { let p = rep_sum e;
       b ← fst_pair p; p_rest ← snd_pair p;
       e1 ← fst_pair p_rest; e2 ← snd_pair p_rest;
       le ← f1 e1; re ← f2 e2;
       zip_vals τ (not b) le re }
```

When e = (b, (e1, e2)), neither e1 nor e2 is known to evaluate to TEBot, and the value of b is not known statically, case_sum generates code for the left branch (f1 e1) and the right branch (f2 e2) and applies the transformation zip_vals – the $\bowtie$ relation of Fig. 5 – to the resulting expressions. Indexing the relation are the type τ of e1 and e2 and the boolean conditional **not** b (inl is defined to let b = false, hence the negation). The $\bowtie$ relation maps two TExps e1 and e2 to a result e12 in which the b branch – deciding between e1 and e2 – has been pushed to the leaves of the syntax tree, enforcing the invariant that TExps of nonbase-type such as TSum or TProd are represented as symbolic locations during elaboration. The relation itself is defined by case analysis on the structure of τ. In the definitions of case_sum and $\bowtie$, the coercions

rep_sum :: TExp ('TSum τ_1 τ_2) $\to$ TExp ('TProd 'TBool ('TProd τ_1 τ_2))
unrep_sum :: TExp ('TProd 'TBool ('TProd τ_1 τ_2)) $\to$ TExp ('TSum τ_1 τ_2)

cast between sums as products (rep_sum), and back again (unrep_sum).

SNÅRKL supports recursive functions through the use of a (bounded) fixpoint combinator fix whose type is:

fix :: ((TExp τ_1 $\to$ Comp τ_2) $\to$ (TExp τ_1 $\to$ Comp τ_2)) $\to$ TExp τ_1 $\to$ Comp τ_2

At a user-configurable depth[5] d the expression fix f e returns TEBot, indicating delayed error; if the output of the resulting circuit, given user inputs, depends on the TEBot expression (it exceeds the recursion bound – perhaps the user input is the serialization of a list of size $d + 1$), the circuit evaluation will go wrong.

3.3   From TExps to R1CS

Compiling TExps to Rank-1 Constraint Systems is more straightforward, and in general follows previous work on arithmetizing general-purpose programs. The main difference is that between TExp and R1CS we employ an intermediate constraint representation CONSTRAINTS that is more suitable than R1CS for optimization. We present R1CS first, then CONSTRAINTS and the encoding of select TExps into CONSTRAINTS. Section 4 shows how to optimize CONSTRAINTS.

The input specification language of libsnark, Rank-1 Constraint Systems (R1CS), builds on the QAP arithmetic constraint representation of GGPR [11]. A rank-1 constraint system is a system of constraints on degree-1 polynomials over a finite field, e.g.:

$$A \quad * \quad B \quad = \quad C$$
$$(2x_0 + 3x_1) * (-3x_1) = 2x_0 + 4x_1$$

The variables x_0, x_1 range over a finite field $\mathcal{F}_p$ of prime characteristic p. A system of such constraints encodes the behavior of an arithmetic circuit (cf. GGPR [11] for additional details).

Listing 3.1. SNÅRKL's representation of Rank-1 Constraint Systems (R1CS)

```
1  type Assgn a = Map.IntMap a
2  data Poly a where Poly :: Field a ⇒ Assgn a → Poly a
3  data R1C a where R1C :: Field a ⇒ (Poly a, Poly a, Poly a) → R1C a
4  data R1CS a = R1CS {
5    rlcs_clauses :: [R1C a], rlcs_num_vars :: Int,
6    rlcs_in_vars :: [Var], rlcs_out_vars :: [Var],
7    rlcs_gen_witness :: Assgn a → Assgn a }
```

[5] The recursion bound is necessary to ensure that elaboration terminates.

SNÅRKL's representation of R1CS is given in Listing 3.1. An assignment (line 1, Assgn a) maps variables (type Var = Int) to values of type a. A rank-1 polynomial (line 2) is just an assignment in which a has the operators of a field and variable -1 is by convention the constant term. A rank-1 constraint (line 3) is a polynomial constraint $A * B = C$ in which A, B, and C are all polynomials. The R1CS type collects a list of rank-1 constraints, the number of variables appearing in the constraints, which variables are inputs and outputs, and a function, r1cs_gen_witness, that maps input assignments to satisfying witnesses.

SNÅRKL's constraint language presents an abstraction layer on top of R1CS, making it easier to optimize R1CS-style encodings. The main datatype is:

```
data Constraint a =
    CAdd a [(Var,a)]
  | CMult (a,Var) (a,Var) (a,Maybe Var)
  | CMagic Var [Var] ([Var] → State (SEnv a) Bool).
```

$$\llbracket\ e\ \rrbracket_{out} = [CAdd\ ...,...]$$

$$\llbracket\ EVar\ x\ \rrbracket_{out} = [CAdd\ 0\ (fromList\ [(out, 1),\ (x, -1)])]$$
$$\llbracket\ EVal\ c\ \rrbracket_{out} = [CAdd\ c\ (fromList\ [(out, -1)])]$$
$$\llbracket\ EAssert\ (EVar\ x1)\ e2\ \rrbracket_{out} = \llbracket\ e2\ \rrbracket_{x1}$$
$$\llbracket\ EBinop\ Or\ e1\ e2\ \rrbracket_{out} = \llbracket\ e1\ \rrbracket_{e1\_out} +\!\!+ \llbracket\ e2\ \rrbracket_{e2\_out}$$
$$+\!\!+ \llbracket\ EBinop\ Mult\ (EVar\ e1\_out)\ (EVar\ e2\_out)\ \rrbracket_{e12\_out}$$
$$+\!\!+ \llbracket\ EBinop\ Sub\ (EBinop\ Add\ (EVar\ e1\_out)\ (EVar\ e2\_out))\ (EVar\ out)\ \rrbracket_{e12\_out}$$

Fig. 6. TExps to CONSTRAINTS (excerpts)

The type a is usually specialized to field elements. The additive constraint CAdd a [(Var, a)] asserts that the linear combination of a constant (of type a) with the variable–coefficient terms ([(Var, a)]) equals 0. For example, the constraint CAdd 2 [(x,1), (y,−3)] is $2 + 1x - 3y = 0$. Multiplicative constraints CMult ... encode facts like $2x*3y = -7z$. In general, CMult (c,x) (d,y) (e,**Just** z) means $cx * dy = ez$. When the second element of the third pair is **Nothing**, the interpretation is $cx * dy = e$.

Compiling both additive and multiplicative constraints to R1CS is straightforward. For example, the additive constraint CAdd 3 [(y,−5), (z,23)] yields:

R1C (const_poly one) (Poly (fromList [$(x_c, 3)$, (y,−5), (z,23)])) (const_poly **zero**).

The variable $x_c = -1$ is reserved for the polynomial's constant term. The function const_poly c constructs the constant polynomial equal c. Multiplicative constraints are equally straightforward. For example, CMult (3,x) (4,y) (5,**Just** z) results in the rank-1 constraint $3x * 4y = 5z$.

So-called CMagic constraints are hints to SNÅRKL's constraint solver that encode nondeterministic "advice" – used to resolve the values of variables introduced by the nondeterministic encodings of expressions such as disequality tests (about which we say more below).

Listing 4.1. Constraint minimization

```
1   simplify_rec :: Field a ⇒ ConstraintSet a → State (SEnv a) (ConstraintSet a)
2   simplify_rec S = do
3     S' ← simplify_once S
4     if size S' < size S then simplify_rec S'
5     else if S − S' ⊆ ∅ then return S' else simplify_rec S'
6   where simplify_once S =
7     do {S' ← go ∅ S; remove_tauts S'}
8       go W U | size U == 0 = return W
9       go W U | otherwise =
10        let (given, U') = deleteFindMin U in do
11        in do given' ← subst_constr given
12              given_taut ← is_taut given'
13              if given_taut then go W U'
14              else do {learn given';
15                       go (W ∪ {given'}) U'}
```

Compiling TExps to constraints follows previous work (e.g., [16,18]), yet some of the encodings are nonobvious. Consider boolean disjunction in TExps of the form TEBinop (TOp Or) e1 e2. The encoding – after types have been erased – is given in Fig. 6, along with that of variables, values, and assertions. The compilation relation $[\![\cdot]\!]_{out}$ is indexed by an output variable out that corresponds one-to-one with the output "wire" of the resulting arithmetic circuit, itself encoded as a list of constraints of type Constraint a. For example, compilation of EVar x, with output variable out, constructs the polynomial constraint $0 + 1*out + -1x = 0$ asserting that out = x. The encoding EVal c is similar.

To compile boolean disjunction EBinop Or e1 e2, we first recursively compile e1 and e2 – sending their values through fresh output variables e1_out and e2_out. Then we compile the TExp that encodes the constraint

$$e1\_out + e2\_out − out = e1\_out * e2\_out.$$

As long as e1_out, e2_out, and out range over boolean values 0, 1 – a constraint we encode separately as the additional fact $x*x = x$ for each boolean variable x – the equality above is satisfiable iff out = e1_out ∨ e2_out.

Many of the remaining compilation rules are straightforward (we do not show them in Fig. 6). One exception is disequality testing. Here SNÅRKL uses a nondeterministic encoding borrowed from PINOCCHIO [16] and Setty et al. [18] that relies on CMagic constraints to resolve the values of a nondeterministic witness variable. Assume the expression is y = x!=0 ? 1 : 0, which we represent in C-style syntax. Both x and y are variables. The encoding is, there exists an m such that both $x*m = y$ and $(1−y)*x = 0$. Since m is not uniquely determined by the above two facts, we use a CMagic constraint to resolve its value when solving for the witnesses of Fig. 1: if x = 0 then let m = 0. Otherwise, let m equal the modular multiplicative inverse x^{-1} of x in the underlying field $\mathcal{F}_p$.

4   Constraint Minimization

Key generation and proving times in VC systems typically depend on the size, e.g., in number of constraints, of the arithmetization of the source program. Previous work (e.g., [3,8,16]) uses clever encodings of individual program constructs to optimize encoding size but no system we know of applies systematic constraint minimization.

Why is systematic optimization problematic? If the original source program is interpreted in order to find satisfying assignments, as in systems such as GEP-PETTO [8], then optimizing the constraint system makes it more difficult to map particular variables and constraints back to program points in the source program; minimization may remove variables and constraints entirely. We solve this problem by having the constraint minimizer perform double duty; for a particular problem instance with concrete inputs provided by the verifying party, simply rerun the constraint minimizer with those concrete initial values. The result, using the constraint minimization algorithm we describe in this section, is a satisfying assignment for the entire constraint system.

Both constraint minimization and solving happen at the level of SNÅRKL's CONSTRAINTS intermediate language. The main data structure is an environment SEnv a = SEnv { eqs :: UnionFind a, solve_mode :: SolveMode } that stores a union-find instance, for mapping variables to their equivalence classes (or to constants) as new variable equalities are learned during optimization, and a flag solve_mode = UseMagic | JustSimplify that tells the simplifier whether to ignore CMagic constraints. If solve_mode = UseMagic (the simplifier is in solve mode), magic constraints are used to resolve the values of nondeterministic witness variables. Otherwise (simplifier mode), the simplifier ignores CMagic constraints.[6]

The main minimization routines, operating over a set of constraints S, are given in Listing 4.1. The idea (simplify_rec, line 2) is to repeatedly apply the simplification procedure simplify_once (line 7) as long as each application (line 4) successfully removes at least one constraint from the set S, because it was able to determine that the constraint was tautological. It is also possible (line 5) that some constraint has been simplified, yet the total number of constraints remains the same. In this case, we continue simplifying. If no new constraints are removed or simplified, we halt with S'.

The function go (beginning at line 8) operates over two sets, a working set of constraints W and an unselected set U. Originally, all constraints are in U. At each iteration, the function deletes the smallest constraint from U (under a particular total order, line 10), simplifies the constraint (line 11) under the equalities currently recorded in the simplification environment, SEnv, then checks whether the resulting constraint is tautological (line 13). If it is, the tautological constraint is removed and go continues to the next iteration, throwing the clause away (line 13). Otherwise (line 14), we attempt to learn new equalities from the constraint (between variables and variables, and variables and constants) and continue (line 15) with the new clause in W.

---

[6] It would be unsound to rely on these constraints to learn new facts.

The function learn (called in line 14) implements just a few simplification rules. For example, from constraints CAdd − 1[(x,c)] (expressing $-1 + cx = 0$) we learn $x = c^{-1}$ as long as c is invertible. Likewise, from CAdd 0 [(xc), (y,d)] (expressing $0 + cx + dy = 0$) we learn $x = y$ as long as c = −d and c is nonzero. The function subst_constr, which substitutes the equalities currently in context into a constraint, is also straightforward. When applied to, e.g., CAdd constraints it replaces all variables by their union-find roots, replaces certain variables by constants, folds constants, and filters out terms with coefficient 0.

5   Measurements

Since SNÅRKL uses a standard VC backend, our analysis in this section forgoes a direct evaluation of the practicality of the underlying cryptography[7] in favor of answering the following questions:

1. Does SNÅRKL's general-purpose constraint minimizer (Sect. 4) produce circuits of comparable size to those encoded by hand in systems like PINOCCHIO?
2. How much overhead is imposed, over proof generation in libsnark, by using the constraint minimizer of Sect. 4 to generate circuit witnesses?

We consider the four benchmarks described in Fig. 8. For benchmarks that have been implemented in PINOCCHIO (**Fixed Matrix** and **Input Matrices**) we report (Fig. 7a) the number of constraints generated by SNÅRKL vs. those in PINOCCHIO's manual encoding, as reported in [16]. In each case, we generate just one additional constraint, resulting from the fact that we return the sum of the resulting matrix in addition to performing the multiplication (thus preventing over-optimization of the resulting circuit by the SNÅRKL compiler).

#**Constraints**	SNÅRKL	PINOCCHIO
Fixed Matrix	601	600
Input Matrices	347,901	347,900

(a) Constraints per benchmark

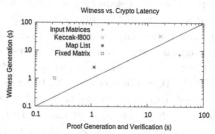

(b) Witness generation vs. cryptographic proof generation and verification latency

Fig. 7. Results

For each benchmark, we also measured (using Citerion [15]; confidence intervals were small) the relative latency of witness generation as performed by the constraint minimizer of Sect. 4 versus cryptographic proof generation and verification in libsnark (Fig. 7b). Both of these procedures must be performed online once per problem instance. The results here are more mixed. Only one benchmark (**Input Matrices**) falls below the line, and therefore has lower witness generation than proof generation and verification latency. In the remaining

---

[7] libsnark was evaluated in [3].

Fixed Matrix Multiply a fixed $n \times n$ matrix M (known at compile time) by an n-length input vector A, resulting in the n-length output vector $M \cdot A$. Output the sum of the elements in $M \cdot A$. This microbenchmark reproduces the "Fixed Matrix, Medium" benchmark of PINOCCHIO [16, Sect.4.3], with parameter $n = 600$.

Input Matrices Multiply an $n \times n$ input matrix M_1 by a second $n \times n$ input matrix M_2. Output the sum of the elements in $M_1 \cdot M_2$. This microbenchmark reproduces PINOCCHIO's "Two Matrices, Medium" benchmark [16, Sect.4.3] with $n = 70$.

Keccak-f(800) The main function of SHA3's "sponge" construction. The lane width ($= 32$) is a parameter known at compile time. As input, Keccak-f(800) takes a 3-dimensional array of size $5 \times 5 \times 32$ bits. It outputs the exclusive or of the 800-bit array that results after applying 22 rounds of Keccak-f.

Map List Map the function $(\lambda x.x + 1)$ over a list of field elements of size 50 and return the list's last element. The size and contents of the list are circuit inputs. The generated circuit supports input lists up to size 100 elements.

Fig. 8. Description of the benchmarks

benchmarks, the cost of witness generation exceeds that of proof generation but the difference is usually small. This is despite the fact that our constraint minimizer has not yet been highly optimized.

6 Related Work

There has been a great deal of work in verifiable computing over the past few years [3,4,7–10,16,18,21]. With PINOCCHIO [16] and its most recent incarnation GEPPETTO [8], researchers at MSR and elsewhere have built VC systems that incorporate novel techniques like MultiQAPs for sharing state between reusable circuit components, and energy-saving circuits for reducing cryptographic costs in programs with conditional branches. These new techniques are complementary to the work we present in this paper. Because SNÅRKL compiles to the clearly defined R1CS interface (Fig. 3), future improvements to libsnark resulting from cross-fertilization by tools such as PINOCCHIO and GEPPETTO will bring immediate benefit, even without change to the compiler.

In parallel to systems like PINOCCHIO, PANTRY [7] and its successor BUFFET [21] (both refinements of previous systems GINGER [18] and PEPPER [19]) showed new techniques for efficiently compiling RAM programs. BUFFET, for example, adapts the RAM abstraction of TINYRAM to the compilation model of PANTRY, resulting in large cryptographic speedups over previous systems. That said, BUFFET's imperative input language is still a subset of C; while other tools support other (generally, subsets of) imperative languages like LLVM [8], no tool we know of directly supports functional programs as in SNÅRKL.

The work on TINYRAM [3,4], which is implemented as an extension of core libsnark, represents an interesting third point in the design spectrum: instead of directly compiling C programs to constraints, TINYRAM modifies gcc to output assembly programs in a small bespoke assembly language, then "executes" the programs by encoding the semantics of the TINYRAM ISA as arithmetic constraints. This execution strategy is implementable in SNÅRKL. In fact, one immediate goal of future work is the implementation of other kinds of abstract machines beyond just ISAs – such as interpreters and type-checkers for lambda calculi. With such tools, it may be possible to recast, e.g., dependent type systems in a VC mold: the proof that term e has type τ is a VC proof π that the arithmetization of a type-checking function f applied to e evaluates to Some τ. Finally, the design of SNÅRKL's frontend has benefited from long lines of work on embedded DSLs (e.g., [14]) and on multi-stage programming (e.g., [20]). Recent work on specialized type rules for DSLs (e.g., [17]) may provide a method for improving the reporting of type errors in SNÅRKL's embedded type system.

7   Conclusion

Verifiable computing is approaching practicality. But there is still work to do. In this paper, we report on SNÅRKL ("Snorkel"), a DSL embedded in Haskell for functional programming against a verifiable computing backend. We demonstrate that simple constraint minimization techniques – when applied systematically to a carefully designed intermediate representation – are an effective means of generating small circuits. Our DSL and implementation support familiar features from functional programming such as sums, products, inductive datatypes, and case analysis.

References

1. Arora, S., Lund, C., Motwani, R., Sudan, M., Szegedy, M.: Proof verification and the hardness of approximation problems. JACM **45**(3), 501–555 (1998)
2. Arora, S., Safra, S.: Probabilistic checking of proofs: a new characterization of NP. JACM **45**(1), 70–122 (1998)
3. Ben-Sasson, E., Chiesa, A., Genkin, D., Tromer, E., Virza, M.: SNARKs for C: verifying program executions succinctly and in zero knowledge. In: Canetti, R., Garay, J.A. (eds.) CRYPTO 2013. LNCS, vol. 8043, pp. 90–108. Springer, Heidelberg (2013). https://doi.org/10.1007/978-3-642-40084-1_6
4. Ben-Sasson, E., Chiesa, A., Tromer, E., Virza, M.: Succinct non-interactive zero knowledge for a von Neumann architecture. In: USENIX Security (2014)
5. Ben-Sasson, E., et al.: The libsnark library. https://github.com/scipr-lab/libsnark. Accessed 23 Sep 2015
6. Brassard, G., Chaum, D., Crépeau, C.: Minimum disclosure proofs of knowledge. J. Comput. Syst. Sci. **37**(2), 156–189 (1988)
7. Braun, B., Feldman, A.J., Ren, Z., Setty, S., Blumberg, A.J., Walfish, M.: Verifying computations with state. In: SOSP, pp. 341–357. ACM (2013)
8. Costello, C., et al.: Geppetto: versatile verifiable computation. In: Proceedings of the 36th IEEE Symposium on Security and Privacy, vol. 15. IEEE (2014)
9. Fournet, C., Kohlweiss, M., Danezis, G., Luo, Z.: ZQL: a compiler for privacy-preserving data processing. In: USENIX Security, pp. 163–178 (2013)
10. Fredrikson, M., Livshits, B.: ZØ: an optimizing distributing zero-knowledge compiler. In: USENIX Security (2014)

11. Gennaro, R., Gentry, C., Parno, B., Raykova, M.: Quadratic span programs and succinct NIZKs without PCPs. In: Johansson, T., Nguyen, P.Q. (eds.) EURO-CRYPT 2013. LNCS, vol. 7881, pp. 626–645. Springer, Heidelberg (2013). https://doi.org/10.1007/978-3-642-38348-9_37
12. GHC Team. The glorious Glasgow Haskell compilation system user's guide (2005)
13. Goldwasser, S., Micali, S., Rackoff, C.: The knowledge complexity of interactive proof-systems. In: Proceedings of the Seventeenth Annual ACM Symposium on Theory of Computing, pp. 291–304. ACM (1985)
14. Mainland, G., Morrisett, G., Welsh, M.: Flask: staged functional programming for sensor networks. In: ICFP 2008 (2008)
15. O'Sullivan, B.: The Criterion library. http://www.serpentine.com/criterion. Accessed 23 Sep 2015
16. Parno, B., Howell, J., Gentry, C., Raykova, M.: Pinocchio: nearly practical verifiable computation. In: Proceedings of the 35th IEEE Symposium on Security and Privacy, pp. 238–252. IEEE (2013)
17. Serrano, A., Hage, J.: Type error diagnosis for embedded DSLs by two-stage specialized type rules. In: Thiemann, P. (ed.) ESOP 2016. LNCS, vol. 9632, pp. 672–698. Springer, Heidelberg (2016). https://doi.org/10.1007/978-3-662-49498-1_26
18. Setty, S.T., et al.: Taking proof-based verified computation a few steps closer to practicality. In: USENIX Security (2012)
19. Setty, S.T., McPherson, R., Blumberg, A.J., Walfish, M.: Making argument systems for outsourced computation practical (sometimes). In: NDSS (2012)
20. Taha, W., Sheard, T.: Multi-stage programming with explicit annotations. In: PEPM (1997)
21. Wahby, R.S., Setty, S., Ren, Z., Blumberg, A.J., Walfish, M.: Efficient RAM and control flow in verifiable outsourced computation. In: NDSS (2015)
22. Walfish, M., Blumberg, A.J.: Verifying computations without reexecuting them. CACM 58(2), 74–84 (2015)
23. Xi, H., Chen, C., Chen, G.: Guarded recursive datatype constructors. In: POPL, pp. 224–235. ACM (2003)

Hygienic Source-Code Generation
Using Functors
(Extended Abstract)

Karl Crary[(⊠)]

Carnegie Mellon University, Pittsburgh, USA
crary@cs.cmu.edu

Abstract. Existing source-code-generating tools such as Lex and Yacc
suffer from practical inconveniences because they use disembodied code
to implement actions. To prevent this problem, such tools could generate closed functors that are then instantiated by the programmer with
appropriate action code. This results in all code being type checked in its
appropriate context, and it assists the type checker in localizing errors
correctly. We have implemented a lexer generator and parser generator
based on this technique for both Standard ML and Haskell.

1 Introduction

Compiler implementers have a love-hate relationship with source-code-
generating tools such as Lex [6] (which generates lexers from regular expressions)
and Yacc [4] (which generates shift-reduce parsers from context-free grammars).
These tools automate the some of the most tedious parts of implementing a
parser, but they can be awkward to use.

One of the main awkward aspects of such tools is the *disembodied code problem.* To build a lexer or a parser, these tools cobble together snippets of code
(each implementing an action of the lexer/parser) supplied by the programmer
in a lexer/parser specification file. Unfortunately, the code snippets, as they
appear in the specification file, are divorced from their ultimate context. The
tools manipulate them as simple strings.[1]

This makes programming awkward in several ways. Functions and other values are passed into the snippets using identifiers that are bound nowhere in
the programmer's code, nor even introduced by a pseudo-binding such as **open**.
Rather, the snippet is copied into a context in which such identifiers are in scope.
This can make code difficult to read.

More importantly, disembodied code makes debugging challenging, because
the code seen by the compiler bears little resemblance to the code written by

---

[1] Such strings may even include syntax errors, which are duly copied into the output
code. Typically the tool does not even ensure that delimiters are matched.

© Springer International Publishing AG 2018
F. Calimeri et al. (Eds.): PADL 2018, LNCS 10702, pp. 53–60, 2018.
https://doi.org/10.1007/978-3-319-73305-0_4

the programmer. For example, consider the following line from an ML-Lex [1] specification:

```
{whitespace}+ => ( lex () );
```

This line tells the lexer to skip any whitespace it encounters by matching it and then calling itself recursively to continue. (Note that `lex` is an example of an identifier introduced implicitly when the snippet is copied.) ML-Lex converts the line into the Standard ML code:

```
fun yyAction0 (strm, lastMatch : yymatch) =
    (yystrm := strm; ( lex () ))
```

This output code already is not very easy to read. However, the problem is greatly exacerbated by the familiar phenomenon in typed functional languages that type checkers are often bad at identifying the true source of a type error. Suppose we introduce an error into the specification by omitting the argument to `lex`:

```
{whitespace}+ => ( lex );
```

We now obtain[2] several pages of error messages looking like:

```
foo.lex.sml:1526.25-1526.70 Error: operator and
operand don't agree [tycon mismatch]

  operator domain: yyInput.stream * action * yymatch
  operand:         yyInput.stream *
                   (yyInput.stream * yymatch -> unit
                   -> (?.svalue,int) ?.token)
                   * yymatch
in expression:
  yyMATCH (strm,yyAction0,yyNO_MATCH)
```

and none of the errors is anywhere near the copied snippet containing the error.

The problem is related to the issue of variable hygiene in macro expansion [5]. In both cases, the programmer writes code (a lexer/parser action, or macro argument) divorced from its ultimate context and then—after processing—that code is dropped verbatim into its ultimate context. In the setting of macros, this sets the scene for variable capture to occur, which is nearly always erroneous. In lexer generators, variable capture often is actually desired (consider the `lex` identifier), but, as observed above, it is nevertheless difficult to reason about and to debug.

Accordingly, we are interested in source-code generation in which all code is type-checked in the same context in which it is written. We call this *hygienic source-code generation* by analogy to hygienic macro expansion, which ensures the same thing for macros.

---

[2] Using Standard ML of New Jersey v100.68.

An obvious way to accomplish hygienic source-code generation is to have the tool type-check every snippet before it assembles them into output code. But, this approach is unattractive in practice, because it necessitates including all the apparatus of parsing, elaboration, and type-checking as part of a tool that does not otherwise need all that apparatus.

We propose a simpler and cleaner alternative: Rather than type-check disembodied code in context, we dispense with disembodied code altogether. To accomplish this, the tool—rather than assembling snippets of source code into a program—generates a functor that abstracts over the code that used to reside in snippets. The programmer then applies the functor in order to instantiate the lexer or parser with specific action implementations.

A third alternative, arguably more principled than ours, is to implement the lexer/parser generator in a type-safe metaprogramming language such as MetaML [8] or its cousins. With such an approach, as in ours, the action implementations would be type-checked in context, without any need to duplicate compiler apparatus. Furthermore, it would remove the need to write the lexer/parser specification and action implementations in two separate places, as our proposal requires. On the other hand, this alternative requires one to use a special programming language. We want an approach compatible with pre-existing, conventional functional programming languages, specifically Standard ML and Haskell.

Finally, in some problem domains one may consider avoiding generated source code entirely. For example, in parsing, some programmers find parser combinators [2,3] to be a suitable or even preferable alternative to Yacc-like tools. Nevertheless, many programmers prefer traditional LR parser generators for various reasons including error reporting and recovery, and ambiguity diagnostics. In this work we take it as given that source-code generation is preferred, for whatever reason.

At first blush, our proposal might seem to replace one sort of disembodied code with another. This is true in a sense, but there is a key difference. The code in which the functor is applied is *ordinary code,* submitted to an ordinary compiler. That compiler then type checks the action code (that formerly resided in snippets) in the context in which it now appears, which is the functor's argument.

As a practical matter, each action becomes a distinct field of the functor argument, and consequently each action is type-checked independently, as desired. The type of the functor is already known, so an error in one action will not be misinterpreted as an error in all the other actions.

Employing this design, we have implemented a lexer generator, called CM-Lex, and a parser generator, called CM-Yacc. Each tool supports Standard ML and Haskell.[3] Both tools are available on-line at:

www.cs.cmu.edu/~crary/cmtool/

In the remainder of this abstract we illustrate the concept using the lexer generator for Standard ML. The full paper discusses the problem of actions that

---

[3] The Haskell version generates Haskell code, but is implemented in Standard ML and shares most of its implementation with the Standard ML version.

call the lexer recursively, and it discusses the parser generator and how the tools are adapted to Haskell. It can be found on-line at:

www.cs.cmu.edu/~crary/papers/2018/cmtool.pdf

2 Lexing Functor Generation

The following is a very simple CM-Lex specification:

```
name LexerFun
alphabet 128

function f : t =
   (seq 'a 'a) => aa
   (seq 'a (* 'b) 'c) => abc
```

The specification's first two lines indicate that CM-Lex should produce a functor named **LexerFun**, and that it should generate a 7-bit parser (any symbols outside the range $0 \ldots 127$ will be rejected automatically).

The remainder gives the specification of a lexing function named **f**. The function will return a value of type **t**, and it is defined by two regular expressions. Regular expressions are given as S-expressions using the Scheme Shell's SRE notation[4] [7].

Thus, the first arm activates an action named **aa** when the regular expression aa is recognized. The second activates an action named **abc** when the regular expression ab^*c is recognized.

Observe that the specification contains no disembodied code. The actions are simply given names, which are instantiated when the resulting functor is applied.

From this specification, CM-Lex generates the following Standard ML code:[5]

```
functor LexerFun
   (structure Arg :
      sig
        type t

        type info = { match : char list,
                      follow : char stream }

        val aa : info -> t
        val abc : info -> t
      end)
   :>
   sig
      val f : char stream -> Arg.t
   end
 = ... implementation ...
```

---

[4] Although SREs are less compact than some other notations, we find their syntax is much easier to remember.

[5] We simplify here and in the following examples for the sake of exposition.

When the programmer calls the functor, he provides the type t and the actions aa and abc, both of which produce a t from a record of matching information. The functor then returns a lexing function f, which produces a t from a stream of characters.

Although the programmer-supplied actions can have side effects, the lexer itself is purely functional. The input is processed using lazy streams (the signature for which appears in Fig. 1). Each action is given the portion of the stream that follows the matched string as part of the matching information.

```
signature STREAM =
  sig
    type 'a stream
    datatype 'a front =
        Nil
      | Cons of 'a * 'a stream

    val front : 'a stream -> 'a front
    val lazy : (unit -> 'a front) -> 'a stream
  end
```

Fig. 1. Lazy streams

As an illustration of how the functor might be applied, the following program processes an input stream, printing a message each time it recognizes a string:

```
structure Lexer =
  LexerFun
  (structure Arg =
    struct
      type t = char stream

      type info = { match : char list,
                    follow : char stream }

      fun aa ({follow, ...}:info) =
        ( print"matched aa\n"; follow )

      fun abc ({follow, ...}:info) =
        ( print "matched ab*c\n"; follow )
    end)

fun loop (strm : char stream) =
  (case front strm of
     Nil => ()
   | Cons _ => loop (Lexer.f strm))
```

The function `Lexer.f` matches its argument against the two regular expressions and calls the indicated action, each of which prints a message and returns the remainder of the stream.

Observe that the implementations of the actions (the fields `aa` and `abc` of the argument structure) are ordinary Standard ML code. As one consequence, the action code faces the standard type checker. Moreover, each action's required type is unambiguously given by `LexerFun`'s signature and the type argument `t`, so error identification is much more accurate.

For example, suppose we replace the `aa` action with an erroneous implementation that fails to return the remainder of the stream:

```
fun aa ({follow, ...}:info) =
  ( print "matched aa\n" )
```

The type checker is able to identify the source of the error precisely, finding that `aa` has the type `unit` instead of `t`:

```
example.sml:8.4-29.12 Error: value type in
structure doesn't match signature spec
    name: aa
  spec:   ?.Arg.info -> ?.Arg.t
  actual: ?.Arg.info -> unit
```

2.1 An Expanded Specification

We may add a second function to the lexer by simply adding another function specification:

```
function g : u =
  (or (seq 'b 'c) (seq 'b 'd)) => bcbd
  epsilon => error
```

In the parlance of existing lexer generators, multiple functions are typically referred to as multiple *start conditions* or *start states,* but we find it easier to think about them as distinct functions that might or might not share some actions. In this case, the function `g` is specified to return a value of type `u`. Since `u` might not be the same type as `t`, `g` cannot share any actions with `f`.

The first arm activates an action named `bcbd` when the regular expression $bc + bd$ is recognized. The second arm activates an action named `error` when the empty string is recognized. Like other lexer generators, CM-Lex prefers the longest possible match, so an epsilon arm will only be used when the input string fails to match any other arm. Thus, the latter arm serves as an error handler.[6]

---

[6] In contrast, the specification for `f` was inexhaustive, so CM-Lex added a default error handler that raises an exception.

From the expanded specification, CM-Lex generates the functor:

```
functor LexerFun
   (structure Arg :
      sig
         type t
         type u

         type info = { match : char list,
                       follow : char stream }

         val aa : info -> t
         val abc : info -> t
         val bcbd : info -> u
         val error : info -> u
      end)
   :>
   sig
     val f : char stream -> Arg.t
     val g : char stream -> Arg.u
   end
 = ...implementation...
```

3   Conclusion

We argue that functor generation is a cleaner mechanism for source-code-generating tools than assembling snippets of disembodied code. The resulting functor makes no demands on the surrounding code (other than a few standard libraries), and so it is guaranteed to type check.[7] The programmer never need look at the generated code.

In contrast, with a snippet-assembling tool, an error in any snippet will — even in the best case — require the programmer to look at generated code containing the snippet. More commonly, the programmer will need to look at lots of generated code having nothing to do with the erroneous snippet.

We have demonstrated the technique for lexer and parser generation, but there do not seem to be any limitations that would preclude its use for any other application of source-code generation.

---

[7] More precisely, it is guaranteed to type check in an initial context containing standard libraries and other module definitions. Unfortunately, Standard ML does not quite enjoy the weakening property, so the resulting functor is not guaranteed to type check in *any* context. Pollution of the namespace with datatype constructors and/or infix declarations for identifiers that are used within the generated functor will prevent it from parsing correctly. This is one reason why it is considered good practice in SML for all code to reside within modules.

References

1. Appel, A.W., Mattson, J.S., Tarditi, D.R.: A lexical analyzer generator for Standard ML, October 1994. www.smlnj.org/doc/ML-Lex/manual.html
2. Frost, R., Launchbury, J.: Constructing natural language interpreters in a lazy functional language. Comput. J. **32**(2), 108–121 (1989)
3. Hutton, G.: Higher-order functions for parsing. J. Funct. Program. **2**(3), 323–343 (1992)
4. Johnson, S.C.: Yacc – yet another compiler compiler. Technical Report 32, Bell Laboratories Computing Science, Murray Hill, New Jersey, July 1975
5. Kohlbecker, E., Friedman, D.P., Felleisen, M., Duba, B.: Hygienic macro expansion. In: 1986 ACM Conference on Lisp and Functional Programming, p. 161 (1986)
6. Lesk, M.E.: Lex – a lexical analyzer generator. Technical Report 39, Bell Laboratories Computing Science, Murray Hill, New Jersey, October 1975
7. Shivers, O.: The SRE regular-expression notation, August 1998. Post to the comp.lang.scheme newsgroup, now archived at http://www.scsh.net/docu/post/sre.html
8. Taha, W., Sheard, T.: MetaML and multi-stage programming with explicit annotations. Theor. Comput. Sci. **248**(1–2), 211–242 (2000)

Constraint Programming and Business Rules

Three Is a Crowd: SAT, SMT and CLP on a Chessboard

Sebastian Krings[1]([✉]) [iD], Michael Leuschel[1] [iD], Philipp Körner[1] [iD],
Stefan Hallerstede[2] [iD], and Miran Hasanagić[2] [iD]

[1] Institut für Informatik, Universität Düsseldorf,
Universitätsstr. 1, 40225 Düsseldorf, Germany
{krings,leuschel}@cs.uni-duesseldorf.de, p.koerner@uni-duesseldorf.de
[2] Department of Engineering, Aarhus University, Aarhus, Denmark
{sha,miran.hasanagic}@eng.au.dk

Abstract. Constraint solving technology for declarative formal models has made considerable progress in recent years, and has many applications such as animation of high-level specifications, test case generation, or symbolic model checking. In this article we evaluate the idea of using very high-level declarative models themselves to express constraint satisfaction problems. In particular, we study an old mathematical puzzle from 100 years ago, called the crowded chessboard. We study various high-level and low-level encodings and solutions, covering SAT, SMT and CLP-based solutions of the puzzle. Additionally, we present a new technique combining SAT-solving with CLP which is able to solve the puzzle efficiently.

1 Motivation: Model-Based Constraint Solving

Logic programming and constraint programming are key members of the declarative language paradigm. Logic programs and constraint (logic) programs tend to be much more declarative than traditional imperative programs, but developers still have to consider considerable operational aspects. High-level formal methods languages like B, TLA⁺, or Z, are more declarative still: they were developed to be specification languages, with little concern for execution.[1] In between logic programs and formal methods are logic-based encodings like SMT-LIB.

In this paper, we study a non-trivial constraint satisfaction problem, investigating both the ease of expressing the problem and the solving performance for a range of declarative languages, from Prolog, onto SAT, SMT and high-level formal specification languages. One popular specification language is B [1], which has its roots in first-order predicate logic, with (higher-order) set theory and arithmetic. In that respect, it is quite similar to other formal methods such as TLA⁺, Z or even VDM. Constraint solvers have made a big impact for formal methods in general and B or TLA⁺ in particular, by providing validation technology for *proof* [8,18], *animation* [15], *bounded or symbolic model checking* [13], and *test case generation* [21].

---

[1] Some even argue that formal specifications should be non-executable [11].

© Springer International Publishing AG 2018
F. Calimeri et al. (Eds.): PADL 2018, LNCS 10702, pp. 63–79, 2018.
https://doi.org/10.1007/978-3-319-73305-0_5

We want to turn our focus from constraint solving technology for validating models towards using formal models to express constraint satisfaction problems. The idea is to use the expressivity of the B language and logic to express practical problems, and to use constraint solving technology on these high level models. In [16], we already argued that B is well suited for expressing constraint satisfaction problems in other domains as well. This was illustrated on the Jobs puzzle challenge [24] and we are now solving various time tabling problems [23].

In this paper, we want to present one particular benchmark puzzle, and various ways to solve it. One motivation was that the puzzle was formulated exactly 100 years ago. A more academic motivation is that the puzzle is relatively easy to explain and hence should be relatively easy for other researchers to provide their own solutions in their favorite declarative formalism and compare it with ours.

Indeed, a real-life problem such as the time-tabling problem in [23] is very arduous to describe in an article, and would require considerable investment to write a solution in another formalism, requiring many weeks or months of effort. A puzzle such as the N-queens puzzle, on the other hand, is too simple and allows many very special encodings, which cannot be easily used in real-life, practical problems. The encoding is not really a challenge, and a solution to the N-queens puzzle only provides limited insights into practicality of a formalism.

We feel that the crowded chessboard problem provides the almost perfect middle ground, even though it is a combinatorical problem: the problem can still be explained in a paper, and has some entertaining aspects as well. Furthermore, solutions can be easily checked by a human, provided the solution is rendered graphically. In the following, we investigate different declarative encodings of the problem, considering ease of understanding, correspondance to the problem statement and solving performance. Constraint solving technology can be classified into the following broad categories, which we all experiment with:

- Constraint programming, used in Sects. 3 and 4 and used by PROB's default solver in Sect. 2.1,
- Translation to boolean satisfiability and using SAT solvers in Sect. 5,
- Translation to SMT-LIB and using SMT solvers in Sect. 6.

All models used in this paper are available at: https://github.com/leuschel/crowded-chessboard.

2   The Crowded Chessboard Problem and Its B Solution

The Crowded Chessboard Problem. The crowded chessboard is a 100 year old problem appearing as problem 306 in Dudeney's book [9]. The book provides the following description of the problem:

> "The puzzle is to rearrange the fifty-one pieces on the chessboard so that no queen shall attack another queen, no rook attack another rook, no bishop attack another bishop, and no knight attack another knight. No

notice is to be taken of the intervention of pieces of another type from that under consideration - that is, two queens will be considered to attack one another although there may be, say, a rook, a bishop, and a knight between them. And so with the rooks and bishops. It is not difficult to dispose of each type of piece separately; the difficulty comes in when you have to find room for all the arrangements on the board simultaneously."

Table 1 shows the maximum number of pieces for which the puzzle can still be solved. To gain unsatisfiable benchmarks, we will increment the number of knights.

Table 1. Configurations

board size	♛	♜	♝	♞
5	5	5	8	5
6	6	6	10	9
7	7	7	12	11
8	8	8	14	21
9	9	9	16	29
10	10	10	18	37
11	11	11	20	47
12	12	12	22	57
13	13	13	24	69
14	14	14	26	81
15	15	15	28	94
16	16	16	30	109

2.1 B Solution

We now try to formalise this problem in the B language, as clearly as possible. Our goal here is to make a human readable formalisation of the model, where a human can be convinced that the problem has been modelled correctly. Indeed, in constraint programming it is quite often the case that subtle errors creep into a formalisation, which can go unnoticed for quite some time. Thus, below we also intersperse the formal model with a few visualisations and other sanity checks, to ensure that the model is correct. The LATEX of this section has been derived by executing the model, see [14].

For the visualisations, we first set the dimension n of the board to 5 and thus have the following set of possible indexes on the chessboard: $Idx = \{1, 2, 3, 4, 5\}$. Furthermore, we define the set of chess pieces, including a special piece $Empty$ for empty squares: $PIECES = \{Queen, Bishop, Rook, Knight, Empty\}$.

2.2 Specifying Movements

First, we compute for every position on the board which squares can be reached by a horizontal or vertical move, i.e., a function which returns a set of coordinates that can be attacked from a given position. For example, we have $moveHV(2 \mapsto 3) = \{(1 \mapsto 3), (2 \mapsto 1), (2 \mapsto 2), (2 \mapsto 4), (2 \mapsto 5), (3 \mapsto 3), (4 \mapsto 3), (5 \mapsto 3)\}$, visualised in Fig. 1. This can be expressed in B using a lambda function:

$$moveHV = \lambda(i,j).(\{i,j\} \subseteq Idx \mid \{k,l \mid \{k,l\} \subseteq Idx \land (i,j) \neq (k,l) \land (i = k \lor j = l)\})$$

Now, we compute the diagonal moves, e.g., we have $moveDiag(2 \mapsto 3) = \{(1 \mapsto 2), (1 \mapsto 4), (3 \mapsto 2), (3 \mapsto 4), (4 \mapsto 1), (4 \mapsto 5)\}$, visualised in Fig. 2.

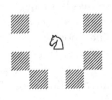

Fig. 1. Rook attack   **Fig. 2.** Bishop attack   **Fig. 3.** Knight attack

$$moveDiag = \lambda(i,j).(\{i,j\} \subseteq Idx \mid \{k,l \mid \{k,l\} \subseteq Idx \wedge (i,j) \neq (k,l) \wedge$$
$$(k-i = l-j \vee i-k = l-j)\})$$

To describe the moves of the knight, we introduce the following auxiliary function to compute the absolute distance between indices:

$$dist = \lambda(i,j).(i \in \mathbb{Z} \wedge j \in \mathbb{Z} \mid \text{IF } i \geq j \text{ THEN } i-j \text{ ELSE } j-i \text{ END}).$$

Using it, the knight's moves can now be described as follows:

$$moveK = \lambda(i,j).(\{i,j\} \subseteq Idx \mid \{k,l \mid \{k,l\} \subseteq Idx \wedge i \neq k \wedge$$
$$j \neq l \wedge dist(i,k) + dist(j,l) = 3\})$$

For example, we have $moveK(2 \mapsto 3) = \{(1 \mapsto 1),(1 \mapsto 5),(3 \mapsto 1),(3 \mapsto 5),(4 \mapsto 2),(4 \mapsto 4)\}$, visualized in Fig. 3. We can now assemble all of these into a single higher-order function, which for each piece returns the attacking function (which in turn for each position on the board returns the set of attacked positions):

$$attack = \{(Rook \mapsto moveHV),(Bishop \mapsto moveDiag),(Knight \mapsto moveK),$$
$$(Queen \mapsto \lambda(p).(p \in (Idx \times Idx) \mid moveHV(p) \cup moveDiag(p))),$$
$$(Empty \mapsto ((Idx) \times (Idx)) \times \{\varnothing\})\}$$

2.3   Specifying the Number of Pieces

After having modelled how the pieces move, we now describe how many pieces of each type we want to place on the board as follows. Note that the second conjunct asserts the number of all placed figures, including the empty field, to be n^2. That is, it computes the number of empty squares from the given figures. The only hard-coded part is the number of knights (5 in this case):

$$nrPcs \in PIECES \rightarrow 0 \ldots n^2 \wedge \Sigma(p).(p \in PIECES \mid nrPcs(p)) = n^2 \wedge$$
$$((Queen \mapsto n) \in nrPcs \wedge (Rook \mapsto n) \in nrPcs \wedge$$
$$(Bishop \mapsto 2*n-2) \in nrPcs \wedge (Knight \mapsto 5) \in nrPcs)$$

This gives rise to the following solution for $n = 5$:

$$nrPcs = \{(Queen \mapsto 5), (Rook \mapsto 5), (Bishop \mapsto 8),$$
$$(Knight \mapsto 5), (Empty \mapsto 2)\}$$

2.4   Solving the Crowded Chessboard Puzzle

Solving the crowded chessboard puzzle now amounts to solving the predicates:

$board \in Idx \times Idx \to PIECES$

$\forall P.(P \in PIECES \Rightarrow card(\{p | p \in dom(board) \wedge board(p) = P\}) = nrPcs(P))$

$\forall(pos, piece).((pos \mapsto piece) \in board$
$$\Rightarrow \forall pos2.(pos2 \in attack(piece)(pos) \Rightarrow board(pos2) \neq piece))$$

Observe how compact the core B representation of the problem is. The first predicate sets up the board and specifies the possible pieces that can be put on the board. The second predicate specifies how many pieces of each kind should be placed on the board. The third predicate posits that no piece can attack another piece of the same kind. In case we want to add a new kind of piece or change the rules for an existing piece, these three predicates would remain unchanged; one would only have to adapt the definition of the *attack* function. The first solution found by PROB for n = 5 is visualized in Fig. 4.

Fig. 4. Solution

Of course, the model could be improved by adding further (implied) constraints, e.g., by asserting that bishops have to be placed on border cells. However, by doing so, we would decrease correspondence to the original problem formulation, sacrificing comprehensibility for solving speed.

2.5   New CLP and SAT Integration

We believe that the above encoding is compact, elegant, easy to understand, validate and adapt by a human. Unfortunately, as it stands, this encoding can be solved by PROB only for small values of n. Given the success of the SAT approach later in Sect. 5, one may wonder why PROB's SAT backend [20] cannot be applied to the B model instead of the default CLP solver.

The reason is the higher order nature of the model: the SAT backend relies on Kodkod [26], a relational model finder translating its input language to SAT. However, Kodkod can only translate certain first-order constructs and data structures. For this reason, the technique in [20] statically splits a predicate P to be solved into a part P_{SAT} that can be translated by Kodkod and another one P_{CLP} that will be solved by PROB's default solver. The solving now proceeds by first performing deterministic propagation in P_{CLP}, possibly instantiating values in P_{SAT}. Then, P_{SAT} is solved, the solution of which is fed into PROB for solving P_{CLP}. The core problem is that, when solving P_{CLP} we cannot generate new constraints to be shipped to the SAT solver. This is exactly what we would need in our case: let PROB evaluate the higher-order *attack* function from Sect. 2.2, unroll the involved quantifiers and then ship simple first-order constraints to a SAT solver.

We have implemented exactly this style of integration in reaction to the challenge posed by the crowded chessboard. The idea is to allow the user to annotate parts of the constraint as to be treated by a SAT solver. Note that these parts can be inside quantifiers, in which case *ProB* would expand these quantifiers and (possibly) compute relevant values using higher-order datastructures.

We annotate implications, equalities, inequalities and cardinality constraints for SAT and let PROB deal with the rest, e.g., determining and applying the higher-order *attack* function. Doing so, the first two predicates given in Sect. 2.4 can completely be given to a SAT solver via Kodkod. The third one however is unrolled by PROB, only the inner predicate gets solved by Kodkod:

$$\overbrace{\forall(piece, i, j, i2, j2).(i \mapsto j \in (1\ldots n)\times(1\ldots n) \wedge i2 \mapsto j2 \in attack(piece)(i \mapsto j)}^{ProB(CLP)}$$
$$\underbrace{\Rightarrow board1((i-1)*n+j) = piece \Rightarrow board1((i2-1)*n+j2) \neq piece)}_{Kodkod(SAT)}$$

Observe that we have rewritten the quantification over $(piece, i, j, i2, j2)$ slightly, to enable PROB to completely expand the quantifier and apply the higher-order function *attack*.

3   A Prolog CLP(FD) Solution

Given that PROB's default CLP solver does not scale for the high-level B model, we have written a direct encoding of the crowded chessboard problem in SICStus Prolog using the finite domain library CLP(FD) [5]. As the following code snippet shows, the chessboard is encoded as a list of length n of lists of n finite domain variables each, in the range 0 to 4. The value 0 denotes an empty square, 1 a queen, 2 a rook, 3 a bishop, and 4 a knight. The entry predicate is solve(N,K,Sol), where N specifies the size of the board and K the number of knights to be placed. The solution is returned in *Sol*; by backtracking all solutions can be found.

```
solve(N,Knights,Sol) :-
    length(Sol,N),
    maplist(pieces(N),Sol),
    append(Sol,AllPieces),
    ... constraint setup ...
    labeling([ffc],AllPieces).
pieces(N,L) :- length(L,N), clpfd:domain(L,0,4).
```

Above, *AllPieces* is a flattened list of the domain variables. Below, we explain the most important part of the constraint setup. To ensure that we place the correct number of pieces of each type onto the board we use the `global_cardinality` constraint of CLP(FD):

```
Bishops is 2*N-2,
Empty is N*N - 2*N - Bishops - Knights,
global_cardinality(AllPieces,[0-Empty,1-N,2-N,3-Bishops,4-Knights])
```

We use the following auxiliary predicates for rows, columns and diagonals to ensure that queens, rooks and bishops do not attack each other:

```
exactly_one(Piece,List)  :- count(Piece,List,'#=',1).
at_most_one(Piece,List)  :- count(Piece,List,'#<',2).
```

For example, `maplist(exactly_one(1),Sol)` ensures that no queens attack each other on rows. We can see that this is a lower-level encoding than the B-solution: There is special code for knights, which are treated quite differently from the other pieces. Furthermore, the model checks explicitly that there is exactly one queen on every row and column.

4   OSCAR/Scala Solution

As an additional solution, we have written an encoding in Scala using the OSCAR Constraint Programming library [19]. This library supports a CLP(FD) modelling approach combined with various search heuristics. Compared to PROB, OSCAR usually sacrifices completeness for efficiency, while also providing support for built-in constraint functions. Such functions have dedicated and optimised domain restriction and search algorithms. Variables in OSCAR are explicitly declared with their domains, e.g., `val Pieces = Set(0 to k)`. The representation of the problem in the OSCAR model follows closely that of the B model. However, implementation concerns need to be considered in OSCAR. For instance, when dereferencing a 2-dimensional array, the first index must be of type `int` (but not of type `CPIntVar`). Hence, to refer to rows and columns usually the 2-dimensional array and its transpose are required. E.g., in OSCAR the board is modelled by

```
val board = Array.fill(n, n)(CPIntVar(Pieces))
val board_t = board.transpose
```

Constraints are added to the constraint store by means of a function `add(c)`, where `c` is a constraint. Constraints may not contain quantifiers. As a consequence, OSCAR models are less abstract than B models as well as not as easy to read and understand, e.g., concerning knight attacks:

```
for(i<-0 until n; j<-0 until n)
  (for(u<-Seq(-2, -1); v<-Seq(-2, -1, 1, 2);
    if(u.abs!=v.abs && i+u>=0 && i+u<n && j+v>=0 && j+v<n))
  yield board(i+u)(j+v)).foreach
    {t=>add(board(i)(j).isEq(k)==>t.isDiff(k))}
```

We have analyzed two differently structured versions of the model.

1. A monolithic version where constraints are propagated between the four sub-problems, similarly to the B and Prolog models.
2. A layered version where the sub-problems are solved in a predetermined order (first bishops, then rooks, then queens, finally knights) where constraints are propagated within the sub-problems and allocated positions are passed as constants from one to the next sub-problem. The only way the sub-problems communicate is by backtracking.

Three similar sets Bset, Rset and Qset are used in the layered model to pass the already allocated board positions to the next sub-problem dealing with bishops, rooks and queens, respectively. E.g., Bset is declared as

```
val Bset = scala.collection.mutable.Set[(Int, Int)]()
```

When the solver for the bishops problem has found a solution, the positions of the bishops are copied into Bset,

```
for(i<-0 until n; j <- 0 until n)
  if(board(i)(j).value.toInt!=0) Bset += (i, j)
```

The sub-model for the rooks contains constraints to block these positions,

```
for(i<-Bset) add(board(i._1)(i._2)!==r)
```

and adds the constraints for the placement of the rooks using global cardinality constraints gcc

```
for(i <- 0 until n){
  add(gcc(board(i), Array((r,CPIntVar(0 to 1)))))
  add(gcc(board_t(i), Array((r,CPIntVar(0 to 1)))))
}
add(gcc(board.flatten.toArray, Array((r,CPIntVar(nR)))))
```

The same scheme is followed for the queens and knights subproblems.

We have varied the order of the sub-problems discussed above and the alternatives have a worse performance than the one presented here. This is likely due to the degrees of liberty when placing the figures, influenced by the possible moves and the number of figures. As an example, for models starting with the bishops sub-problem, the search performed better than for those starting with the queens sub-problem. This could be a consequence of having to place almost twice as many bishops as queens, i.e., we reduce the search space more when passing the positions occupied by bishops while still having enough liberty in placing the queens on the board.

The layered approach is not suitable for testing of unsatisfiability even for small board sizes: backtracking is more costly than direct constraint propagation. In addition, the search uses limits on the permitted number of iterations. In the benchmarks this is not an issue, because the runtime is dominated by the sub-problems. The ability to experiment easily with model representations and search heuristics is an advantage of OSCAR. The price to pay for this is the lower level of abstraction which makes it more difficult to validate the model against the problem statement.

We have also experimented with modelling variants using a piece-centric model instead of a board-centric model. The models were generally less performant than the two discussed above. We see two reasons for this: (1) when the models are to be considered jointly, some optimisations usually applied to piece-centric models were not possible because they depend on specific data-models, (2) it requires replacing a few arithmetic calculations and comparisons with many boolean comparisons. Due to the small board sizes used there are no performance issues due to memory management. We also observed that when trying to break symmetries in these models, the low level of the programming and the restrictions on referencing arrays obscured the added constraints. This reduces the legibility of the models further and makes validation more difficult.

5 SAT Encoding

A different approach towards solving the crowded chessboard puzzle is to encode it using pure propositional calculus and employ SAT solvers such as Minisat [10]. The general idea is as follows: For each kind of chess figure to be placed we introduce $n \times n$ boolean variables to encode the chessboard, e.g., $queen_{2,5}$. We set a variable to true to represent a figure on a certain square, while false represents an empty square.

Most placement rules can be encoded easily. First, we encode that no two figures can be placed on the same square. This is done by enforcing, that for each combination of indices i, j the fields encoded as $queens_{i,j}$, $rooks_{i,j}$, $bishops_{i,j}$ and $knights_{i,j}$ should not be true simultaneously. For example, for $queens$ and $rooks$ we assert $\forall i \in 1 \ldots n, j \in 1 \ldots n \cdot queens_{i,j} = \top \Rightarrow rooks_{i,j} = \bot$. Of course, using universal quantification is not allowed in the input of a common SAT solver. Thus, we have to unroll the formula and set the constraint up explicitly for all combinations of chess pieces, i and j.

Next, we have to encode the movement of figures. For a solution to be correct, we require that no two figures of the same kind can capture each other. Again, this can be encoded using implications, e.g., for the case of linear movement we assert $\forall i \in 1 \ldots n, j \in 1 \ldots n, x \in 1 \ldots n, x \neq j \cdot queens_{i,j} = \top \Rightarrow queens_{i,x} = \bot$. Obviously, diagonal movement can be encoded similarly. Again, we have to unroll the resulting constraints to remove the universal quantification.

Encoding the knights movement is more complicated and can not be expressed as easily using quantification. They key idea however remains the same: we iterate over all possible fields a knight can reach and set up implications preventing other knights from being placed there. To do so, we compute the set of fields a knight can reach from a current field i, j:

$$reachable_{i,j} = \{(i+1, j+2), (i-1, j+2), (i+1, j-2), (i-1, j-2),$$
$$(i+2, j+1), (i+2, j-1), (i-2, j+1), (i-2, j-1)\}.$$

Of course, we have to keep in mind not to violate the borders of the chess board:

$$reachable2_{i,j,n} = \{(x,y)|(x,y) \in reachable_{i,j} \wedge x \in 1\ldots n \wedge y \in 1\ldots n\}.$$

Following, we can prevent knights from attacking each other:

$$\forall i \in 1\ldots n, j \in 1\ldots n, (x,y) \in reachable2_{i,j,n} knights_{i,j} = \top \Rightarrow knights_{x,y} = \bot$$

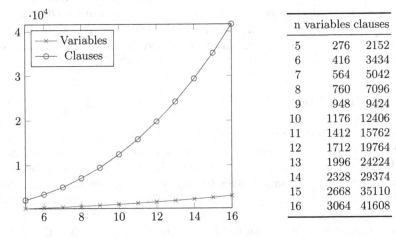

n	variables	clauses
5	276	2152
6	416	3434
7	564	5042
8	760	7096
9	948	9424
10	1176	12406
11	1412	15762
12	1712	19764
13	1996	24224
14	2328	29374
15	2668	35110
16	3064	41608

Fig. 5. Board size vs. variables/clauses (Maximum number of knights)

In contrast to movement, encoding the number of figures to be placed is quite involved. This is due to the fact the very low-level SAT encoding does not feature constructs like cardinality computation. There are extensions to SAT introducing *quantified Boolean satisfiability*, or QSAT for short. When the quantification of variables is not existential, SAT becomes PSPACE-complete.

To summarize, we have two possible ways to proceed: use a solver for quantified boolean formulas or encode the cardinality constraints ourselves. As we intended to present a low-level alternative to the high-level encoding in B and PROB, we went with the second alternative. Essentially, there are three ways to encode the sum of boolean variables by means of pure propositional calculus:

- Encode a bit-wise adder and treat every boolean variable as an input bit. The result can be compared to the required cardinality using bit-level arithmetic. This is the approach we will use in our benchmarks.
- An improved encoding of bitwise addition called the *totalizer* [3]. In contrast to the naive encoding it provides improved unit propagation. However, for the problem at hand we did not observe any speedup.
- Use a sorting network as outlined in [2].

As can be seen in Fig. 5, encoding the crowded chessboard puzzle using pure propositional calculus involves introducing numerous variables and connecting them by a high number of relatively simple constraints. In particular, the number of clauses rises quadratically, as expected due to the pairwise constraints.

6   SMT Encoding

In contrast to the very low-level encoding needed for SAT solvers, SMT solvers support a much richer logic. In particular, cardinality constraints can be expressed by means of addition. Furthermore, we can again use quantifiers to express the relations between chess pieces. We investigated three possible encodings of the crowded chessboard puzzle into SMT:

1. The board-centric approach, where we try to find a function mapping positions to chess pieces occupying them.
2. The piece-centric approach, where we try to find a function mapping pieces to their position on the chess board.
3. A low-level approach using a boolean encoding similar to Sect. 5. This time however, cardinality is expressed using integer arithmetic.

For the first two approaches, fields are encoded as pairs of two integers ranging from 1 to n. The two functions $first$ and $second$ are used to access the first and second entry. A set of common predicates is used to set up the constraints:

$$on\_board(x) \Leftrightarrow 1 \leq first(x) \leq n \wedge 1 \leq second(x) \leq n$$
$$not\_same\_row(x,y) \Leftrightarrow first(x) \neq first(y)$$
$$not\_same\_col(x,y) \Leftrightarrow second(x) \neq second(y)$$
$$not\_same\_diag(x,y) \Leftrightarrow |first(x) - first(y)| \neq |second(x) - second(y)|$$

All of them can directly be encoded using SMT-LIB, the common input language of SMT solvers. For the first approach, we try to find $board$, a mapping of pairs to integers ranging from -1 to 3, where -1 represents an empty square, 0 a queen, 1 a rook, 2 a bishop and 3 a knight. We assert that the board may not hold other values and that a figure may not be placed outside of the field:
$$\forall x \cdot -1 \leq board(x) \leq 3 \wedge \neg on\_board(x) \Rightarrow board(x) = -1.$$

Movement and attacking is also modeled using universal quantification. For instance, the fact that two rooks may not attack each other is encoded as follows:

$$\forall x, y \cdot board(x) = 1 \wedge board(y) = 1 \wedge x \neq y$$
$$\Rightarrow not\_same\_row(x,y) \wedge not\_same\_col(x,y)$$

Cardinality is encoded by enforcing the existence of n pairs where a queen is placed. The first universal quantification can be expressed efficiently in SMT-LIB by a *distinct* constraint:

$$\exists q_1, \ldots, q_n \cdot \left((\forall i, j \in [1, n], i \neq j \cdot q_i \neq q_j) \wedge (\forall i \in [1, n] \cdot board(q_i) = 0) \right)$$

This first approach was not successful, as it could not compete with the SAT approach even for small board sizes. While the usage of SMT instead of SAT greatly increases expressiveness and therefore understandability of the encoded problem, it also causes a performance decline if used as above.

The second approach, the piece-centric view of the puzzle can be extracted out of the first one by unrolling *board*. Essentially, we set up a variable for each queen, rook, bishop and knight. In consequence, we do not have to consider empty squares anymore. Furthermore, by using the correct number of variables, checking cardinality boils down to checking inequality.

Now that we have immediate access to the different figures, we can hardcode some simple symmetry reductions directly into the constraints. For instance, we know that the queens cannot share a row at all. Hence, we can sort them by asserting $\forall i \in [1, n] \cdot first(q_i) = i$.

We could again use quantifiers for the attack relation. For instance, in case of the queens we could reuse the *not_same_diag* predicate defined above:

$$\forall x, y \cdot \left(\bigvee_{i=1}^{n} x = q_i \right) \wedge \left(\bigvee_{i=1}^{n} y = q_i \right) \wedge x \neq y \Rightarrow not\_same\_diag(x, y).$$

However, SMT solvers such as Z3 [7] and CVC4 [4] currently do not detect saturation of the left hand side, i.e., they do not realize that the quantifier in fact handles all combinations of two queens. In consequence, we decided to unroll the universal quantifier and assert all *not_same_diag* combinations individually.

7   Related Work and Other Encodings

There are well-known approaches (e.g., [12]) to encoding constraint problems using integer programming (IP). Instead of asking for logical satisfaction one asks for the solution to a minimisation problem. An IP formulation for the crowded chessboard problem has been proposed in [6] where two approaches are discussed: (i) counting the number of attacks or (ii) a direct binary model for the logical constraints. The objective function for model (i) is binary discarding the extra information provided by counting the number of attacks. The XPRESS-MP models that are mentioned are not accessible. However, a MiniZinc model and a Picat encoding based on the direct binary model of [6] is available. For the MiniZinc version, a comment in the model states that for $n = 8$ the computation of a solution takes 108 seconds using ECLiPSe/eplex [22,25], however, in our benchmarks solutions were found much faster. A more low-level implementation of the direct binary model has been implemented directly in ECLiPSe/eplex. As one would expect, this implementation obscures the clear abstract description of [6] when using a Prolog-like notation.

8 Empirical Evaluation

In this section, we evaluate the performance of the different approaches. Each encoding is executed once for several board sizes. The amount of knights is varied in order to check both a satisfiable and unsatisfiable instance. All benchmarks were run on an AMD Opteron with 2 GHz and 4 physical cores. Up to 3 benchmarks were run in parallel. After 30 min without a result, the execution was aborted. Results are given in Table 2 and Fig. 6, showing the runtimes in seconds.

We benchmarked the CLP(FD) encoding introduced in Sect. 3 using SICStus Prolog. For $n = 5$ and 5 knights, solving takes 2.6 s. For $n = 6$ and 9 knights it takes only 2 s, but to determine that there is no solution for 10 knights it takes >30 min. For $n = 7$ and 12 knights however, unsatisfiability is detected in 11 s. We did not manage to solve the full puzzle for $n = 8$ and 21 knights.

In summary, this encoding is more efficient than the higher level one written in B in Sect. 2, as the high level one can only solve the puzzle for $n = 5$. This shows that there is still scope to reduce the overhead of ProB's default CLP backend, given that it is based on CLP(FD) and SICStus as well. However, it is disappointing not to be able to solve the original puzzle for $n = 8$. In the future, we will investigate whether we can replace the global_cardinality constraint by a more effective encoding.

Table 2. Solving times (in seconds), * means unsat, empty means timeout

n k	B		CLP(FD)	OscaR		SAT	SMT			ECLiPSe		Picat
	plain	+Kodkod		plain	split		board	figure	SAT	plain	MiniZinc	
5 5	6.1	8.3	2.6	2.8	1.5	0.7	117.6	1.9	0.4	0.6	0.3	1.3
*5 6	28.4	8.3		2.2		0.8			0.7	0.6	0.3	3.0
6 9		10.8	2.0	85.9	3.0	0.8		636.4	1.7	0.6	0.5	3.5
*6 10		11.9		485.6		0.7			3.8	3.9	1.2	12.8
7 11		16.7	42.8		7.4	0.9			41.4	1.1	0.6	4.0
*7 12		16.1	10.9			0.2			48.6	0.7	0.5	3.3
8 21		75.5			41.5	13.2			402.1	1.0	4.8	8.5
*8 22		374.1				160.1			1535.0	54.9	93.7	516.0
9 29		709.5				184.7				16.9	13.5	11.7
*9 30		1385.1				1257.4				59.8	1633.1	245.0
10 37		1408.9				189.6				1.2	153.6	23.6
*10 38		1413.5								300.6		726.2
11 47		1449.5								38.2		56.1
*11 48		1455.3								275.2		
12 57		1509.1								46.0		81.2
*12 58		1516.6								1106.4		
13 69		1599.5								201.2		
*13 70		1615.0								430.2		
14 81		1768.4								59.5		
*14 82		1755.4										
15 94											2.5	
*15 95												

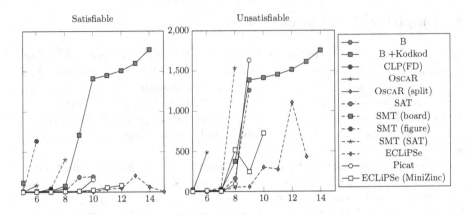

Fig. 6. Runtimes for satisfiable and unsatisfiable instances

Furthermore, integrating PROB's default backend with other solvers is beneficial. Thanks to the improved integration with Kodkod presented in Sect. 2.5, PROB can solve all satisfiable and unsatisfiable instances with $n \leq 14$. Combining SAT and CLP proves to be stronger than both working independently.

In Sect. 4, we presented another attempt at a constraint programming solution to this problem; this time using the OSCAR library in Scala. Unfortunately, the monolithic solution also does not scale to $n = 8$, but an optimized layered version, splitting the constraints and sacrificing completeness for efficiency, does scale (but is in principle not guaranteed to find a solution if there is one).

With respect to the search, the layered approach showed a superior performance. For $n = 5$, the execution time was roughly split in half, while for $n = 6$ the layered version was nearly 30 times faster. Until $n = 8$ the performance is very high in comparison, which is likely down to the small amount of backtracking that occurs during the search up to this point.

For the low-level encoding into SAT, we benchmarked using the winner of the SAT competition 2017, Maple [17]. Despite the blowup in complexity the resulting performance of a translation to SAT is often better than the one exhibited by our other encoding for large n. Both for satisfiable and unsatisfiable benchmarks Maple outperforms CLP(FD), PROB and OSCAR. In particular, for $n = 8$ and 22 knights, the low-level SAT encoding using Maple reports unsatisfiability after 160.1 s. Furthermore, it can compute solutions for $n = 10$.

Our last approach, replacing the cardinality constraint by integer arithmetic, proves not to be an advantage over the plain SAT encoding. In fact, the context switch between SAT and Z3's arithmetic solver causes overhead and, in consequence, reduces performance. For $n = 8$, Z3 takes 402 s to find a model. If the number of knights is increased to 22, Z3 detects unsatisfiability in 1535 s.

The related encodings discussed in Sect. 7 perform surprisingly well: Using the MiniZinc encoding we find a solution for $n = 8$ and 21 knights in 8.5 s. We are not sure what caused the speedup since the model was introduced in [6], but suspect a combination of improvements in ECLiPSe/eplex and faster CPUs.

The performance of the Picat and the MiniZinc model differs, although they are based on the same encoding. While Picat is slower for $n \leq 8$, it is faster for larger instances. The direct encodings in ECLiPSe and Picat show that tailoring towards the particular strengths of solvers is beneficial regarding performance. ECLiPSe outperforms the more general solution written in MiniZinc on the larger benchmarks. In particular, it is the only combination of encoding and solver able to solve the puzzle for $n \geq 14$. However, as argued above, the price is readability.

9 Conclusion, Outlook and Discussion

In conclusion, the crowded chessboard problem turned out to be surprisingly difficult to solve. The problem also allowed us to compare a variety of approaches.

- The high-level B model from Sect. 2.1 is a very readable, mathematical formulation of the problem. It cannot be solved for $n = 8$ using the current CLP(FD)-based backend of PROB, but it can be used to validate solutions found by other approaches. Other backends of PROB based on SAT [20] or SMT cannot be applied, due to the higher-order nature of the model.
- The lower-level, direct CLP(FD) encoding in Sect. 3 is faster, but also cannot scale to $n = 8$.
- The monolithic encoding using the OSCAR constraint library in Sect. 4 also does not scale, but an optimized, layered version, sacrificing completeness for efficiency, does.
- Various attempts at a lower-level direct SMT-LIB encoding in Sect. 6, also cannot be solved for $n = 8$ using Z3.
- The high-level B model from Sect. 2.5 is slightly less declarative than the B model from Sect. 2.1, but scales surprisingly well.
- Among the fastest of our solutions is a direct SAT encoding, generated by a Python program in Sect. 5. However, this solution is hardest to read by a human: neither the SAT encoding nor the Python program are ideal for human validation and reviewing.

The ultimate goal is to be able to solve the high-level, readable model from Sect. 2.1, fully automatically. We hope that further refinements of the approaches in Sects. 2.5 and 4 will enable this, and pave the road for very declarative but tractable modelling of complex constraint problems.

References

1. Abrial, J.-R.: The B-Book. Cambridge University Press, Cambridge (1996)
2. Asín, R., Nieuwenhuis, R., Oliveras, A., Rodríguez-Carbonell, E.: Cardinality networks and their applications. In: Kullmann, O. (ed.) SAT 2009. LNCS, vol. 5584, pp. 167–180. Springer, Heidelberg (2009). https://doi.org/10.1007/978-3-642-02777-2_18

3. Bailleux, O., Boufkhad, Y.: Efficient CNF encoding of boolean cardinality constraints. In: Rossi, F. (ed.) CP 2003. LNCS, vol. 2833, pp. 108–122. Springer, Heidelberg (2003). https://doi.org/10.1007/978-3-540-45193-8_8

4. Barrett, C., Conway, C.L., Deters, M., Hadarean, L., Jovanović, D., King, T., Reynolds, A., Tinelli, C.: CVC4. In: Gopalakrishnan, G., Qadeer, S. (eds.) CAV 2011. LNCS, vol. 6806, pp. 171–177. Springer, Heidelberg (2011). https://doi.org/10.1007/978-3-642-22110-1_14

5. Carlsson, M., Ottosson, G., Carlson, B.: An open-ended finite domain constraint solver. In: Glaser, H., Hartel, P., Kuchen, H. (eds.) PLILP 1997. LNCS, vol. 1292, pp. 191–206. Springer, Heidelberg (1997). https://doi.org/10.1007/BFb0033845

6. Chlond, M.J.: IP modeling of chessboard placements and related puzzles. INFORMS Trans. Educ. 2(2), 56–57 (2002)

7. de Moura, L., Bjørner, N.: Z3: an efficient SMT solver. In: Ramakrishnan, C.R., Rehof, J. (eds.) TACAS 2008. LNCS, vol. 4963, pp. 337–340. Springer, Heidelberg (2008). https://doi.org/10.1007/978-3-540-78800-3_24

8. Déharbe, D., Fontaine, P., Guyot, Y., Voisin, L.: SMT solvers for Rodin. In: Derrick, J., Fitzgerald, J., Gnesi, S., Khurshid, S., Leuschel, M., Reeves, S., Riccobene, E. (eds.) ABZ 2012. LNCS, vol. 7316, pp. 194–207. Springer, Heidelberg (2012). https://doi.org/10.1007/978-3-642-30885-7_14

9. Dudeney, H.E.: Amusements in Mathematics (1917). https://www.gutenberg.org/ebooks/16713

10. Eén, N., Sörensson, N.: An extensible SAT-solver. In: Giunchiglia, E., Tacchella, A. (eds.) SAT 2003. LNCS, vol. 2919, pp. 502–518. Springer, Heidelberg (2004). https://doi.org/10.1007/978-3-540-24605-3_37

11. Hayes, I., Jones, C.: Specifications are not (necessarily) executable. Softw. Eng. J. 4(6), 330–338 (1989)

12. Hooker, J.N.: Logic-Based Methods for Optimization: Combining Optimization and Constraint Satisfaction. John Wiley, New York (2000)

13. Krings, S., Leuschel, M.: Proof assisted symbolic model checking for B and event-B. In: Butler, M., Schewe, K.-D., Mashkoor, A., Biro, M. (eds.) ABZ 2016. LNCS, vol. 9675, pp. 135–150. Springer, Cham (2016). https://doi.org/10.1007/978-3-319-33600-8_8

14. Leuschel, M.: Formal model-based constraint solving and document generation. In: Ribeiro, L., Lecomte, T. (eds.) SBMF 2016. LNCS, vol. 10090, pp. 3–20. Springer, Cham (2016). https://doi.org/10.1007/978-3-319-49815-7_1

15. Leuschel, M., Butler, M.J.: ProB: an automated analysis toolset for the B method. STTT 10(2), 185–203 (2008)

16. Leuschel, M., Schneider, D.: Towards B as a high-level constraint modelling language. In: Ait Ameur, Y., Schewe, K.D. (eds.) ABZ 2014. LNCS, vol. 8477, pp. 101–116. Springer, Heidelberg (2014). https://doi.org/10.1007/978-3-662-43652-3_8

17. Luo, M., Li, C.-M., Xiao, F., Manyà, F., Lü, Z.: An effective learnt clause minimization approach for CDCL SAT solvers. In: Proceedings IJCAI-2017, pp. 703–711 (2017)

18. Merz, S., Vanzetto, H.: Automatic verification of TLA$^+$ proof obligations with SMT solvers. In: Bjørner, N., Voronkov, A. (eds.) LPAR 2012. LNCS, vol. 7180, pp. 289–303. Springer, Heidelberg (2012). https://doi.org/10.1007/978-3-642-28717-6_23

19. OscaR Team. OscaR: Scala in OR (2012). https://bitbucket.org/oscarlib/oscar

20. Plagge, D., Leuschel, M.: Validating B, Z and TLA$^+$ using PROB and Kodkod. In: Giannakopoulou, D., Méry, D. (eds.) FM 2012. LNCS, vol. 7436, pp. 372–386. Springer, Heidelberg (2012). https://doi.org/10.1007/978-3-642-32759-9_31

21. Savary, A., Frappier, M., Leuschel, M., Lanet, J.-L.: Model-based robustness testing in EVENT-B using mutation. In: Calinescu, R., Rumpe, B. (eds.) SEFM 2015. LNCS, vol. 9276, pp. 132–147. Springer, Cham (2015). https://doi.org/10.1007/978-3-319-22969-0_10
22. Schimpf, J., Shen, K.: ECLiPSe - from LP to CLP. TPLP **12**(1–2), 127–156 (2012)
23. Schneider, D., Leuschel, M., Witt, T.: Model-based problem solving for university timetable validation and improvement. In: Bjørner, N., de Boer, F. (eds.) FM 2015. LNCS, vol. 9109, pp. 487–495. Springer, Cham (2015). https://doi.org/10.1007/978-3-319-19249-9_30
24. Shapiro, S.C.: The jobs puzzle: a challenge for logical expressibility and automated reasoning. In: AAAI SS (2011)
25. Shen, K., Schimpf, J.: Eplex: harnessing mathematical programming solvers for constraint logic programming. In: van Beek, P. (ed.) CP 2005. LNCS, vol. 3709, pp. 622–636. Springer, Heidelberg (2005). https://doi.org/10.1007/11564751_46
26. Torlak, E., Jackson, D.: Kodkod: a relational model finder. In: Grumberg, O., Huth, M. (eds.) TACAS 2007. LNCS, vol. 4424, pp. 632–647. Springer, Heidelberg (2007). https://doi.org/10.1007/978-3-540-71209-1_49

An Automated Detection of Inconsistencies in SBVR-based Business Rules Using Many-sorted Logic

Kritika Anand⬤, Pavan Kumar Chittimalli$^{(\boxtimes)}$⬤, and Ravindra Naik⬤

TCS Innovation Labs, Pune, India
{kritika.anand,pavan.chittimalli,rd.naik}@tcs.com

Abstract. Business rules control and constrain the behavior and structure of the business system in terms of its policies and principles. Business rules are restructured frequently as per the internal or external circumstances based on market opportunities, statutory regulations, and business focus. The current practice in industry, of detecting inconsistencies manually, is error prone, due to the size, complexity and ambiguity in representation using natural language.

Our work detects inconsistencies in business rules based on model checking that exploits the FOL basis of SBVR specification. We aim to reduce the burden on solvers and obtain effective system level test data, leading to the development of a novel inconsistency rule checker based on extracting the unsatisfiable cores using solvers like Z3, CVC4, etc. We introduce the concept of graphical clusters, to partition SBVR vocabularies and represent the former exploiting the many-sorted logic and graph reachability algorithm, thus reducing the domain of quantification and the number of uninterpreted functions. The translation of SBVR to SMT-LIBv2 is implemented as part of our tool BuRRiTo. Experimental results are shown on industrial level rule sets.

Keywords: Business rules · First order logic · SBVR · SMT solvers

1 Introduction

Enterprise business organizations regulate their business activities by imposing certain logical constraints, often termed as business rules, that apply across the process and procedures. Business rules are embedded in the source code of legacy systems, governing policies, work flow descriptions, process flows, decision tables or databases. Business strategies are subject to redesign depending upon the external market conditions, government policies or with the attempt of maximizing revenue. Laws and business policies are changed regularly by the government, as a result of which businesses continually have to respond to changes in the legal framework e.g. the "Sarbanes-Oxley Act of 2002" is a United States federal law that was passed in response to a number of corporate accounting scandals that occurred between 2000 and 2002 [1]. Both legislation amendments

© Springer International Publishing AG 2018
F. Calimeri et al. (Eds.): PADL 2018, LNCS 10702, pp. 80–96, 2018.
https://doi.org/10.1007/978-3-319-73305-0_6

and business transformation force the enterprises to revisit their business rules, highlighting the need for automatic testing of business rules. Consistency checking also aids in the study of effect of addition of a new rule or policy on the already existing set of rules. Also, the compliance checking within the rules is a prerequisite for verifying the business process models against the regulations. Thus, checking for ambiguities within individual rules, and between different rules, both syntactically and semantically is of paramount importance.

The procedural process languages like BPMN, EPC and BPEL are concerned with the control-flow perspective of business processes. On the other hand, business rules capture the declarative aspects of business processes like constraints, complex decisions and relationships between variables [2]. Our current approach focuses on checking the consistency of the business rules which are expressed in Semantics of Business Vocabulary and Rules (SBVR) [3], an OMG standard for representing business rules. SBVR is a Controlled Natural Language (CNL), that works as a bridge between business and IT, aiming to provide a way to express business knowledge (requirements, operational procedures etc.) to the IT community. The main reason for choosing SBVR for the rule modelling is due to its declarative nature, natural language representation and support for the first order logic. The SBVR meta-model is used to represent business knowledge as (1) Specifying business vocabularies, (2) Specifying business rules. The business vocabulary is a cohesive set of interconnected concepts using which the organizations or communities specify the conduct of business. These concepts are entities represented through *name, term,* and *verb*. The SBVR business rule is created by combining *name, term,,* and *verb* with the built-in keywords (quantification, modality or logical operators).

In this paper, we exploit the First Order Logic (FOL) basis of SBVR representation and develop a framework that automatically converts the SBVR rules to the SMT-LIBv2 [4,5] formulas and check the latter for inconsistencies using solvers like Z3 [6], CVC4 [7], etc. In our earlier work [8], we have proposed a method to detect inconsistencies amongst the rules using the above mentioned solvers. In this paper, we introduce a new technique based on many-sorted logic of FOL and the graph reachability algorithm to alleviate the shortcomings of the paper [8] and to deal with the complex rules which are unhandled by the previous works [8–13] on consistency checking. In the work [14], the authors used many-sorted logic for the verification of web application data models via translation to FOL.

The rest of the paper is organized as follows. Section 2 presents the background and the list of challenges that motivated the need of the work. Section 2.1 provides an introduction to many-sorted logic of FOL followed by Sect. 3 which describes the proposed approach in detail through examples. Section 4 illustrates implementation of the technique and the type of inconsistencies that can be detected by our approach. Finally, experimental studies and discussions are provided in Sect. 5.

2   Motivation

Figure 1 represents a set of business rules that motivated the need of our work. The real world business rules provides the facility to take one or more actions (consequent) based on the specification of one or more conditions (antecedant). The multiple conditions can be enumerated using the *AND* or *OR* operators and business rule is processed according to fulfillment of all conditions (*AND*) or any one of the condition (*OR*). The major percentage of business rules in real life data is of the form:

"if $cond_1$ and $cond_2$ and.....$cond_n$ then $action_1$ and $action_2$ and....$action_m$" or
"if $cond_1$ or $cond_2$ or.....$cond_n$ then $action_1$ and $action_2$ and....$action_m$"

The previous works on consistency checking of business rules [8–13] are not able to find inconsistencies in all the rules of such form involved in the business process which are successfully addressed in our approach. Secondly, our approach handles the inconsistencies present in complex rules which are not addressed in any of the previous works.

By complex rules, we mean the fact types associated with the rule falls under one of the following categories.

(i) Rule having the keyword '*that*' which is used after a designation for a noun concept and before a designation for a verb concept. Rule r_3 is one such instance.
(ii) Rule involving the keyword '*of*' that associates a property with a noun concept like rule r_4 in Fig. 1.
(iii) Rule that is combination of (*i*) and (*ii*).

Complex rules can also contain logical operators like negation, conjunction, disjunction or implication. Rule r_5 in Fig. 1 is a complex rule of the form "$f1$ if $f2$" where $f1$, $f2$ are fact types where $f2$ is of the category (*iii*).

We also handle SBVR rules and definitions (e.g., r_6 in Fig. 1) that consists of aspects in which a thing or property associated with a noun concept is measurable in terms of 'greater than' or 'less than' or 'equal to', that are not addressed in previous works on consistency checking of business rules.

In paper [8], the SBVR terms that do not belong to the predefined sort like Integer, Real, Boolean, *etc.* are mapped as constants of 'Thing' *sort*. Every function or predicate in FOL takes the argument or returns the value of type 'Thing' or predefined sort resulting in following limitations.

---

r_1: It is obligatory that each <u>rental</u> *has* at most 3 <u>additional drivers.</u>
r_2: It is obligatory that each **<u>EURent</u>** *has* at least 4 <u>additional drivers.</u>
r_3: It is obligatory that <u>driver</u> that *is authorized in* country, has <u>driving license</u> that *is valid.*
r_4: It is obligatory that <u>rented car</u> of the <u>rental</u> *is stored at* the <u>pick-up branch</u> of the <u>rental</u>.
r_5: It is permitted that a <u>rental</u> *is open* if an <u>estimated rental charge</u> *is provisionally charged to* a <u>credit card</u> of <u>renter</u> that *is responsible for* the <u>rental</u>.
r_6: It is obligatory that the <u>rental duration</u> of each <u>rental</u> *is less than* 90 rental days.

Fig. 1. SBVR rules from EURent [15] that motivated the need of the work.

1. The existential and universal quantification is applied on the whole universe of sort 'Thing', causing an increase in the count of quantifier instantiations, along with excessive deduction on predicate, thereby increasing the complexity of the solver while finding the unsatisfiable cores. In many cases, SMT solvers returned 'UNKNOWN' when they failed to prove a set of SMT-LIBv2 formulas involving quantified variables as unsatisfiable.
2. The analysis of the model, generated from the SBVR using the '**get-value**' or '**get-model**' results in a lot of uninterpreted functions, which takes arbitrary values to make the model satisfiable, thereby generating an incorrect model.
3. The cardinality constraints in SBVR rule is represented using *'at least'*, *'at most'*, or *'exactly'* quantification. The translation of rules (e.g., r_1 and r_2) as depicted in Fig. 1 into SMT-LIBv2 formulas is incorrect semantically, resulting in generation of erroneous test data.

The work [9–12] mapped many SBVR concepts to the consistent ontologies which the authors claim can be used for consistency checking, due to the presence of supported reasoners like Hermit, Pellet [16,17], but no work was able to give any concrete case study for detecting the inconsistent rules with the help of the transformed formal knowledge base.

2.1 Introduction to Many-sorted Logic

Many-sorted logic is the generalization of FOL in which the domain of universe is classified into disjunct sorts (or types). The sorts in many-sorted logic are similar to the types in the conventional programming languages. The structure (signature) of many-sorted logic is defined as:

$$\sigma = (S, C, F, P)$$

where

- S is the enumerable set of sorts $\{S_1, S_1, ..., S_n\}$ and S_i is non-empty, $\sum$ is n-sorted.
- C is countable set of constant symbols $\{c_1, c_2, ..., c_k\}$ of sort S_i.
- F is the countable set of function symbols $\{f_1, f_2, ..., f_m\}$ taking sorts as the arguments.
- P is the countable set of predicate symbols $\{p_1, p_2, ..., p_j\}$ taking sorts as the arguments.

Many-sorted logic is defined by means of the following information.

1. Many-sorted logic allows the arguments of functions and predicates to have different sorts. Every constant symbol or function return types is associated with a defined sort before its usage.
2. Many-sorted logic facilitates to perform quantification over a given sorts instead of entire domain of universe.

3. Sorts in many-sorted logic are mutually exclusive, i.e., a constant in FOL shall always be associated with a single sort and the constants that belong to different sorts can never be equal [14].
4. In contrast to the set theory, the sorts in many-sorted logic do not support the subset relation.

The introduction of many-sorted logic in translation to SMTLIBv2 formulas from SBVR aims to reduce the number of generated uninterpreted functions, thereby reducing the amount of deductions performed by SMT solvers on the quantified variables and objects. The use of many-sorted logic increases the computational efficiency and reduces the search space as compared with the unsorted logic [18]. Many-sorted logic finds the model in an efficient way by applying symmetry reduction techniques for each sort separately. Also, we apply the graph based algorithms in the mappings with the aim to generate correct test data and model.

3   Proposed Approach

Figure 2 shows the high-level block diagram of the proposed solution approach (called as *Inconsistency Rule Checker*). The proposed approach is a multi-step process primarily consists of 3 phases: Pre-transformation, Transformation and Verification. The source or the input to tool is the SBVR which is processed into machine readable format i.e. SBVR XMI and the output is the set of all inconsistent rules in the SBVR format.

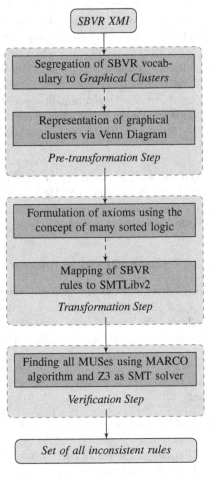

Fig. 2. Block diagram to detect inconsistencies in SBVR based business rules.

1. Phase I: In Pre-transformation phase, we segregate the *term, verb, noun, and fact type* concepts, which form the core of SBVR vocabulary to graphical clusters and latter represent the graphical clusters to Venn Diagram.
2. Phase II: The transformation phase describes our approach of translation from SBVR vocabularies and rules to SMT-LIBv2 formulas using the logical structure and semantics of many-sorted logic.
3. Phase III: The generated SMT-LIBv2 formulas are fed as an input to the verification phase which aims at detecting all set of inconsistencies in business rules using SMT solvers like Z3, CVC4. Internally, the problem of finding all

set of inconsistent rules is reduced to that of finding all minimally unsatisfiable subformulas (MUS) which is explained in detail in Sect. 3.3. To illustrate the approach, we consider the SBVR vocabulary shown in Fig. 3.

3.1   Pre-transformation Step

In this phase, we construct the *forest* of *directed trees* from the SBVR vocabulary as shown in Fig. 4. The individual noun concept '*Sweden_airport_branch*' and noun concepts '*airport_branch*' and '*branch*' are related through inheritance. A possible approach is to use distinct sorts for every SBVR concept.

Many-sorted logic does not support the subsort relation and an element can only belong to one sort at a time. It is evident that '*Sweden_airport_branch*' is an instance of '*airport_branch*' and also of '*branch*' transitively. To overcome this hurdle, we propose the idea of *graphical clusters*. We form a *graphical cluster* for each *directed tree* of the *forest*. To schematically represent the logic formula and relations in the *graphical cluster*, **Venn diagram** is used. We create the sets (or classes) for every SBVR noun concept and sub-set relationship between the sets is predicted from parent-child relationship (inheritance) present in the SBVR vocabulary.

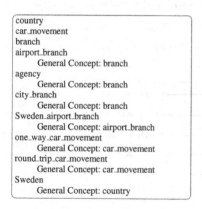

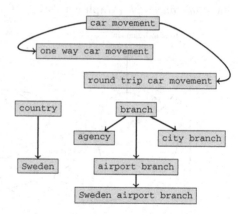

Fig. 3. Sample SBVR vocabulary.   **Fig. 4.** Forest of directed trees for SBVR vocabulary shown in Fig. 3.

We define *graphical cluster* with the following properties:

1. A sub-set relation in **Venn diagram** associated with *graphical cluster* is a logical way to represent directed edge in directed tree or inheritance in SBVR vocabulary.
2. The number of classes in a *graphical cluster* is equal to the number of general noun concept terms present in the directed tree corresponding to that cluster.
3. All the nodes of a *directed tree* of the *forest* are declared as constants or the members of the corresponding *graphical cluster*.

4. Each set of **Venn diagram** associated with *graphical cluster* is non-empty (every SBVR noun concept is a member of its set).
5. The parent(B)-child(A) relation is depicted with the notion of *proper-subset* in Venn diagram ($A \subset B$).
6. The SBVR noun concepts having the concept type as *synonym* are represented using the equality of sets.

A distinct sort is introduced for each graphical cluster. We obtain three graphical clusters, labelled with the sorts *'Cluster_Country'*, *'Cluster_Car_Movement'* and *'Cluster_Branch'* for the above SBVR example whose SMT-LIBv2 translation is depicted by formulas as:

```
(declare-sort Cluster_Country 0 )
(declare-sort Cluster_Branch 0 )
(declare-sort Cluster_Car_Movement 0 )
```

Figure 5 represents the Venn diagram of the graphical cluster associated with the sort *'Cluster_Branch'*. It constitutes the set *'branch_domain'* having the subsets *'agency_domain'*, *'city_branch_domain'*, and *'airport_branch_domain'*. It is important to note that a general noun concept that is not hierarchically related to another general noun concept in the SBVR vocabulary will have only one set in the graphical cluster but the directed tree corresponding to the cluster may not be a *singleton graph* (graph consisting of a single isolated node with no edges).

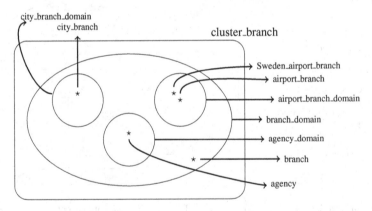

Fig. 5. Graphical Cluster associated with sort *'Cluster_Branch'*.

The command **declare-const** declares a constant of a given type or sort e.g., SMT-LIBv2 formula to assign *airportBranch* to the sort *Cluster_Branch* is represented as:

```
(declare-const airportBranch Cluster_Branch)
```

To represent in SMT-LIBv2, for each set, we declare a predicate which takes as an argument the sort of its graphical cluster and returns a Boolean value. The formula to represent the predicate axiom for the set *'airport_branch'* is:

```
(declare-fun airport_branch_domain (Cluster_Branch) Bool)
```

To represent the knowledge present in Venn diagram, we formulate axioms. Axioms constrain the interpretation of classes, their relationships and contents. We define the following axioms to represent the graphical clusters into FOL:

1. *Inclusion Axiom*: It allows 'subclass of' relationships to be established between class (set) expressions. $C \subseteq D$ implies that each instance of one C is also an instance of D, thus constructing a hierarchy of classes. Let '$n2$' be a noun concept derived from another noun concept '$n1$' in SBVR and the sort of the *graphical cluster* corresponding to '$n1$' and '$n2$' be *Cluster_A*, then *inclusion axiom* is defined as:

$$\forall x \in Cluster\_A, n2\_domain(x) \rightarrow n1\_domain(x)$$

where $n1\_domain$ and $n2\_domain$ are the predicates that corresponds to the sets in Venn diagram for $n1$ and $n2$ respectively.

2. *Class Assertion Axiom*: It allows to state whether SBVR term is an element of the set e.g., the SMT-LIBv2 formula to assert '*airport_branch*' and '*Sweden_airport_branch*' to the set '*airport_branch_domain*' is:

```
(assert (airport_branch_domain airport_branch))
(assert (airport_branch_domain Sweden_airport_branch))
```

3. *Disjoint Class Axiom*: It states that the sets in the *graphical cluster* which are not related through inclusion axiom are disjoint, i.e., no SBVR term is an element of two or more sets at a time.

   Given a *graphical cluster* of sort *Cluster_n*, the immediate children of noun concept $n_l = \{n_1, n_2, ..., n_k\}$. Then, the disjoint class axiom is defined as:

$$\forall x \in Cluster\_n, \ n_i\_domain(x) \rightarrow \neg(n_1\_domain(x)) \wedge ... \wedge \neg(n_{(i-1)}\_domain(x))$$
$$\wedge \neg(n_{(i+1)}\_domain(x)) \wedge ... \wedge \neg(n_{(k)}\_domain(x))$$
$$\wedge \neg(n_l = x)$$

We use graph reachability algorithm [19] to identify the sets in the Venn diagram which are to be logically negated. For example, consider the graph shown in Fig. 4, *agency* and *city_branch* are not reachable from *airport_branch* while the *term concepts* in Fig. 4 which are reachable, e.g., *branch*, are added as negation, that conveys the idea that branch does not belong to the set *airport_branch_domain*.

For the cluster '*Cluster_branch*', the Disjoint class axiom is represented as:

$$\forall x \in Cluster\_n, \ airport\_branch\_domain(x) \rightarrow \neg(city\_branch\_domain(x)) \wedge$$
$$\neg(agency\_domain(x)) \wedge \neg(x = branch)$$

By default, this holds true. But if the sets in the graphical structure are overlapping, this axiom is not satisfied. This can occur when the definition or rule in SBVR explicitly reveals that an SBVR element is child of two or more concepts.

4. *Equivalent Class Axiom*: Consider a noun concept 'n1' as a synonym to noun concept 'n2'. Equivalent Class Axiom allows the two sets of Venn diagram to be equal.

$$\forall x \in Cluster\_A, n2\_domain(x) = n1\_domain(x)$$

5. *Disjoint Union Axiom*: SBVR provides a way to categorize the individuals belonging to certain entity according to a set of different criteria using '*categorization*' and '*segmentation*' capabilities. *Segmentation* is the categorization scheme whose contained categories are complete (total) and disjoint with respect to the general concept containing the categorization scheme. Consider the following SBVR vocabulary which is an extension of vocabulary shown in Fig. 3:

> Branches by Type
> Definition: segmentation that *is for concept* branch and *subdivides* branch *based on* branch type
> Necessity: Branches by Type *includes the categories* airport branch *and* city branch *and* agency

Here '*branch type*' is the '*categorization*' type, on the basis of which the '*branch*' is partitioned into mutually exclusive classes. The corresponding FOL generated for the above example is shown below:

$\forall x \in Cluster\_branch,$

$branch\_domain(x) \rightarrow (x = branch)$

$\vee\ ((airport\_branch\_domain(x)) \wedge \neg(agency\_domain(x)) \wedge \neg(city\_branch\_domain(x)))$

$\vee\ ((agency\_domain(x)) \wedge \neg(airport\_branch\_domain(x)) \wedge \neg(city\_branch\_domain(x)))$

$\vee\ ((city\_branch\_domain(x)) \wedge \neg(airport\_branch\_domain(x)) \wedge \neg(agency\_domain(x)))$

3.2 Transformation Step

Semantic formulations of the SBVR rule include:

(a) modal formulations (*necessary, obligatory, impossible, prohibited*, etc.)
(b) quantifications (*universal, existential, at-most-n, at-least-n* and *exactly-n*)
(c) logical operators (*logical negation, conjunction, disjunction* and *implication*)

> r_1: It is obligatory that each car rental *is owned by* atleast 2 branches.
> r_2: It is obligatory that driver that *is authorized in* Sweden, *has* a driving license that *is valid*.

Fig. 6. Sample SBVR rules.

To illustrate the class of rules r_1 and r_2 (Fig. 6), we consider the SBVR vocabulary shown in Fig. 7. To capture the information present in the SBVR rule, we formulate the mappings based on axioms explained in Sect. 3.1.

It can be seen that rule r_2 is based on facts f_1, f_2, and f_3 (Fig. 7). To represent fact types in SBVR, we create a new sort *BoolVal* which can take three values t (similar to *true*), f (similar to *false*) or NA (not assigned). Let bf be the binary fact defined as $bf \rightarrow n_1 v_1 n_2$, where n_1 (subject) and n_2 (object) are noun concept related through verb concept v_1. The corresponding mapping to SMT-LIBv2 is specified as:

```
n₁: driver
n₂: country
IN₁: Sweden

    General Concept: country
IN₂: Germany
    General Concept: country
n₃: branch
n₄: car_rental
n₅: driving_license

    General Concept: license
n₆: Rental_A
    General Concept: car_rental
n₇: pick_up_location
f₁: driver is authorized in country
f₂: driving_license is valid
f₃: driver has license
f₄: car_rental is owned by branch.
```

Fig. 7. SBVR vocabulary for the rules depicted in Fig. 6.

$$(\texttt{declare-const } v_1 \ (\texttt{Array Sort\_A \ Sort\_B BoolVal}))$$

where *Sort_A* and *Sort_B* are the clusters associated with $n1$ and $n2$ respectively. We assign default value NA to the predicate for the elements (of sorts) that are not explicitly related in the rules. The SMT-LIBv2 for $f1$ is generated as:

```
(declare-datatypes () ((BoolVal NA t f))
(declare-const
isAuthorizedIn(Array Cluster_Driver Cluster_Country BoolVal))
(assert (=(default isAuthorizedIn)NA))
```

The rule r_1 in Fig. 6 encompasses the *obligation formulation* which ranges over an *universal quantification*. This *universal quantification* introduces a variable '*car rental*' that scopes over an *atleast-n quantification* of cardinality 2. *At-least-n quantification* (*at-most-n quantification*) is the quantification that has a minimum (maximum) cardinality n and the number of referents of the variable introduced by this quantification is more (less) than or equal to n. This *atleast-n quantification* in turn ranges over the concept '*branch*'. A sample *at-least-n quantification* can be generalized as 'It is obligatory that $n1$ $v1$ at-least n $n2$'. Rule r_1 can be seen as an instance of such quantification which is mapped in SMT-LIBv2 representation with the following formula:

```
(assert    (forall ((x Cluster_Rental))
       (exists ((a Cluster_Branch)(b Cluster_Branch))
          (and (branch_domain a) (branch_domain b)
             (implies (car_rental_domain x )
                (and   (= (select isOwnedBy x a ) t)
                       (= (select isOwnedBy x b ) t))
                   (distinct a b ))))))
```

In a SBVR rule, sometimes the keyword '*that*' is used after the designation for a noun concept and before a designation for a verb concept. It introduces a restriction on the noun concept which is based on the facts defined in the vocabulary. Consider rule r_2 in Fig. 6, the concept *driver* is restricted by the fact *"driver is authorized in country"*.

Rule r_2 is semantically interpreted as "If driver is authorized in Sweden, then that driver has a driving license that is valid.", thereby the corresponding SMT-LIBv2 representation is generated as:

```
(assert(forall ((x Cluster_Driver)(z Cluster_Country))
  (exists ((y Cluster_License))
    (and (driving_license_domain y)
        (implies
            (and (driver_domain x)
      (driving_license_domain y)
                (= Sweden z) (=(select isAuthorizedIn x z) t))
            (and (= (select has x y ) t)
                (= (select isValidIn y ) t))))))))
```

BuRRiTo tool provides the provision to automatically transform SBVR vocabulary and rules into SMT-LIBv2 format. SBVR rules or definitions can contain the aspects in which a thing is measurable in terms of *'greater than'*, *'less than'* or *'equal to'*. It is also used to categorize the concepts belonging to certain entity according to a set of different criteria using 'categorization' capabilities. It can be interpreted from the SBVR vocabulary in Fig. 8 that *'duration'* is the property associated with the *'rental'* which can accept the values of type *Integer*. To map such scenarios in SMT, we declare a constant of a 2-D array which takes sort associated with the concept *'rental'* and the *Integer* sort as the parameters. Due to space limitation, we only show SMT-LIBv2 generated for the concept *'medium duration rental'*.

n_1: rental
n_2: duration
n_3: low duration rental
        Definition: rental that *has* duration *less than* or *equal to* 4 days
n_4: medium duration rental
        Definition: rental that *has* duration *greater than* 4 days and *less than* 6 days
n_5: high duration rental
        Definition: rental that *has* duration *greater than* or *equal to* 6 days

Fig. 8. A sample SBVR vocabulary.

```
(declare-const durationInt (Array Cluster_Rental Int))
(assert
(forall ((x Cluster_Rental)(a Cluster_Duration))
    (implies
        (and (medium_duration_rental_domain x) (duration_domain a))
        (and (= (select has x a ) t)
            (> (select durationInt x ) 4)
            (< (select durationInt x ) 6) ))))
```

3.3 Verification Step

SMT solvers will find the conflicting set of rules in the form of unsatisfiable cores. The unsatisfiable core will return a subset of the named formulas. We add labels to the assertions so that the command 'get-unsat-core' can use these labels in UNSAT core output. Let f_i be a function for rule r_i that exists in the system and X_i be the name to it. The conflict can be found by putting assert statement and check-sat for each such function.

To the best of our knowledge, unsat core generation is supported by MATH-SAT [20], Yices [21], CVC3, and Z3 solvers. In our work, we conduct experiments with Z3 as SMT solver. But the 'get-unsat-core' finds only one set of unsatisfiable constraints. After removing or correcting the conflicting rule, we again run the solver to find next set of unsatisfiable constraints. But we are interested in finding all sets of conflicting rules at a time. The problem of finding all set of inconsistent rules can be reduced to that of finding all minimally unsatisfiable subformulas. To illustrate such scenario, consider the following set of rules.

$$R = \{R_1, R_2, R_3, ..., R_n\}$$

If there exists some assignment to the values of the function and predicate symbols that satisfies every rule, then R is said to be satisfiable or SAT, otherwise it is unsatisfiable. We are interested in finding all the minimal sets of rules from R that are inconsistent with respect to each other. We consider the model M represented by the formula:

$$F = \{f(R_1), f(R_2), f(R_3)........., f(R_n)\}$$

where $f(R_i)$ is the boolean FOL formula corresponding to the rule R_i.

For the model M, MUSes(Minimal unsatisfiable subformulas) can be defined as

$$MUSes(M) = mu = \begin{cases} mu \subseteq F \text{ and } mu \text{ is } UNSAT \\ \forall x \in mu, mu \backslash x \text{ is } SAT \end{cases}$$

To find all the sets of inconsistent rules, we use Z3's Python-based API [22] features which extracts all minimal unsatisfiable cores together with all maximal satisfying subsets. It is based on Marco Algorithm which aims at enumerating all MUSes of an unsatisfiable constraint [23]. The technique to find all unsatisfiable cores uses the concept of a *Map Solver*. The basic *'grow'* and *'shrink'* algorithms are used for finding an Maximal Satisfying Subset (MSS) or an MUS respectively of constraint set.

4   Implementation

We built an *Inconsistency Rule Checker* on top of SBVR rule editor in our BUR-RITO tool. The SBVR rule editor facilitates an easy way to business analysts for specifying the SBVR vocabularies and rules. The tool is allowed to generate the SBVR XMI based on the SBVR 1.2 meta-model, that can be provided as an input to the *Rule Checker*. The user interface for SBVR editor is shown in Fig. 9. The tool presents all sets of inconsistent rules encountered at the end of the process, as illustrated in Fig. 10.

```
⊖ Product_A
  ⊖      General Concept:product
⊖ Product_B
  ⊖      General Concept:product
⊖ Product_B has group_code
⊖ rental
⊖ luxury_rental
  ⊖      General Concept:rental
⊖ rental is insured by credit_card
⊖ car is assigned to rental
   //--------Business Rules----------------------
⊖ It is obligatory that
⊖ if
        car is physically present in EURent_branch
     then
        car is assigned to rental.
   It is necessary that group_code of Product_B is Motor_Home.
   It is obligatory that rental is insured by atleast 2 credit_card.
   It is necessary that group_code of Product_B is Motor_Home_Plus.
   It is obligatory that luxury_rental is insured by atmost 1 credit_card.
   It is necessary that driver owns a license that is valid.
```

Fig. 9. Snapshot of the business rule editor of the BuRRiTo tool

Fig. 10. Snapshot of the conflicting rules detected by **Inconsistency Rule Checker** of the BuRRiTo tool

It can be seen that from the set of 6 business rules given as input in SBVR rule editor in Fig. 9, the inconsistency checker detects two classes of ambiguous rules as shown in Fig. 10.

Figure 11 depicts a sample set of inconsistencies that can be detected with our approach. The rule r_8, r_9 and r_{10} are inconsistent as in the SBVR vocabulary, the concept 'one way car movement' is segmented into three disjoint concepts: 'local car movement', 'in country car movement' and 'international car movement'. Consider the rule r_{11} and r_{12}, the verb concept 'specifies' and 'is specified by' are inverse verb concepts of one another, leading to ambiguities between r_{11} and r_{12}.

Case 1	r_1: it is necessary that each car rental is insured by exactly 1 credit card.
	r_2: it is necessary that each luxury car rental is car rental.
	r_3: it is necessary that each luxury car rental is insured by atleast 2 credit cards.
Case 2	r_4: it is obligatory that if car is physically present in EU-Rent branch then car is assigned to rental.
	r_5: it is impossible that if car is physically present in EU-Rent branch or car is assigned to rental.
Case 3	r_6: it is necessary that lowest cost group of car rental is **GROUP A.**
	r_7: it is necessary that lowest cost group of car rental is **GROUP B.**
Case 4	r_8: it is obligatory that India-Burma car movement is one-way car movement.
	r_9: it is obligatory that India-Burma car movement is local car movement.
	r_{10}: it is obligatory that India-Burma car movement is international car movement.
Case 5	r_{11}: it is obligatory that car movement specifies car group.
	r_{12}: it is impossible that car group is specified by car movement.
Case 6	r_{13}: it is obligatory that duration of each rental is less than 90 days.
	r_{14}: it is obligatory that duration of Rental.A is equal to 100 days.

Fig. 11. Set of inconsistent rules detected by **Inconsistency Rule Checker** using BuRRiTo tool.

5 Experimental Studies and Discussions

We manually validated the generated SMT-LIBv2 for each mapping to verify the correctness of translation. In addition, we conducted experiments on 2 case studies.

1. EU Rent Car Rental [15]:
   It contains the set of concepts of general and specific things of importance to the EURent car rental business. It consists of 64 rules ranging over 14 different modules. We created the SBVR rules and manually embedded the inconsistencies in each module. We then provided the rules as an input to *Inconsistency Rule Checker* implemented in BURRITO tool. In this study, the tool successfully identified all 14 injected conflicts.

Table 1. Comparison of work for knowledge representation and consistency checking of SBVR.

SBVR concepts	Our work	Chittimalli and Anand [8]	Karpovič [12]	Kendal and Linehan [9]	Reynares [10]
General noun concept	✓	✓	✓	Incorrect	✓
Individual noun concept	✓	✓	✓	✓	✓
Facts	✓	✓	✓	✗	✗
Property association	✓	✓	✓	✓	✗
Concept1 specialiczes concept2	✓	✓	✓	✓	✓
Segmentation	✓	✓	✓	✓	✓
Categorization	✓	✓	✓	✓	✓
Inverse verb concept	✓	✓	✓	✓	✓
Universal quantification and existential quantification	✓	✓	✓	✗	✓
Quantification involving 'at-least-n', 'at-most-n' and 'exactly-n'	✓	Incorrectly mapped	✓	✗	✓
Simple rules	✓	✓	✓	✓	✓
Rules involving conjunction	✓	✓	✓	✗	✓
Rules involving disjunction	✓	✓	✓	✗	✓
Rules involving implication	✓	Only in some cases	Only in some cases	✗	✗
Logical negation of logical formulation	✓	✓	✓	✗	✗
Quantity1 'is less than' or 'greater than' or 'equal to' quantity2	✓	✗	✓	✗	✗
Complex rules involving restriction on noun concept	✓	✗	✗	✗	✗
Complex rules involving keyword 'of' associating property to noun concept	✓	✗	✗	✗	✗
Concept1 is coextensive with concept2 (Synonym)	✓	✓	✓	✗	✗
Alethic and Deontic modalities	✗	✗	✗	✗	✗

2. Rules from Industrial Insurance Application:
   We obtained a set of 110 rules from the Industrial case-study belonging to insurance domain. The rules were complex containing the data related to liability and package policy. The business experts added 15 inconsistencies in a sample set of such rules that were converted to SBVR. Our tool successfully identified 12 inconsistent rules. The rules involving arithmetic calculations and mathematical operations (sum of, product of, percentage calculation, etc.) were not mapped to the SMT-LIBv2 in our current approach, thereby unable to detect 3 inconsistencies.

In the study, we investigate following research questions:

RQ1: How many concepts of SBVR are covered in our mappings?
RQ2: Is our approach of knowledge representation of SBVR and detecting inconsistent rules better compared with the previous works?
RQ3: What are the existing gaps in present solutions and possible opportunities for future research?

The first research question deals with the completeness of our mappings with respect to SBVR. The results of **RQ1** are presented in Table 1, where the important SBVR concepts are listed depicting the capability of the tool to capture them in the mappings and consistency check. This table is an extension of the results presented by Karpovič in his paper [12]. Mitra and Chittimalli conducted a systematic literature review on the existing consistency checking of business rules presented in the SBVR format [24].

Apart from generation of correct model and effective system level test data, our work reduced the deductions performed by the solver by minimizing the number of un-interpreted functions. Let there be m terms present in SBVR vocabulary where m is the sum of *general noun concept* terms and *individual noun concept* terms and sorts can have the elements from the defined vocabulary, then the number of uninterpreted functions produced using paper [8] for unary fact types is $O(m)$, for binary fact types is $O(m \times m)$ and for n-ary is $O(m^n)$. The work presented in the paper reduced the uninterpreted functions to $O(p)$ for unary where p is the terms present in the graphical cluster corresponding to the sort associated with the argument of predicate. And for n-ary, the number of uninterpreted functions produced is $O(p_1 \times p_2 \times \ldots \times p_n)$ where p_i is the number of terms present in the graphical cluster corresponding to the sort associated with the i_{th} argument of function. Thereby, the current approach has reduced burden on the 3 core components of Z3 [6]: (1) DPLL-based SAT solver, (2) Satellite solvers (arithmetic, arrays, etc.), (3) E-matching abstract machine (quantifiers).

The work presented in the paper makes the following novel contributions:

1. While there has been work done in detecting inconsistencies in business rules, we are the first to introduce the concept of many sorted logic and graph reachability in translation of SBVR to SMT-LIBv2, thereby efficiently exploiting the FOL basis of SBVR specification.

2. The technique presented in [8] finds only one set of unsatisfiable constraints at one time. We reduced the problem finding all set of inconsistent rules to that of finding all minimally unsatisfiable subformulas to finding all sets of conflicting rules at a time. We built an *Inconsistency Rule Checker* on top of SBVR rule editor in our BuRRiTo tool which successfully finds all set of inconsistent rules.

3. We proposed 60 different mappings for automatic translation of SBVR based rules, vocabulary, definitions and other concepts (e.g. synonym, synonymous form, inverse verb concept, etc.) overcoming the limitations of the previous works mentioned in Sect. 2. Although BuRRiTo performs well in the experiments, but the future research in the field of inconsistency rule checking should take into consideration the alethic and deontic modalities captured in the rules.

References

1. Sarbanes Oxley Act: Sarbanes Oxley Act. https://www.thebalance.com/sarbanes-oxley-act-and-the-enron-scandal-393497
2. Zeginis, C., Plexousakis, D.: Business Process Modelling. http://www.csd.uoc.gr/~hy565/lectures/Lecture-2-BP%20Modeling.pdf
3. Semantics of Business Vocabulary and Rules (SBVR). http://www.omg.org/spec/SBVR/. Accessed 29 Sept 2015
4. Barrett, C., Fontaine, P., Tinelli, C.: The Satisfiability Modulo Theories Library (SMT-LIB) (2016). www.SMT-LIB.org
5. Cok, D.R., et al.: The SMT-LIBv2 language and tools: a tutorial. Language C 2010–2011 (2011)
6. de Moura, L., Bjørner, N.: Z3: an efficient SMT solver. In: Ramakrishnan, C.R., Rehof, J. (eds.) TACAS 2008. LNCS, vol. 4963, pp. 337–340. Springer, Heidelberg (2008). https://doi.org/10.1007/978-3-540-78800-3_24
7. Barrett, C., Conway, C.L., Deters, M., Hadarean, L., Jovanović, D., King, T., Reynolds, A., Tinelli, C.: CVC4. In: Gopalakrishnan, G., Qadeer, S. (eds.) CAV 2011. LNCS, vol. 6806, pp. 171–177. Springer, Heidelberg (2011). https://doi.org/10.1007/978-3-642-22110-1_14
8. Chittimalli, P.K., Anand, K.: Domain-independent method of detecting inconsistencies in SBVR-based business rules. In: Proceedings of the International Workshop on Formal Methods for Analysis of Business Systems, pp. 9–16. ACM (2016)
9. Kendall, E., Linehan, M.H.: Mapping SBVR to OWL2. Technical report, IBM Research Report, RC25363 (WAT1303-040), March 2013
10. Reynares, E., et al.: SBVR to OWL 2 mappings: an automatable and structural-rooted approach. CLEI Electron. J. **17**(3), 3 (2014)
11. Karpovič, J., et al.: The comprehensive mapping of semantics of business vocabulary and business rules (SBVR) to OWL 2 ontologies. Inf. Technol. Control **43**(3), 289–302 (2014)
12. Karpovič, J., et al.: Experimental investigation of transformations from SBVR business vocabularies and business rules to OWL 2 ontologies. Inf. Technol. Control **45**(2), 195–207 (2016)
13. Jackson, D.: Alloy: a Language & Tool for Relational Models (2012). http://alloy.mit.edu/alloy/applications.html

14. Bocic, I., Bultan, T.: Efficient data model verification with many-sorted logic (T). In: 2015 30th IEEE/ACM International Conference on Automated Software Engineering (ASE), pp. 42–52. IEEE (2015)
15. Business Rules Group: EU-Rent Car Rental case study. http://www.businessrulesgroup.org/first_paper/br01ad.htm
16. Glimm, B., et al.: HermiT: an OWL 2 reasoner. J. Autom. Reasoning **53**(3), 245–269 (2014)
17. Sirin, E., et al.: Pellet: a practical OWL-DL reasoner. Web Semant. Sci. Serv. Agents World Wide Web **5**, 51–53 (2007)
18. Cohn, A.G.: A many sorted logic with possibly empty sorts. In: Kapur, D. (ed.) CADE 1992. LNCS, vol. 607, pp. 633–647. Springer, Heidelberg (1992). https://doi.org/10.1007/3-540-55602-8_197
19. Cormen, T.H., Leiserson, C.E., Rivest, R.L., Stein, C.: Graph algorithms. Introduction Algorithms **6** (1992)
20. Bruttomesso, R., Cimatti, A., Franzén, A., Griggio, A., Sebastiani, R.: The MATH-SAT 4 SMT solver. In: Gupta, A., Malik, S. (eds.) CAV 2008. LNCS, vol. 5123, pp. 299–303. Springer, Heidelberg (2008). https://doi.org/10.1007/978-3-540-70545-1_28
21. Dutertre, B., De Moura, L.: The yices smt solver. Tool Paper **2**(2), 1-2 (2006). http://yices.csl.sri.com/tool-paper.pdf
22. Bjorner, N.: Enumeration of Minimal Unsatisfiable Cores and Maximal Satisfying Subsets. https://github.com/Z3Prover/z3/blob/master/examples/python/mus/marco.py
23. Liffiton, M.H., Malik, A.: Enumerating infeasibility: finding multiple MUSes quickly. In: Gomes, C., Sellmann, M. (eds.) CPAIOR 2013. LNCS, vol. 7874, pp. 160–175. Springer, Heidelberg (2013). https://doi.org/10.1007/978-3-642-38171-3_11
24. Mitra, S., Chittimalli, P.K.: A systematic review of methods for consistency checking in SBVR-based business rules (2017)

Prolog and Optimizations

Exploiting Term Hiding to Reduce Run-Time Checking Overhead

Nataliia Stulova[1,2]() (iD), José F. Morales[1] (iD), and Manuel V. Hermenegildo[1,2] (iD)

[1] IMDEA Software Institute, Madrid, Spain
{nataliia.stulova,josef.morales,manuel.hermenegildo}@imdea.org
[2] ETSI Informáticos, Universidad Politécnica de Madrid (UPM), Madrid, Spain

Abstract. One of the most attractive features of untyped languages is the flexibility in term creation and manipulation. However, with such power comes the responsibility of ensuring the correctness of these operations. A solution is adding run-time checks to the program via assertions, but this can introduce overheads that are in many cases impractical. While static analysis can greatly reduce such overheads, the gains depend strongly on the quality of the information inferred. Reusable libraries, i.e., library modules that are pre-compiled independently of the client, pose special challenges in this context. We propose a technique which takes advantage of module systems which can hide a selected set of functor symbols to significantly enrich the shape information that can be inferred for reusable libraries, as well as an improved run-time checking approach that leverages the proposed mechanisms to achieve large reductions in overhead, closer to those of static languages, even in the reusable-library context. While the approach is general and system-independent, we present it for concreteness in the context of the Ciao assertion language and combined static/dynamic checking framework. Our method maintains the full expressiveness of the assertion language in this context. In contrast to other approaches it does not introduce the need to switch the language to a (static) type system, which is known to change the semantics in languages like Prolog. We also study the approach experimentally and evaluate the overhead reduction achieved in the run-time checks.

Keywords: Logic programming · Module systems
Practicality of run-time checking
Assertion-based debugging and validation · Static analysis

1 Introduction

Modular programming has become widely adopted due to the benefits it provides in code reuse and structuring data flow between program components.

Research partially funded by Spanish MINECO TIN2015-67522-C3-1-R grant *TRACES* and the Madrid M141047003 *N-GREENS* program. We also thank Dylan McDermott, Alan Mycroft, and the anonymous reviewers for their comments. An extended abstract on this work was published as [1].

© Springer International Publishing AG 2018
F. Calimeri et al. (Eds.): PADL 2018, LNCS 10702, pp. 99–115, 2018.
https://doi.org/10.1007/978-3-319-73305-0_7

A tightly related concept is the principle of *information hiding* that allows concealing the concrete implementation details behind a well-defined interface and thus allows for cleaner abstractions. Different programming languages implement these concepts in different ways, some examples being the encapsulation mechanism of classes in object-oriented programming and opaque data types. In the (constraint) logic programming context, most mature language implementations incorporate module systems, some of which allow programmers to restrict the visibility of some functor symbols to the module where they are defined, thus both hiding the concrete implementation details of terms from other modules and providing guarantees that only the predicates of that particular module can use those functor symbols as term constructors or matchers.

One of the most attractive features of untyped languages for programmers is the flexibility they offer in term creation and manipulation. However, with such power comes the responsibility of ensuring correctness in the manipulation of data, and this is specially relevant when data can come from unknown clients. A popular solution for ensuring safety is to enhance the language with optional assertions that allow specifying correctness conditions both at the module boundaries and internally to modules. These assertions can be checked dynamically by adding run-time checks to the program, but this can introduce overheads that are in many cases impractical. Such overheads can be greatly reduced with static analysis, but the gains then depend strongly on the quality of the analysis information inferred. Unfortunately, there are some common scenarios where shape/type analyses are necessarily imprecise. A motivational example is the case of reusable libraries, i.e., the case of analyzing, verifying, and compiling a library for general use, without access to the client code or analysis information on it. This includes for example the important case of servers accessed via remote procedure calls. Static analysis faces challenges in this context, since the unknown clients can fake data that is really intended to be internal to the library. Ensuring safety then requires sanitizing input data with potentially expensive run-time checks.

In order to alleviate this problem, we present techniques that, by exploiting term hiding and the strict visibility rules of the module system, can greatly improve the quality of the shape information inferred by static analysis and reduce the run-time overhead for the calls across module boundaries by several orders of magnitude. These techniques can result in improvements in the number and size of checks that allow bringing guarantees and overheads to levels close to those of statically-typed approaches, but without imposing on programs the restriction of being well-typed. For concreteness, we use in this work the relevant parts of the Ciao system [2], which pioneered the assertion-based, combined static+dynamic checking approach: the module system, the assertion language –which allows providing optional program specifications with various kinds of information, such as modes, shapes/types, non-determinism, etc.–, and the overall framework. However, our results are general and we believe they can be applied to many dynamic languages. In particular, we present a semantics for modular logic programs where the mapping of module symbols is abstract and implementation-agnostic, i.e., independent of the visibility rules of particular module systems.

2 Preliminaries

We first recall some basic notation and the standard program semantics, following the formalization of [3]. An *atom* A is a syntactic construction of the form $f(t_1, \ldots, t_n)$ where f is a symbol of arity n and the t_i are *terms*. Terms are inductively defined as variable symbols or constructions of the form $f(t_1, \ldots, t_n)$ where f is a symbol of arity n $(n \geq 0)$ and the t_i are terms. Note that we do not (yet) distinguish between predicate symbols and functors (uninterpreted function symbols), denoting the global set of *symbols* as FS. A *constraint* is a conjunction of expressions built from predefined predicates (such as term equations or inequalities over the reals) whose arguments are constructed using predefined functions (such as real addition). A *literal* is either an atom or a constraint. *Constants* are introduced as 0-ary symbols. A *goal* is a conjunction of literals. A *clause* is defined as $H \leftarrow B$, where H is an atom (the head) and B is a goal (the body). A *definite program* is a finite set of clauses. The *definition* of an atom A in a program, $\mathsf{cls}(A)$, is the set of program clauses whose head has the same predicate symbol and arity as A, renamed-apart. We assume that all clause heads are *normalized*, i.e., H is of the form $f(X_1, \ldots, X_n)$ where the $X_1, \ldots, X_n$ are distinct free variables.

We recall the classic operational semantics of (non-modular) definite programs, given in terms of program *derivations*, which are sequences of *reductions* between *states*. We use :: to denote concatenation of sequences. A *state* $\langle G \mid \theta \rangle$ consists of a goal sequence G and a constraint store (or *store* for short) θ. A *query* is a pair (L, θ), where L is a literal and θ a store, for which the (constraint) logic programming system starts a computation from state $\langle L \mid \theta \rangle$. The set of all derivations from the query Q is denoted $\mathsf{derivs}(Q)$. A finite derivation from a query (L, θ) is *finished* if the last state in the derivation cannot be reduced, and it is *successful* if the last state is of the form $\langle \square \mid \theta' \rangle$, where $\square$ denotes the empty goal sequence. In that case, the constraint $\exists_L \theta'$ (denoting the projection of θ onto the variables of L) is an *answer* to (L, θ). Else, the derivation is *failed*. We denote by $\mathsf{answers}(Q)$ the set of answers to a query Q.

3 An Abstract Approach to Modular Logic Programs

There have been several proposals to date for supporting modularity in logic programs, all of which are based on performing a partition of the set of program symbols into modules. As mentioned before, the two most widely adopted approaches are referred to as *predicate-based* and *atom-based* module systems. In predicate-based module systems all symbols involved in terms are global, i.e., they belong to a single global user module –a special module from which all modules import the symbols and to which all modules can add symbols. In atom-based module systems [4] only constants and explicitly exported symbols are global, while the rest of the symbols are local to their modules. Ciao [5] adopts a hybrid approach which is as in predicate-based systems but with the possibility of marking a selected set of symbols as local (we will use this model in the examples in Sect. 5). Despite the differences among these module systems, by performing module resolution applying the appropriate visibility rules, programs are reducible in all systems to a form that can be interpreted using the same Prolog-style semantics. We will use this property in order to abstract our results away from particular module systems and their symbol visibility rules. To this end we present a formalization of the "flattened" version of a modular program, where visibility is explicit and is thus independent of the visibility conventions of specific module systems. Let MS denote the set of all *module symbols*. The *flattened* form of a modular definite program is defined as follows:

Definition 1 (Modular Program). *A modular program is a pair* $(P, \text{mod}(\cdot))$, *where* P *is a definite program and* $\text{mod}(\cdot)$ *is a mapping that assigns for each symbol* $f \in \text{FS}$ *a unique module symbol* $m \in \text{MS}$. *Let* C *be a clause* $H \leftarrow B$ *in* P, $\text{mod}(C) \triangleq \text{mod}(H)$. *Let* A *be an atom*[1] *or a term of the form* $f(\ldots)$. *Then* $\text{mod}(A) \triangleq \text{mod}(f)$.

The $\text{mod}(\cdot)$ mapping creates a partition of the clauses in the definite program P. We refer to each resulting equivalence class as a module, and represent it with the module symbol shared by all clauses in that class. The set of all symbols defined by a module m is $\text{def}(m) = \{f | f \in \text{FS}, \text{mod}(f) = m, m \in \text{MS}\}$.

Definition 2 (Interface of a Module). *The* interface *of a module* m *is given by the disjoint sets* $\text{exp}(m)$ *and* $\text{imp}(m)$, *s.t.* $\text{exp}(m) \subseteq \text{def}(m)$ *is the subset of the symbols defined in* m *that can appear in other modules, referred to as the* export list *of* m, *and* $\text{imp}(m) = \{f | f \in \text{FS}, f \text{ is in symbols of } \text{cls}(p), p \in \text{def}(m)\} \setminus \text{def}(m)$ *is a superset of symbols in the bodies of the predicates of* m, *that are not defined in* m, *referred to as the* import list *of* m.

To track calls across module boundaries we introduce the notion of *clause end literal*, a marker of the form $\text{ret}(H)$, where H stands for the head of the parent clause, as given in the following definition:

Definition 3 (Operational Semantics of Modular Programs). *We redefine the derivation semantics such that goal sequences are of the form* $(L, m) :: G$ *where* L *is a literal, and* m *is the module from which* L *was introduced, as shown below. Then, a state* $S = \langle (L, m) :: G \mid \theta \rangle$ *can be reduced to a state* S' *as follows:*

1. $\langle (L, m) :: G \mid \theta \rangle \rightsquigarrow \langle G \mid \theta \wedge L \rangle$ *if* L *is a constraint and* $\theta \wedge L$ *is satisfiable.*
2. $\langle (L, m) :: G \mid \theta \rangle \rightsquigarrow \langle (B_1, n) :: \ldots :: (B_k, n) :: (\text{ret}(L), n) :: G \mid \theta \rangle$ *if* L *is an atom and* $\exists (L \leftarrow B_1, \ldots, B_k) \in \text{cls}(L)$ *where* $\text{mod}(L) = n$ *and it holds that* $(L \in \text{def}(n) \wedge n = m) \bigvee (L \in \text{exp}(n) \wedge L \in \text{imp}(m) \wedge n \neq m)$.
3. $\langle (L, m) :: G \mid \theta \rangle \rightsquigarrow \langle G \mid \theta \rangle$ *if* L *is a clause return literal* $\text{ret}(\_)$.

Basically, for reduction step 2 to succeed, the L literal should either be defined in module m (and then $n = m$) or it should belong to the export list of module n and be in the import list of module m.

---

[1] In practice constraints are also located in modules. It is trivial to extend the formalization to include this, we do not write it explicitly for simplicity.

4   Run-Time Checking of Modular Programs

Assertion Language. We assume that program specifications are provided by means of assertions: linguistic constructions that allow expressing properties of programs. For concreteness we will use the **pred** assertions of the Ciao assertion language [2,6,7], following the formalization of [3,8]. Such **pred** assertions define the set of all admissible preconditions for a given predicate, and for each such pre-condition, a corresponding post-condition. These pre- and post-conditions are formulas containing literals defined by predicates that are specially labeled as *properties*. Properties and the other predicates composing the program are written in the same language. This approach is motivated by the direct correspondence between the declarative and operational semantics of constraint logic programs. In what follows we refer to these literals corresponding to properties as *prop* literals. The predicate symbols of *prop* literals are module-qualified in the same way as those of the other program literals.

Example 1 (Property). The following property describes a sorted list:

```
sorted([]). sorted([_]). sorted([X,Y|L]) :- X =< Y, sorted([Y|L]).
```

i.e., $[\![sorted(A)]\!] = \{A = [], A = [B], A = [B,C|D] \wedge B \leq C \wedge E = [C|D] \wedge sorted(E)\}$.

The left part of Fig. 1 shows a set of assertions for a predicate (identified by a normalized atom $Head$). The Pre_i and $Post_i$ fields are conjunctions[2] of *prop* literals that refer to the variables of $Head$. Informally, such a set of assertions states that in any execution state $\langle (Head, m) :: G \mid \theta \rangle$ at least one of the Pre_i conditions should hold, and that, given the $(Pre_i, Post_i)$ pair(s) Pre_i holds, then, if the predicate succeeds, the corresponding $Post_i$ should hold upon success. We denote the set of assertions for a predicate represented by $Head$ by $\mathcal{A}(Head)$, and the set of all assertions in a program by $\mathcal{A}$.

```
:- pred Head : Pre₁ => Post₁.
...
:- pred Head : Preₙ => Postₙ.
```

$$C_i = \begin{cases} c_i.\mathsf{calls}(Head, \bigvee_{j=1}^{n} Pre_j) & i = 0 \\ c_i.\mathsf{success}(Head, Pre_i, Post_i) & i = 1..n \end{cases}$$

Fig. 1. Correspondence between assertions and assertion conditions.

In our formalization, rather than using the assertions for a predicate directly, we use instead a normalized form which we refer to as the set of *assertion conditions* for that predicate, denoted as $\mathcal{A}_C(Head) = \{C_0, C_1, \ldots, C_n\}$, as shown in Fig. 1, right. The c_i are identifiers which are unique for each assertion condition. The calls($Head, \ldots$) conditions encode the check that ensures that the calls to the predicate represented by the $Head$ literal are within those admissible by the set of assertions, and we thus call them the *calls assertion conditions*. The success($Head, Pre_i, Post_i$) conditions encode the checks for compliance of the

---

[2] In the general case *Pre* and *Post* can be DNF formulas of *prop* literals but we limit them to conjunctions herein for simplicity of presentation.

successes for particular sets of calls, and we thus call them the *success assertion conditions*. If there are no assertions associated with $Head$ then the corresponding set of assertion conditions is empty. The set of assertion conditions for a program, denoted $\mathcal{A}_C$ is the union of the assertion conditions for each of the predicates in the program, and is derived from the set $\mathcal{A}$ of all assertions in the program.

Semantics with Run-time Checking of Assertions and Modules. We now present the operational semantics with assertions for modular programs, which checks whether assertion conditions hold or not while computing the derivations from a query in a modular program. The identifiers of the assertion conditions (the c_i) are used to keep track of any violated assertion conditions. The $\mathsf{err}(c)$ literal denotes a special goal that marks a derivation finished because of the violation of the assertion condition with identifier c. A finished derivation from a query (L, θ) is now *successful* if the last state is of the form $\langle \Box \mid \theta' \rangle$, *erroneous* if the last state is of the form $\langle \mathsf{err}(c) \mid \theta' \rangle$, or *failed* otherwise. The set of derivations for a program from its set of queries $\mathcal{Q}$ using the semantics with run-time checking of assertions is denoted by $\mathsf{rtc\text{-}derivs}(\mathcal{Q})$. We also extend the clause return literal to the form $\mathsf{ret}(H, \mathcal{C})$, where $\mathcal{C}$ is the set of identifiers c_i of the assertion conditions that should be checked at that derivation point. A literal L *succeeds trivially* for θ in program P, denoted $\theta \Rightarrow_P L$, iff $\exists \theta' \in \mathsf{answers}((L, \theta))$ such that $\theta \models \theta'$. Intuitively, a literal L succeeds trivially if L succeeds for θ without adding new constraints to θ. This notion captures the checking of properties and we will thus often refer to this operation as "checking L in the context of θ."[3]

Definition 4 (Operational Semantics for Modular Programs with Run-Time Checking). *A state $S = \langle (L, m) :: G \mid \theta \rangle$ can be reduced to a state S', denoted $S \leadsto_{\mathsf{rtc}} S'$, as follows:*

1. *If L is a constraint then $S' = \langle G \mid \theta \wedge L \rangle$ if $\theta \wedge L$ is satisfiable.*
2. *If L is an atom and $\exists (L \leftarrow B_1, \ldots, B_k) \in \mathsf{cls}(L)$, then the new state is*

$$S' = \begin{cases} \langle \mathsf{err}(c) \mid \theta \rangle & \text{if } \exists c.\mathsf{calls}(L, Pre) \in \mathcal{A}_C(L) \wedge \theta \not\Rightarrow_P Pre \\ \langle (B_1, n) :: \ldots :: (B_k, n) :: (\mathsf{ret}(L, \mathcal{C}), n) :: G \mid \theta \rangle & \text{otherwise} \end{cases}$$

s.t. $\mathcal{C} = \{c_i \mid c_i.\mathsf{success}(L, Pre_i, Post_i) \in \mathcal{A}_C(L) \wedge \theta \Rightarrow_P Pre_i\}$ where $\mathsf{mod}(L) = n$ and it holds that $(L \in \mathsf{def}(n) \wedge n = m) \bigvee (L \in \mathsf{exp}(n) \wedge L \in \mathsf{imp}(m) \wedge n \neq m)$
3. *If L is a clause return literal $\mathsf{ret}(\_, \mathcal{C})$, then*

$$S' = \begin{cases} \langle \mathsf{err}(c) \mid \theta \rangle & \text{if } \exists c \in \mathcal{C} \text{ s.t. } c.\mathsf{success}(L', \_, Post) \in \mathcal{A}_C(L') \wedge \theta \not\Rightarrow_P Post \\ \langle G \mid \theta \rangle & \text{otherwise} \end{cases}$$

---

[3] Note that even if several assertion conditions may be violated at the same time, we consider only the first one of them. The ordering is only imposed by the implementation and does not affect the semantics.

Theorem 1 below on the correctness of the operational semantics with run-time checking can be straightforwardly adapted from [8].[4] The completeness of this operational semantics as presented in Theorem 2 below can only be proved for *partial* program derivations, as the new semantics introduces the err() literal that directly replaces the goal sequence of a state in which a violation of an assertion condition occurs.

Theorem 1 (Correctness Under Assertion Checking). *For any tuple* $(P, \mathcal{Q}, \mathcal{A})$ *it holds that* $\forall D' \in$ *rtc-derivs*$(\mathcal{Q}) \exists D \in$ *derivs*$(\mathcal{Q})$ *s.t.* D' *is equivalent to* D *(including partial derivations).*

Theorem 2 (Partial Completeness Under Assertion Checking). *For any tuple* $(P, \mathcal{Q}, \mathcal{A})$ *it holds that* $\forall D = (S_1, \ldots, S_k, S_{k+1}, \ldots, S_n) \in$ *derivs*$(\mathcal{Q})$ $\exists D' \in$ *rtc-derivs*$(\mathcal{Q})$ *s.t.* D' *is equivalent to* D *or* $(S_1, \ldots, S_k, \langle err(c) \mid \_\rangle).$

5   Shallow Run-Time Checking

As mentioned before, the main advantage of modular programming is that it allows safe local reasoning on modules, since two different modules are not allowed to contribute clauses to the same predicate.[5] Our purpose herein is to study how in systems where the visibility of function symbols can be controlled, similar reasoning can be performed at the level of terms, and in particular how such reasoning can be applied to reducing the overhead of run-time checks. We will refer to these reduced checks as *shallow* run-time checks, which we will formally define later in this section. We start by recalling how in cases where the visibility of terms function symbols can be controlled, this reasoning is impossible without global (inter-modular) program analysis, using the following example:

Example 1. Consider a module $m1$ that exports a single predicate p/1 that constructs point/1 terms:

```
:- module(m1, [p/1, r/0]).      % m1 declared, p/1 and r/0 are exported
p(A) :- A = point(B), B = 1.    % A = user:point(1)
:- use_module(m2,[q/1]).        % import q/1 from a module m2
r :- X = point(2), q(X).        % X = user:point(2)
```

Here, we want to reason about the terms that can appear during program execution at several specific program points: (a) before we call p/1 (point at which execution enters module m1); (b) when the call to p/1 succeeds (point at which execution leaves the module); and (c) before we call q/1 (point at which execution enters another module). When we exit the module at points (b) and

---

[4] The formal definition of the equivalence relation on derivations, as well as proofs for the theorems and lemmas can be found in Appendix A of the extended version of this paper available from CoRR at https://arxiv.org/abs/1705.06662 (v3).

[5] In practice, an exception is multifile predicates. However, since they need to be declared explicitly, local reasoning is still valid assuming conservative semantics (e.g., *topmost* abstract values) for them.

(c) we know that in any point(X) constructed in $m1$ either $X = 1$ or $X = 2$. However, when we enter module $m1$ at point (a) A could have been bound by the calling module to any term including, e.g., point([4,2]), point(2), point(a), point(1), etc., since the use of the point/1 functor is not restricted.

Now we will consider the case where the visibility of terms can be controlled. We start by defining the following notion:

Definition 5 (Hidden Functors of a Module). *The set of hidden functors of a module is the set of functors that appear in the module that are local and non-exported.*

Example 2. In this example we mark instead the point/1 symbol as hidden. We use Ciao module system notation [5], where all function symbols belong to user, unless marked with a :- hide f/N declaration. Such symbols are hidden, i.e., local and not exported.[6]

```
:- module(m1, [p/1, r/0]).
:- hide point/1.              % point/0 is restricted to m1
p(A) :- A = point(B), B = 1.  % m1:point(1), not user:point(1)
:- use_module(m2,[q/1]).
r :- X = point(2), q(X).      % m1:point(2) escapes through call to q/1
```

Let us consider the same program points as in Example 1. When we exit the module, we can infer the same results, but with m1:point/1 instead of user:point/1. Now, if we see the m1:point(X) term at point (a) we know that it has been constructed in $m1$, and the X has to be bound to either 1 or 2, because the code that can create bindings for X is only located in $m1$ (and the point/1 terms are passed outside the module at points (b) and (c)).

As mentioned before, these considerations will allow us to use an optimized form of checking that we refer to as *shallow checking*. In order to formalize this notion, we start by defining all possible terms that may exist outside a module m as its *escaping terms*. We will also introduce the notion of *shallow properties* as the specialization of the definition of these properties w.r.t. these escaping terms, and we will present algorithms to compute such shallow versions of properties.

Definition 6 (Visible Terms at a State). *A property that represents all terms that are visible in a state* $S = \langle (L, \_) :: G \mid \theta \rangle$ *of some derivation* $D \in rtc\text{-}derivs(\mathcal{Q})$ *for a tuple* $(P, \mathcal{Q}, \mathcal{A})$ *is* $\text{vis}_S(X) \equiv \bigvee_{V \in \text{Vars}_L} (X = V \wedge \theta)$ *where* Vars_L *denotes the set of variables of literal* L.

Definition 7 (Escaping terms). *Consider all states* S *in all derivations* $D \in rtc\text{-}derivs(\mathcal{Q})$ *of any tuple* $(P, \mathcal{Q}, \mathcal{A})$ *where* P *imports a given module* m. *A property that represents escaping terms w.r.t.* m *is* $\text{esc}_m(X) \equiv \bigvee \text{vis}_S(X)$ *for each* $S = \langle (\_, n) :: \_ \mid \_ \rangle$ *with* $n \neq m$.

---

[6] Note that this can be achieved in other systems: e.g., in XSB [4] it can be done with a :- local/1 declaration, combined with not exporting the symbol.

Algorithm 1. ESCAPING_TERMS

1: **function** ESCAPING_TERMS(M)
2:      $Def := \mathsf{usr}(X)$
3:      **for all** L exported from M **do**
4:          **for all** $c.\mathsf{success}(L, \_, Post) \in \mathcal{A}_C(L)$ **do**
5:              **for all** $P \in$ LITNAMES($Post, vars(L)$) **do**
6:                  $Def := Def \sqcup P(X)$
7:      **for all** L imported from M **do**
8:          **for all** $c.\mathsf{calls}(L, Pre) \in \mathcal{A}_C(L)$ **do**
9:              **for all** $P \in$ LITNAMES($Pre, vars(L)$) **do**
10:                  $Def := Def \sqcup P(X)$
11:      **return** $(\mathsf{esc}_m(X) \leftarrow Def)$
12: **function** LITNAMES($G, Args$)
13:      **return** set of P such that $A \in Args$ and $G = (\ldots \wedge P(A) \wedge \ldots)$

The set of all public symbols to which a variable X can be bound is denoted as $\mathsf{usr}(X) = \{X | \mathsf{mod}(X) = \mathtt{user}\}$. The following lemma states that it is enough to consider the states at the module boundaries to compute $\mathsf{esc}_m(X)$:

Lemma 1 (Escaping at the Boundaries). *Consider all derivation steps $S_1 \leadsto_{\mathsf{rtc}} S_2$ where $S_1 = \langle (L_1, m) :: \_ | \_ \rangle$ and $S_2 = \langle (L_2, n) :: \_ | \theta \rangle$ with $n \neq m$. That is, the derivation steps when calling a predicate at n from m (if L_1 is a literal) or when returning from m to module n (if L_1 is $\mathsf{ret}(\_)$). Let $\mathsf{esc}_{m'}(X)$ be the* smallest *property (i.e., the property with the smallest model) such that $\theta \Rightarrow_P \mathsf{esc}_{m'}(X)$ for each variable X in the literal L_2, and $\mathsf{usr}(X) \Rightarrow_P \mathsf{esc}_{m'}(X)$. Then $\mathsf{esc}_{m'}(X) \vee \mathsf{usr}(X)$ is equivalent to $\mathsf{esc}_m(X)$.*

Algorithm 1 computes an over-approximation of the $\mathsf{esc}_m(X)$ property. The algorithm has two parts. First, it loops over the exported predicates in module m. For each exported predicate we use $Post$ from the success assertion conditions as a safe over-approximation of the constraints that can be introduced during the execution of the predicate. We compute the union ($\sqcup$, which is equivalent to $\vee$ but it can sometimes simplify the representation) of all properties that restrict any variable argument in $Post$. The second part of the algorithm performs the same operation on all the properties specified in the Pre of the calls assertions conditions. This is a safe approximation of the constraints that can be *leaked* to other modules called from m.

Note that the algorithm can use analysis information to detect more precise calls to the imported predicates, as well as more precise successes of the exported predicates, than those specified in the assertion conditions present in the program.

Lemma 2 (Correctness of ESCAPING_TERMS). The ESCAPING_TERMS algorithm computes a safe (over)approximation to $\mathsf{esc}_m(X)$ (when using the operational semantics with assertions).

Algorithm 2. SHALLOW_INTERFACE

```
 1: function SHALLOW_INTERFACE(M)
 2:     Let M' be M with wrappers for exported predicates
 3:        (to differentiate internal from external calls)
 4:     Let Q(X) := ESCAPING_TERMS(M')
 5:     for all L exported from M do
 6:         for all c.calls(L, Pre) ∈ A_C(L) do
 7:             Update A_C(L) with c.calls(L, Pre#)
 8:         for all c.success(L, Pre, Post) ∈ A_C(L) do
 9:             Update A_C(L) with c.success(L, Pre#, Post)
10:     return M'
```

Shallow Properties. Shallow run-time checking consists in using *shallow* versions of properties in the run-time checks for the calls across module boundaries. While this notion could be added directly to the operational semantics, we will present it as a program transformation based on the generation of shallow versions of the properties, since this also provides a direct implementation path.

Example 3. Assume that the set of escaping terms of m contains `point(1)` and it does not contain the more general `point(_)`. Consider the property: `intpoint(point(X)) :- int(X)`. Checking `intpoint(A)` at any program point outside m must check first that `A` is instantiated to `point(X)` and that `X` is instantiated to an integer (`int(X)`). However, the escaping terms show that it is not possible for a variable to be bound to `point(X)` without `X=1`. Thus, the latter check is redundant. We can compute the optimized – or *shallow* – version of `intpoint/1` in the context of all execution points external to m as `intpoint(point(_))`.

Let SPEC(L, Pre) generate a specialized version L' of predicate L w.r.t. the calls given by Pre (see [9]). It holds that for all θ, $\theta \Rightarrow_P L$ iff $\theta \wedge Pre \Rightarrow_P L'$.

Definition 8 (Shallow property). *The shallow version of a property $L(X)$ w.r.t. module m is denoted as $L(X)^{\#}$, and computed as* SPEC($L(X), Q(X)$), *where $Q(X)$ is a (safe) approximation of the escaping terms of m (*ESCAPING_TERMS(m)).*

Algorithm 2 computes the optimized version of a module interface using shallow checks. It first introduces wrappers for the exported predicates, i.e., predicates `p(X) :- p'(X)`, renaming all internal occurrences of `p` by `p'`. Then it computes an approximation $Q(X)$ of the escaping terms of M. Finally, it updates all Pre in calls and success assertion conditions, for all exported predicates, with their shallow version $Pre^{\#}$. We compute the shallow version of a conjunction of literals $Pre = \bigwedge_i L_i$ as $Pre^{\#} = \bigwedge_i L_i^{\#}$.

Theorem 3 (Correctness of SHALLOW_INTERFACE). Replacing a module m in a larger program by its shallow version does not alter the (run-time checking) operational semantics.

Discussion about precision. The presence of any *top* properties in the calls or success assertion conditions will propagate to the end in the ESCAPING_TERMS algorithm (see Algorithm 1). For a significant class of programs, this is not a problem as long as we can provide or infer precise assertions which do not use this top element. Note that usr(X), since it has a void intersection with any hidden term, does not represent a problem. For example, many generic Prolog term manipulation predicates (e.g., functor/3) typically accept a *top* element in their calls conditions. We restrict these predicates to work only on user (i.e., not hidden) symbols.[7] More sophisticated solutions, that are outside the scope of this paper, include: producing monolithic libraries (creating versions of the imported modules and using abstract interpretation to obtain more precise assertion conditions); or disabling shallow checking (e.g., with a dynamic flag) until the execution exits the context of m (which is correct except for the case when terms are dynamically asserted).

Multi-library scenarios. Recall that properties can be exported and used in assertions from other modules. The shallow version of properties in m are safe to be used not only at the module boundaries but also in any other assertion check outside m. Computing the shallow optimization can be performed per-library, without strictly requiring intermodular analysis. However, in some cases intermodular analysis may improve the precision of escaping terms and allow more aggressive optimizations.

6 Experimental Results

We explore the effectiveness of the combination of term hiding and shallow checking in the reusable library context, i.e., in libraries that use (some) hidden terms in their data structures and offer an interface for clients to access/manipulate such terms. We study the four assertion checking modes of [3]: *Unsafe* (no library assertions are checked), *Client-Safe* (checks are generated only for the assertions of the predicates exported by the library, assertions for the internal library predicates are not checked), *Safe-RT* (checks are generated from assertions both for internal and exported library predicates), and *Safe-CT+RT* (like *RT*, but analysis information is used to clear as many checks as possible at compile-time). We use the lightweight instrumentation scheme from [10] for generating the run-time checks from the program assertions. For eliminating the run-time checks via static analysis we reuse the Ciao verification framework, including the extensions from [3]. We concentrate in these experiments on shape analysis (regular types).

In our experiments each benchmark is composed of a library and a client/driver. We have selected a set of Prolog libraries that implement tree-based data structures. Libraries B-tree and binary tree were taken from the Ciao sources; libraries AVL-tree, RB-tree, and heap were adapted from YAP,

---

[7] This can be implemented very efficiently with a simple bit check on the atom properties and does not impact the execution.

adding similar assertions to those of the Ciao libraries. Table 1 shows some statistics for these libraries: number of lines of code (LOC), size of the object file (Size KB), the number of assertions in the library specification considered (Pred Assertions), and the number of hidden functors per library (# Hidden Symbols).

Table 1. Benchmark metrics.

Name	LOC	Size (KB)	Pred Assertions	# Hidden Symbols
AVL-tree	147	16.7	20	2
B-tree	240	22.1	18	3
Binary tree	58	8.3	6	2
Heap	139	15.1	12	3
RB-tree	678	121.8	20	4

In order to focus on the assertions of the library operations used in the benchmarks (where by an operation we mean the set of predicates implementing it) we do not count in the tables the assertions for library predicates not directly involved in those operations. Library assertions contain instantiation (moded) regular types.[8] For each library we have created two drivers (clients) resulting in two experiments per library. In the first one the library operation has constant ($O(1)$) time complexity and the respective run-time check has $O(N)$ time complexity (e.g., looking up the value stored at the root of a binary tree and checking on each lookup that the input term is a binary tree). Here a major speedup is expected when using *shallow* run-time checks, since the checking time dominates operation execution time and the reduction due to shallow checking should be more noticeable. In the second one the library operation has non-constant ($O(log(N))$) complexity and the respective run-time check $O(N)$ complexity (e.g., inserting an element in a binary tree and checking on each insertion that the input term is a tree). Here obviously a smaller speedup is to be expected with *shallow* checking. All experiments were run on a MacBook Pro, 2.6 GHz Intel Core i5 processor, 8 GB RAM, and under the Mac OS X 10.12.3 operating system.

Static Analysis. Table 2 presents the detailed compile-time analysis and checking times for the *Safe-CT+RT* mode. Numbers in parentheses indicate the percentage of the total compilation time spent on analysis, which stays reasonably low even in the most complicated case (13% for the RB-tree library). Nevertheless, the analysis was able to discharge most of the assertions in our benchmarks, leaving always only 2–3 assertions unchecked (i.e., that will need run-time checks), for the predicates of the library operations being benchmarked.

Run-time Checking. After the static preprocessing phase we have divided our libraries into two groups: (a) libraries where the only unchecked assertions left

---

[8] A simple example of assertions, escaping terms, and shallow checks, as well as full plots for all benchmarks can be found in Appendices B-C of the extended version of this paper available from CoRR at https://arxiv.org/abs/1705.06662 (v3).

Table 2. Static analysis and checking time for benchmarks for the *Safe-CT+RT* mode.

Benchmark	Analysis time, ms					Assertions	
	prep	shfr	prep	eterms	Total	Checking, ms	Unchecked
AVL-tree	2	10	2	31	45 (2%)	59 (2%)	2/20
B-tree	3	9	3	38	53 (2%)	90 (3%)	3/18
Binary tree	1	9	1	14	25 (2%)	33 (2%)	2/6
Heap	2	7	2	24	35 (2%)	71 (4%)	2/12
RB-tree	13	11	14	35	73 (3%)	298 (10%)	3/20

are the ones for the boundary calls (`AVL-tree`, `heap`, and `binary tree`),[9] and (b) libraries with also some unchecked assertions for internal calls (`B-tree` and `RB-tree`). We present run time plots[10] for one library of each group. Since the unchecked assertions in the second group correspond to internal calls of the $O(log(N))$ operation experiment, we only show here a set of plots of the $O(1)$ operation experiment for one library, as these plots are very similar across all benchmarks.

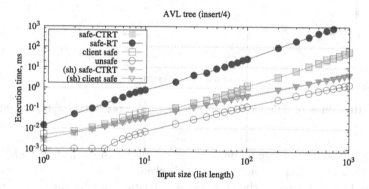

Fig. 2. Run times in different checking modes, `AVL-tree` library, $O(log(N))$ operation.

Figure 2 illustrates the overhead reductions from using the shallow run-time checks in the `AVL-tree` benchmark for the $O(N)$ *insert* operation experiment. This is also the best case that can be achieved for this kind of operations, since in the *Safe-CT+RT* mode all inner assertions are discharged statically. Figure 3 shows the overhead reductions from using the shallow checks in the `B-tree` benchmark for the $O(log(N))$ *insert* operation experiment. In contrast with the previous case, here the overhead reductions achieved by employing shallow checks are dominated by the total check cost, and while the overhead reduction

---

[9] Due to our reusable library scenario the analysis of the libraries is performed without any knowledge of the client and thus the library interface checks must always remain.

[10] The current measurements depend on the C `getrusage()` function, that on Mac OS has microsecond resolution.

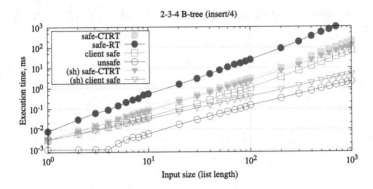

Fig. 3. Run times in different checking modes, `B-tree` library, $O(log(N))$ operation.

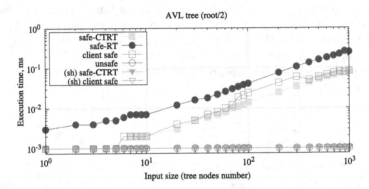

Fig. 4. Run times in different checking modes, `AVL-tree` library, $O(1)$ operation.

is obvious in the *Client-Safe* mode, it is not significant in the *Safe-CT+RT* mode where some internal assertion was being checked.

Figure 4 presents the overhead reductions in run-time checking resulting from the use of the shallow checks in the `AVL-tree` benchmark for the $O(1)$ *peek* operation experiment on the root. As we can see, using shallow checks allows us to obtain constant overhead on the boundary checks for such cheap operations in all execution modes but *Safe-RT*. In summary, the shallow checking technique seems quite effective in reducing the shape-related run-time checking overheads for the reusable-library scenario.

7   Related Work

Modularity. The topic of modules and logic programming has received considerable attention, dating back to [11–13] and resulting in standardization attempts for ISO-Prolog [14]. Currently, most mature Prolog implementations adopt some flavor of a module system, *predicate-based* in SWI [15], SICStus [16], YAP [17], and ECLiPSe [18], and *atom-based* in XSB [4]. As mentioned before, Ciao [2,5] uses a hybrid approach, which behaves by default as in predicate-based systems but with the possibility of marking a selected set of symbols as hidden, making it essentially compatible with that of XSB. Some previous research in the comparative advantages of atom-based module systems can be found in [19].

Parallels with Static Typing and Contracts. While traditionally Prolog is untyped, there have been some proposals for integrating it with type systems, starting with [20]. Several strongly-typed Prolog-based systems have been proposed, notable examples being Mercury [21], Gödel [22], and Visual Prolog [23]. An approach for combining typed and untyped Prolog modules has been proposed in [24]. A conceptually similar approach in the world of functional programming is *gradual typing* [25,26]. The Ciao model offers an (earlier) alternative, closer to *soft typing* [27], but based on safe approximations and abstract interpretation, thus providing a more general and flexible approach than the previous work, since assertions can contain any abstract property – see [28] for a discussion of this topic. This approach has recently also been applied in a number of contract-based systems [29–31], for which we believe our techniques can be relevant.

Run-time Checking Optimization. High run-time overhead is a common problem in systems that include dynamic checking [26]. The impact of global static analysis in reducing run-time checking overhead has been studied in [3]. A complementary approach is improving the instrumentation of the checks and combining it with run-time data caching [10,32] or limiting the points at which tests are performed [33]. While these optimizations can bring significant reductions in overhead, it still remains dependent on the size of the terms being checked. We have shown herein that even in the challenging context of calls across open module boundaries it is sometimes possible to achieve constant run-time overhead.

8 Conclusions

We have described a lightweight modification of a predicate-based module system to support term hiding and explored the optimizations that can be achieved with this technique in the context of combined compile-time/run-time verification. We have studied the challenging case of reusable libraries, i.e., library modules that are pre-compiled independently of the client. We have shown that with our approach the shape information that can be inferred can be enriched significantly and large reductions in overhead can be achieved. The overheads achieved are closer to those of static languages, even in the reusable-library context, without requiring switching to strong typing, which is less natural in Prolog-style languages, where there is a difference between error and failure/backtracking.

References

1. Stulova, N., Morales, J., Hermenegildo, M.: Towards run-time checks simplification via term hiding (extended abstract). In: Technical Communications of ICLP 2017, OASIcs (2017)
2. Hermenegildo, M., Bueno, F., Carro, M., López, P., Mera, E., Morales, J., Puebla, G.: An overview of Ciao and its design philosophy. TPLP **12**(1–2), 219–252 (2012)
3. Stulova, N., Morales, J., Hermenegildo, M.: Reducing the overhead of assertion run-time checks via static analysis. In: PPDP 2016, pp. 90–103. ACM, September 2016
4. Swift, T., Warren, D.S.: XSB: extending Prolog with tabled logic programming. TPLP **12**(1–2), 157–187 (2012)
5. Cabeza, D., Hermenegildo, M.: A new module system for Prolog. In: Lloyd, J., et al. (eds.) CL 2000. LNCS (LNAI), vol. 1861, pp. 131–148. Springer, Heidelberg (2000). https://doi.org/10.1007/3-540-44957-4_9
6. Hermenegildo, M.V., Puebla, G., Bueno, F.: Using global analysis, partial specifications, and an extensible assertion language for program validation and debugging. In: Apt, K.R., Marek, V.W., Truszczynski, M., Warren, D.S. (eds.) The Logic Programming Paradigm, pp. 161–192. Springer, Heidelberg (1999). https://doi.org/10.1007/978-3-642-60085-2_7
7. Puebla, G., Bueno, F., Hermenegildo, M.: Combined static and dynamic assertion-based debugging of constraint logic programs. In: Bossi, A. (ed.) LOPSTR 1999. LNCS, vol. 1817, pp. 273–292. Springer, Heidelberg (2000). https://doi.org/10.1007/10720327_16
8. Stulova, N., Morales, J., Hermenegildo, M.: Assertion-based debugging of higher-order (C)LP programs. In: PPDP 2014, ACM, September 2014
9. Puebla, G., Albert, E., Hermenegildo, M.: Abstract interpretation with specialized definitions. In: Yi, K. (ed.) SAS 2006. LNCS, vol. 4134, pp. 107–126. Springer, Heidelberg (2006). https://doi.org/10.1007/11823230_8
10. Stulova, N., Morales, J., Hermenegildo, M.: Practical run-time checking via unobtrusive property caching. TPLP **15**(04–05), 726–741 (2015)
11. Warren, D., Chen, W.: Formal semantics of a theory of modules. Technical report 87/11, SUNY at Stony Brook (1987)
12. Chen, W.: A theory of modules based on second-order logic. In: 4th IEEE International Symposium on Logic Programming, San Francisco, pp. 24–33 (1987)
13. Miller, D.: A logical analysis of modules in logic programming. J. Logic Program. **6**, 79–108 (1989)
14. ISO: PROLOG: ISO/IEC DIS 13211-2 — Part 2: Modules (2000)
15. Wielemaker, J., Schrijvers, T., Triska, M., Lager, T.: SWI-Prolog. TPLP **12**(1–2), 67–96 (2012)
16. Carlsson, M., Mildner, P.: SICStus Prolog - the first 25 years. TPLP **12**(1–2), 35–66 (2012)
17. Santos Costa, V., Rocha, R., Damas, L.: The YAP Prolog system. TPLP **12**(1–2), 5–34 (2012)
18. Schimpf, J., Shen, K.: ECLiPSe - from LP to CLP. TPLP **12**(1–2), 127–156 (2012)
19. Haemmerlé, R., Fages, F.: Modules for Prolog revisited. In: Etalle, S., Truszczyński, M. (eds.) ICLP 2006. LNCS, vol. 4079, pp. 41–55. Springer, Heidelberg (2006). https://doi.org/10.1007/11799573_6
20. Mycroft, A., O'Keefe, R.: A polymorphic type system for Prolog. Artif. Intell. **23**, 295–307 (1984)

21. Somogyi, Z., Henderson, F., Conway, T.: The execution algorithm of Mercury: an efficient purely declarative logic programming language. J. Logic Program. **29**(1–3), 17–64 (1996)
22. Hill, P., Lloyd, J.: The Gödel Programming Language. MIT Press, Cambridge (1994)
23. Prolog Development Center: Visual Prolog
24. Schrijvers, T., Santos Costa, V., Wielemaker, J., Demoen, B.: Towards typed Prolog. In: Garcia de la Banda, M., Pontelli, E. (eds.) ICLP 2008. LNCS, vol. 5366, pp. 693–697. Springer, Heidelberg (2008). https://doi.org/10.1007/978-3-540-89982-2_59
25. Siek, J.G., Taha, W.: Gradual typing for functional languages. In: Scheme and Functional Programming Workshop, pp. 81–92 (2006)
26. Takikawa, A., Feltey, D., Greenman, B., New, M., Vitek, J., Felleisen, M.: Is sound gradual typing dead? In: POPL 2016, pp. 456–468, January 2016
27. Cartwright, R., Fagan, M.: Soft typing. In: PLDI 1991, SIGPLAN, pp. 278–292. ACM (1991)
28. Hermenegildo, M.V., Bueno, F., Carro, M., López, P., Mera, E., Morales, J., Puebla, G.: The Ciao approach to the dynamic vs. static language dilemma. In: Proceedings of the International WS on Scripts to Programs, STOP 2011. ACM (2011)
29. Fähndrich, M., Logozzo, F.: Static contract checking with abstract interpretation. In: Beckert, B., Marché, C. (eds.) FoVeOOS 2010. LNCS, vol. 6528, pp. 10–30. Springer, Heidelberg (2011). https://doi.org/10.1007/978-3-642-18070-5_2
30. Tobin-Hochstadt, S., Van Horn, D.: Higher-order symbolic execution via contracts. In: OOPSLA, pp. 537–554. ACM (2012)
31. Nguyen, P., Horn, D.V.: Relatively complete counterexamples for higher-order programs. In: PLDI 2015, pp. 446–456. ACM (2015)
32. Koukoutos, E., Kuncak, V.: Checking data structure properties orders of magnitude faster. In: Bonakdarpour, B., Smolka, S.A. (eds.) RV 2014. LNCS, vol. 8734, pp. 263–268. Springer, Cham (2014). https://doi.org/10.1007/978-3-319-11164-3_22
33. Mera, E., Lopez-García, P., Hermenegildo, M.: Integrating software testing and run-time checking in an assertion verification framework. In: Hill, P.M., Warren, D.S. (eds.) ICLP 2009. LNCS, vol. 5649, pp. 281–295. Springer, Heidelberg (2009). https://doi.org/10.1007/978-3-642-02846-5_25

On k-colored Lambda Terms and Their Skeletons

Paul Tarau$^{(\boxtimes)}$ (ID)

Department of Computer Science and Engineering,
University of North Texas, Denton, USA
paul.tarau@unt.edu

Abstract. The paper describes an application of logic programming to the modeling of difficult combinatorial properties of lambda terms, with focus on the class of simply typed terms.

Lambda terms in de Bruijn notation are Motzkin trees (also called binary-unary trees) with indices at their leaves counting up on the path to the root the steps to their lambda binder.

As a generalization of *affine lambda terms*, we introduce *k-colored lambda terms* obtained by labeling their lambda nodes with counts of the variables they bind. We define the *skeleton of a k-colored lambda term* as the Motzkin tree obtained by erasing the de Bruijn indices labeling its leaves. A new bijection between 2-colored skeletons and binary trees reveals their connection to the Catalan family of combinatorial objects.

After a statistical study of properties of *k-colored lambda terms* and their skeletons, we focus on the case of *simply-typed closed k-colored* lambda terms for which a new combinatorial generation algorithm is given and some interesting relations between maximal coloring, size of type expressions and typability are explored.

The paper is structured as a literate Prolog program to facilitate an easily replicable, concise and declarative expression of our concepts and algorithms.

Keywords: Declarative modeling of combinatorial classes
Families of lambda terms · Simply-typed closed lambda terms
Motzkin trees · Bijections between data types

1 Introduction

Lambda terms, in de Bruijn notation [1], can be seen as Motzkin-trees built of unary lambda nodes, binary application nodes and variables at their leaves, labeled with de Bruijn indices pointing toward their lambda binder. We call the *skeleton of a lambda term* the Motzkin tree obtained by erasing its de Bruijn indices.

A useful distinction can be made between lambda constructors that bind variables and those that do not. Among other benefits, distinguishing them makes the analysis of linear and affine terms simpler and puts their skeletons, the 2-colored Motzkin trees, in bijection with the well-known Catalan family of combinatorial objects.

© Springer International Publishing AG 2018
F. Calimeri et al. (Eds.): PADL 2018, LNCS 10702, pp. 116–131, 2018.
https://doi.org/10.1007/978-3-319-73305-0_8

More generally, can we classify lambda nodes by inverting the function from indices at the leaves to their binders?

This leads to the concept of *k-colored lambda terms* where colors classify binders depending on the number of variables they bind. It also brings us to the main focus of this paper, the interaction of k-coloring, skeletons and the class of simply-typed terms, starting with the easy case of always typable affine and linear terms and then empirically approaching some interesting observables for the notoriously difficult general case.

Despite the asymptotically vanishing density of simply-typed lambda terms [2], their all-term and random-term generation has been speeded-up significantly by the use of Prolog-based algorithms that interleave generation and type-inference steps [3,4]. However, the structure of simply-typed lambda terms has so far escaped handling by analytical methods. Basic combinatorial properties like counts for terms of a given size have been obtained so far only by generating all terms, or, as in [4], by mimicking their exhaustive generation with a recursive structure that, while omitting the actual lambda terms, keeps the type-inference mechanism intact.

These difficulties are the main motivation of this paper, which suggests a fresh look at the structure of simply typed terms and their type expressions, via their relations to their k-colored skeletons, revealing insights on the structure of simply-typed closed lambda terms.

The paper is organized as follows. Section 2 describes a new bijection between binary trees and 2-colored Motzkin trees. Section 3 discusses the case of closed, linear and affine lambda terms. Section 4 focuses on the case of k-colored simply typed closed lambda terms and their statistical properties. Section 5 overviews related work and Sect. 6 concludes the paper.

The paper is structured as a literate Prolog program to facilitate an easily replicable, concise and declarative expression of our concepts and algorithms. The code extracted from the paper, together with some related code and utilities for visualization is available at: http://www.cse.unt.edu/~tarau/research/2017/padl18.pro, tested with SWI-Prolog [5] version 7.4.2.

2   A Bijection Between 2-colored Motzkin Trees and Binary Trees

A *Motzkin tree* (also called binary-unary tree) is a rooted ordered tree built from binary nodes, unary nodes and leaf nodes. A *k-colored Motzkin tree* is obtained by labeling its unary nodes with colors from a set of k elements.

As usual in Prolog, we denote, F/N a function symbol F of arity N. Given a set of such function symbols (that we will also call "constructors") one can see the set of terms generated from them as a free algebra using the set of functors as its signature.

We define *2-colored Motzkin trees* (shortly *2-Motzkin trees*) as the free algebra generated by the constructors v/0, l/1, r/1 and a/2. An example of a Prolog term representing a 2-colored Motzkin tree is l(a(l(v),r(v))).

We define lambda terms in de Bruijn form as the free algebra generated by the constructors l/1, r/1 and a/2 with leaves labeled with natural numbers (and seen as wrapped with the constructor v/1 when convenient). When talking about lambda terms, we interpret l/1 constructors as lambda binders a/2 constructors as applications and v/1 constructors as de Bruijn index nodes.

Thus, we can see lambda terms in de Bruijn form as Motzkin trees with leaves labeled with natural numbers. We interpret the labels as pointing to their lambda binder on a path to the root of the tree. If each leaf reaches via its de Bruijn index at least one unary constructor, we call the term closed, otherwise we call it *plain*.

We observe that the constructors marking lambdas may have at least one de Bruijn index pointing to them or have none. We can think about these as *2-colored lambda terms*. Thus, we classify our unary constructors into:

– *binding lambdas*, that are reached by at least one de Bruijn index (denoted l/1)
– *free lambdas*, that cannot be reached by any de Bruijn index (denoted r/1).

We define the *2-colored Motzkin skeleton of a lambda term* (shortly *skeleton*) as the 2-Motzkin tree obtained by erasing the de Bruijn indices labeling their leaves.

It is well-known that 2-Motzkin trees are counted by the Catalan numbers and several bijections between them to members of the Catalan family of combinatorial objects have been identified in the past [6]. We will introduce here a *new* one that is defined inductively in a "compositional way", based on a mapping between small tree components on the two sides. As an application, this allows one to use a uniform random binary tree generation algorithm like [7] to generate random 2-Motzkin trees.

We describe binary trees as the free algebra generated by the constructors e/0 and c/2. Binary trees are a well known member of the Catalan family of combinatorial objects. Our bijection can be seen as connecting any other member of this family to 2-colored Motzkin trees.

We define the bijection between non-empty binary trees and 2-Motzkin trees simply by encoding each of the nodes v/0, l/1, r/1 and a/2 by a unique small binary tree as shown by the reversible bidirectional predicate cat_mot/2, with the binary tree as its first argument and the 2-Motzkin tree as its second.

```
cat_mot(c(e,e),v).
cat_mot(c(X,e),l(A)):-X=c(_,_),cat_mot(X,A).
cat_mot(c(e,Y),r(B)):-Y=c(_,_),cat_mot(Y,B).
cat_mot(c(X,Y),a(A,B)):-X=c(_,_),Y=c(_,_),
  cat_mot(X,A),
  cat_mot(Y,B).
```

Proposition 1. *The predicate* cat_mot/2 *defines a bijection between non-empty binary trees and 2-colored Motzkin trees.*

Proof. It follows by structural induction by observing that the 4 clauses cover via disjoint unification patterns all the 4 possible tree shapes matched one-to-one on the two sides.

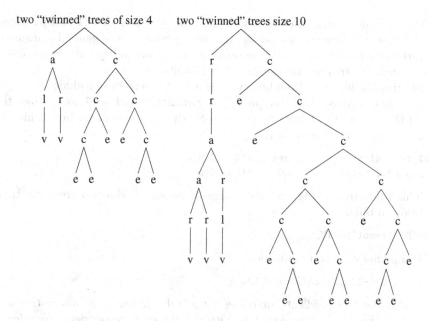

Fig. 1. The 2-colored Motzkin trees to non-empty binary trees bijection

Example 1. *We illustrate the bidirectional Prolog predicate* `cat_mot/2` *with the two trees also shown in Fig. 1, together with two larger trees on the right side, "twinned" in a similar way, Motzkin-tree on the left, binary tree on the right.*

```
?- cat_mot(BinTree,a(l(v),r(v))),cat_mot(BinTree,MotTree).
BinTree = c(c(c(e, e), e), c(e, c(e, e))),
MotTree = a(l(v), r(v)) .
```

As a first application, a linear-time random generator for binary trees (based on instance Rémy's algorithm, [7]) can be "borrowed" in linear time in the size of the terms, to generate 2-colored Motzkin random motzkin trees via the bijection defined by the predicate `cat_mot/2`.

One can also "borrow" the simple binary tree generator `cat(N,T)` which, given a natural number N returns a tree X of size N, assuming a size definition that counts each internal node as 1.

```
cat(N,X):-cat(X,N,0).

cat(e,N,N).
cat(c(A,B),SN,N3):-succ(N1,SN),cat(A,N1,N2),cat(B,N2,N3).
```

Note the use of the bidirectional `succ/2` built-in, which also tests for being larger than 0, when working as predecessor.

By using the generator `cat/2` for binary trees, we derive a generator for 2-colored Motzkin trees via their bijection to non-empty binary trees as follows.

```
mot2(N,M):-cat(N,C),cat_mot(C,M).
```

Given an enumeration of binary trees given by successor `s/1` and predecessor `p/1` (for instance the one in [8] that also provides more general arithmetic operations on them) one can define ranking and unranking operations on binary trees (bijections to/from the set of natural numbers).

Shifting the bijection from binary trees to Motzkin trees to include the *empty binary tree* is achieved with the predicates `cat2mot/2` and `mot2cat/2`. Note the use of the `s/1` and `p/1` operations from [8], that are also given in the literate Prolog program associated in this paper.

```
cat2mot(C,M):-s(C,SuccC),cat_mot(SuccC,M).
mot2cat(M,C):-cat_mot(SuccC,M),p(SuccC,C).
```

This leads to ranking and unranking of 2-colored Motzkin trees via their bijection to binary trees, defined as

```
rank(M,N):-mot2cat(M,C),n(C,N).
```

Unranking can then be defined as:

```
unrank(N,M):-t(N,C),cat2mot(C,M).
```

Note also the `t/2` predicate mapping a natural number to a binary tree and the `n/2` predicate mapping a tree its natural number correspondent. We refer to [8] for their definition and implementation, converting efficiently between binary representations of numbers to/from trees, also replicated in the literate code of this paper.

3   Closed, Affine and Linear Terms

We can see a lambda term in de Bruijn form as a Motzkin tree decorated with natural numbers at its leaves. With a *size definition* (assumed here) that gives 2 units to binary constructors, 1 unit to unary constructors and 0 units to the leaves of the tree, a lambda term and its skeleton can be, conveniently, seen as having the same size, in fact corresponding (up to a constant factor) to its *heap representation* in the runtime system of all programming languages we know of.

Semantically, the labels are understood as pointing to a unary node seen as a lambda binder on the path to the root, starting with 0 for the closest one.

Thus a lambda term is built with the constructors `a/2` representing applications, `l/1` and `r/1` representing lambda nodes and natural numbers marking leaves (possibly wrapped as `v/1` nodes, when convenient).

A 2-Motzkin tree is built with `a/2` representing binary nodes, `l/1` and `r/1` representing unary nodes and `v/0` standing for leaf nodes. Thus we compute a skeleton by replacing the de Bruijn indices at the leaves of a lambda term with the constant `v/0`.

When generating trees of a given size, with several node constructors, it makes sense to have separate counters for each. The predicate `sum_to/3` maintains such counters for nodes of types `l/1`, `r/1` and `a/2`.

```
sum_to(N,c(L,R,A),c(0,0,0)):-N>=0,
  between(0,N,A2),0=:=A2/\1,A is A2>>1,
  LR is N-A2,
  between(0,LR,L),
  R is LR-L.
```

The predicates (suggestively named) `1Dec/2`, `rDec/2` and `aDec/2` define single steps consuming one available unit of size for each of the corresponding constructors. Note the use of the bidirectional built-in predicate `succ/2` that computes in this case the predecessor of a natural number and fails after reaching 0.

```
1Dec(c(SL,R,A),c(L,R,A)):-succ(L,SL).
rDec(c(L,SR,A),c(L,R,A)):-succ(R,SR).
aDec(c(L,R,SA),c(L,R,A)):-succ(A,SA).
```

We will start with generators for closed, affine and linear terms.

As analytic methods are known for computing counts for closed terms as well as closed affine and linear terms [9], we will focus here on some simple properties of their skeletons and on their efficient generators.

3.1 Closed Lambda Terms

A lambda term in de Bruijn form is closed, if for each of its de Bruijn indices, there is a lambda binder to which it points, on the path to the root of the tree representing the term. We call a Motzkin tree *closable* if it is the skeleton of at least one closed lambda term.

It immediately follows that:

Proposition 2. *If a Motzkin tree is a skeleton of a closed lambda term, then it exists at least one lambda binder on each path from the leaf to the root.*

There are slightly more unclosable Motzkin trees than closable ones as size grows:
number of closable skeletons of sizes 0,1,2,... :
0,1,1,2,5,11,26,65,163,417,1086,2858,7599,20391,55127,150028,410719, ...
number of unclosable skeletons of sizes 0,1,2,... :
1,0,1,2,4,10,25,62,160,418,1102,2940,7912,21444,58507,160544,442748, ...

We refer to [10] for an analytic solution proving that asymptotically $\frac{1}{\sqrt{5}}$ of the skeletons are closable.

3.2 Closed Affine Lambda Terms

An *affine lambda term* has one or zero variables bound by each lambda constructor.

Proposition 3. *If a 2-Motzkin tree with n binary nodes is a skeleton of an affine lambda term, then it has exactly $n + 1$ unary 1 nodes, with at least one on each path from the root to its $n + 1$ leaves.*

This suggests generators that separate unary and binary node counts for the skeletons and enforce this constraint on their respective sizes.

The predicate afLam/2, follows closely the one described in detail in [11], except that it handles l/1 and r/1 as separate cases.

```
afLam(N,T):-sum_to(N,Hi,Lo),
  has_enough_lambdas(Hi),
  afLinLam(T,[],Hi,Lo).


has_enough_lambdas(c(L,_,A)):-succ(A,L).
```

The predicate has_enough_lambdas/1 is used to express the constraint that the number of application nodes a/2 should be one less than the number of l/1 constructors (in bijection with the leaves they bind). The predicate afLinLam/4 is defined via Definite Clause Grammars (DCGs) that encapsulate the consumption of the size units[1]. It uses the predicate subset_and_complement_of/3 to direct each lambda binder on either a left or a right path at an application node. Note also the use of the constructor l/2 holding as its first argument the actual variable that it binds.

```
afLinLam(v(X),[X])-->[].
afLinLam(l(X,A),Vs)-->lDec,afLinLam(A,[X|Vs]).
afLinLam(r(A),Vs)-->rDec,afLinLam(A,Vs).
afLinLam(a(A,B),Vs)-->aDec,
  {subset_and_complement_of(Vs,As,Bs)},
  afLinLam(A,As),
  afLinLam(B,Bs).


subset_and_complement_of([],[],[]).
subset_and_complement_of([X|Xs],NewYs,NewZs):-
  subset_and_complement_of(Xs,Ys,Zs),
  place_element(X,Ys,Zs,NewYs,NewZs).


place_element(X,Ys,Zs,[X|Ys],Zs).
place_element(X,Ys,Zs,Ys,[X|Zs]).
```

Erasure of de Bruijn indices turns a 2-colored lambda term into a 2-colored Motzkin tree.

```
toMotSkel(v(_),v).
toMotSkel(l(X),l(Y)):-toMotSkel(X,Y).
toMotSkel(l(_,X),l(Y)):-toMotSkel(X,Y).
toMotSkel(r(X),l(Y)):-toMotSkel(X,Y).
toMotSkel(a(X,Y),a(A,B)):-toMotSkel(X,A),toMotSkel(Y,B).
```

The predicates afSkelGen/2 and linSkelGen/2 transform the generator for lambda terms into generators for their skeletons.

---

[1] Functional programmers might notice here the analogy with the use of monads encapsulating state changes with constructs like Haskell's do notation.

```
afSkelGen(N,S):-afLam(N,T),toMotSkel(T,S).
```

```
linSkelGen(N,S):-linLam(N,T),toMotSkel(T,S).
```

The multiset of skeletons is trimmed to a set of unique skeletons using SWI-Prolog's `distinct/2` built-in.

```
afSkel(N,T):-distinct(T,afSkelGen(N,T)).
```

```
linSkel(N,T):-distinct(T,linSkelGen(N,T)).
```

3.3   Closed Linear Lambda Terms

As lambda binders in linear terms are in bijection with the (uniques) leaves they bind, the following holds.

Proposition 4. *If a Motzkin tree with n binary nodes is a skeleton of a linear lambda term, then it has exactly $n + 1$ unary nodes, with one on each path from the root to its $n + 1$ leaves.*

```
linLam(N,T):-N mod 3=:=1,
  sum_to(N,Hi,Lo),has_no_unused(Hi),
  afLinLam(T,[],Hi,Lo).
```

```
has_no_unused(c(L,0,A)):-succ(A,L).
```

Note the use of the predicate `has_no_unused/1` that expresses, quite concisely, the constraints that `r/1` nodes should not occur in the term and that the set of `l/1` nodes should be in a bijection with the set of leaves.

As (at most) one variable is associated to each binder, no type conflict can arise between occurrences. Thus, all *closed affine and linear terms are well-typed*. The unary nodes of the skeletons of affine term can be seen as having 2 colors, `l/1` and `r/1`. This suggests to investigate next the general case of k-colored terms.

4   k-colored Simply-Typed Closed Lambda Terms

As a natural generalization derived from k-colored Motzkin trees, we define a *k-colored lambda term* having as its lambda constructor `l/1` labeled with the number of variables that it binds. Thus an affine term is a 2-colored lambda term.

The predicate `kColoredClosed/2` generates terms while partitioning lambda binders in k-colored classes. It works by incrementing the count of leaf variables a lambda binds, in a "backtrackable way", by using successor arithmetic with the deepest node kept as a free logical variable at each step.

```
kColoredClosed(N,X):-kColoredClosed(X,[],N,0).

kColoredClosed(v(I),Vs)-->{nthO(I,Vs,V),inc_var(V)}.
kColoredClosed(l(K,A),Vs)-->l,
  kColoredClosed(A,[V|Vs]),
  {close_var(V,K)}.
kColoredClosed(a(A,B),Vs)-->a,
  kColoredClosed(A,Vs),
  kColoredClosed(B,Vs).

l(SX,X):-succ(X,SX).
a-->l,l.

inc_var(X):-var(X),!,X=s(_).
inc_var(s(X)):-inc_var(X).

close_var(X,K):-var(X),!,K=0.
close_var(s(X),SK):-close_var(X,K),l(SK,K).
```

Note also the DCG-mechanism that controls the intended size of the terms via the (conveniently named) predicates 1/2 and a/2 that decrement available size by 1 and respectively 2 units.

Example 2. *3-colored lambda terms of size 3, exhibiting colors 0,1,2.*

```
?- kColoredClosed(3,X).
X = l(0, l(0, l(1, v(0)))) ;
X = l(0, l(1, l(0, v(1)))) ;
X = l(1, l(0, l(0, v(2)))) ;
X = l(2, a(v(0), v(0))) .
```

Given a tree with n application nodes, the counts for all k-colored lambdas in it must sum up to $n+1$. Thus we can generate a binary tree and then decorate it with lambdas satisfying this constraint. Note that the constraint holds for subtrees, recursively. We leave it as future work to find out if this mechanism can reduce the amount of backtracking and accelerate term generation.

4.1   Type Inference for k-colored Terms

The study of the combinatorial properties of simply-typed lambda terms is notoriously hard. The two most striking facts that one might notice when inferring types are:

- *non-monotonicity*, as crossing a lambda increases the size of the type, while crossing an application node trims it down
- *agreement via unification (with occurs check)* between the types of each variable under a lambda

Interestingly, to our best knowledge, no SAT or ASP algorithms exist in the literature that attack the combined type inference and combinatorial generation problem for lambda terms, most likely because of the complexity of emulating unification-with-occurs-check steps in propositional logic. Thus we will follow the interleaving of term generation, checking for closedness and type inference steps shown in [8], but enhance it to also identify variables covered by each lambda binder. In fact, given the surjective function $f : V \to L$ that associates to each leaf variable in a closed lambda term its lambda binder, one can compute the set $f^{-1}(l)$ for each $l \in L$, expressing which variables are mapped to each binder.

Example 3. *We illustrate two 2-colored simply typed terms with lambda nodes shown as* 1/1 *constructors marked with the labels of the variables they bind (if any). We place the inferred type as the right child of a "root" labeled with ": ".*

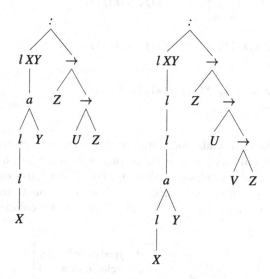

As in [8], our type inference algorithm ensures that variables under the same binder agree on their type via unification with occurs check, to avoid formation of cycles in the types, represented as binary trees with internal nodes "->/2" and logic variables as leaves.

```
simplyTypedColored(N,X,T):-simplyTypedColored(X,T,[],N,0).

simplyTypedColored(v(X),T,Vss)-->{
    member(Vs:T0,Vss),
    unify_with_occurs_check(T,T0),
    addToBinder(Vs,X)
  }.
simplyTypedColored(l(Vs,A),S->T,Vss)-->l,
  simplyTypedColored(A,T,[Vs:S|Vss]),
  {closeBinder(Vs)}.
simplyTypedColored(a(A,B),T,Vss)-->a,
  simplyTypedColored(A,(S->T),Vss),
  simplyTypedColored(B,S,Vss).
```

Note that `addToBinder/2` adds each leaf under a binder to the open end of the list of variable/type pairs list, closed by `closeBinder/1`.

```
addToBinder(Ps,P):-var(Ps),!,Ps=[P|_].
addToBinder([_|Ps],P):-addToBinder(Ps,P).

closeBinder(Xs):-append(Xs,[],_),!.
```

Example 4. *Some terms of size 5 generated by the predicate* `simplyTyped Colored/3` *and their types.*

```
?- simplyTypedColored(5,Term,Type).
Term = l([], l([], l([], l([], l([A], v(A)))))),
Type =  (B->C->D->E->F->F) ;
...
Term = l([A, B], a(l([], v(A)), l([], v(B)))),
Type =  (C->C) ;
...
Term = l([A, B], a(l([], l([], v(A))), v(B))),
Type =  (C->D->C) ;
...
```

We are now ready to make some empirical observations on terms, colors and type sizes. We have noticed that both average and maximum number of colors of lambda terms grow very slowly with size. Figure 2 compares on a log-scale the growths of simply typed closed terms and their closed affine terms subset. As for de Bruijn terms, we can define the *Motzkin skeletons* of k-colored lambda terms

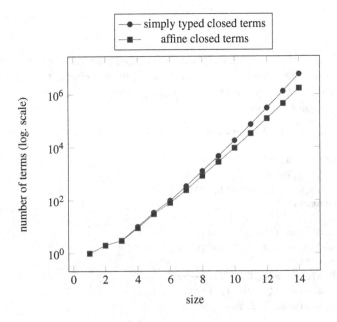

Fig. 2. Counts of simply typed closed terms and affine closed terms by increasing sizes

by erasing the first argument of the l/2 and v/1 constructors. We can also define the *k-colored Motzkin skeletons* of these terms by replacing the variable lists in argument 1 of l/2 constructors by their length and by erasing the arguments of the v/1 constructors.

The predicate toSkels/3 computes the (k-colored) Motzkin skeletons by measuring the length of the list of variables for each binder.

```
toSkels(v(_),v,v).
toSkels(l(Vs,A),l(K,CS),l(S)):-length(Vs,K),toSkels(A,CS,S).
toSkels(a(A,B),a(CA,CB),a(SA,SB)):-
  toSkels(A,CA,SA),
  toSkels(B,CB,SB).
```

We obtain generators for skeletons and k-colored skeletons by combining the generator simplyTypedColored with toSkeleton.

```
genTypedSkels(N,CS,S):-genTypedSkels(N,_,_,CS,S).

genTypedSkels(N,X,T,CS,S):-
  simplyTypedColored(N,X,T),
  toSkels(X,CS,S).

typableColSkels(N,CS):-genTypedSkels(N,CS,_).

typableSkels(N,S):-genTypedSkels(N,_,S).
```

We can generate the set of typable skeletons from the multiset of skeletons by using the built-in distinct/2 that trims duplicate solutions.

```
simpleTypableColSkel(N,CS):-
  distinct(CS,typableColSkels(N,CS)).

simpleTypableColSkel(N,S):-
  distinct(S,typableSkels(N,S)).
```

We define the *type size* of a simply typed term as the number of arrow nodes "->" its type contains, as computed by the predicate tsize/2.

```
tsize(X,S):-var(X),!,S=0.
tsize((A->B),S):-tsize(A,SA),tsize(B,SB),S is 1+SA+SB.
```

Now that we can count, for a given term size, how many k-colored terms exists, one might ask if we can say something about the sizes of their types. This suggests an investigation of the relations between the complexity of type expressions and the number of colors.

Figure 3 shows the significantly slower growths of the average number of colors of colored terms vs. the average size of their types, with a possible log-scale correlation between them.

We call *a most colorful term* of a given size a term that reaches the maximum number of colors.

Figure 4 shows the relation between the number of colors of a most colorful term and a maximum size reached by the type of such a term.

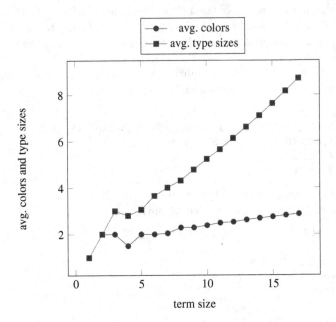

Fig. 3. Growth of colors and type sizes

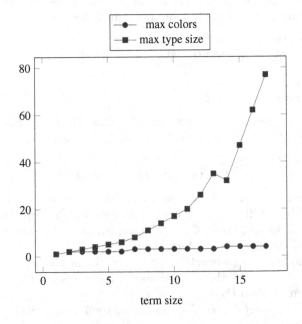

Fig. 4. Colors of a most colorful term vs. its maximum type size

Figure 5 shows the relation between the largest type sizes the most colorful terms of a given size can attain and the maximum possible type size of those terms.

We can observe that the largest most colorful terms reach the largest possible type size for a given term size, most of the time, but as Fig. 5 shows, there are exceptions.

We leave as an open problem to prove or disprove that there's a term size such that for larger terms, the most colorful such terms reach the largest type size possible.

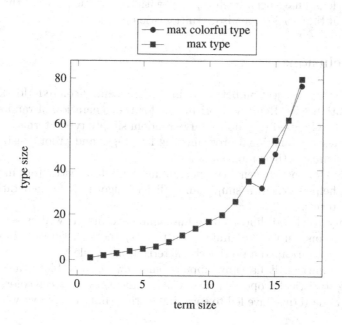

Fig. 5. Largest type size of a most colorful term vs. largest type size

5   Related Work

Several papers exist that define bijections between 2-Motzkin trees and members of the Catalan family of combinatorial objects (e.g., in [6]), typically via depth-first walks in trees connected to Motzkin, Dyck or Schröder paths. However, we have not found any simple and intuitive bijection that connects components of the two families, or one that connects directly binary trees and 2-Motzkin trees, like the one shown in this paper.

The classic reference for lambda calculus is [12]. Various instances of typed lambda calculi are overviewed in [13]. The use of de Bruijn indices for the study of combinatorial properties of lambda terms is introduced in [14].

The combinatorics and asymptotic behavior of various classes of lambda terms are extensively studied in [15]. Distribution and density properties of random lambda terms are described in [16].

The generation and counting of affine and linear lambda terms is extensively covered in [9], with limits for counting larger than in this paper reachable using efficient recurrence formulas. Their asymptotic behavior, in relation with the BCK and BCI combinator systems, as well as bijections to combinatorial maps are studied in [17]. In [10] analytic models are used to solve the problem of the asymptotic density of closable skeletons and their subclass of uniquely closable skeletons.

Asymptotic density properties of simple types (corresponding to tautologies in minimal logic) have been studied in [18] with the surprising result that "almost all" classical tautologies are also intuitionistic ones.

6   Conclusions

The new, intuitive bijection between binary terms and 2-colored Motzkin terms, in combination with Rémy's algorithm [7] for the generation of random binary trees, can also be used to produce large random simply-typed terms, with applications to testing functional programming languages and proof assistants using lambda calculus as their internal language.

The distinction between free and binding lambda constructors in 2-colored terms has helped design a simple and efficient algorithm for generating affine and linear terms.

Contrary to closed, linear and affine lambda terms (as well as several other classes of terms subject to similar constraints) the structure of simply-typed terms has so far escaped a precise characterization. While the focus of the paper is mostly empirical, it has unwrapped some new "observables" that highlight interesting statistical properties. The relations identified between colors and type sizes of lambda terms have led to some interesting (but possibly very hard) open problems.

In a way, our concepts involve abstraction mechanisms that "forget" properties of the difficult class of simply-typed closed lambda terms to reveal equivalence classes that are likely to be easier to grasp with analytic tools. Among them, k-colored terms subsume linear and affine terms and are likely to be usable to fine-tune random generators to more closely match "color-distributions" of lambda terms representing real programs.

Last but not least, we have shown that a language as simple as side-effect-free Prolog, with limited use of impure features and meta-programming, can handle elegantly complex combinatorial generation problems, when the synergy between sound unification, backtracking and DCGs is put at work.

Acknowledgement. This research has been supported by NSF grant 1423324. We thank the reviewers of PADL'18 for their careful reading of the paper and their valuable suggestions to improve its presentation. We thank the participants of the *CLA'2017* workshop (https://cla.tcs.uj.edu.pl/programme.html) for illuminating discussions and their comments on our talk covering the main ideas of this paper.

References

1. de Bruijn, N.G.: Lambda calculus notation with nameless dummies, a tool for automatic formula manipulation, with application to the Church-Rosser theorem. Indagationes Mathematicae **34**, 381–392 (1972)
2. Kostrzycka, Z., Zaionc, M.: Asymptotic densities in logic and type theory. Stud. Logica. **88**(3), 385–403 (2008)
3. Tarau, P.: A hiking trip through the orders of magnitude: deriving efficient generators for closed simply-typed lambda terms and normal forms. In: Hermenegildo, M.V., Lopez-Garcia, P. (eds.) LOPSTR 2016. LNCS, vol. 10184, pp. 240–255. Springer, Cham (2017). https://doi.org/10.1007/978-3-319-63139-4_14. Best paper award
4. Bendkowski, M., Grygiel, K., Tarau, P.: Boltzmann samplers for closed simply-typed lambda terms. In: Lierler, Y., Taha, W. (eds.) PADL 2017. LNCS, vol. 10137, pp. 120–135. Springer, Cham (2017). https://doi.org/10.1007/978-3-319-51676-9_8
5. Wielemaker, J., Schrijvers, T., Triska, M., Lager, T.: SWI-Prolog. Program. Theor. Pract. Logic **12**, 67–96 (2012)
6. Deutsch, E., Shapiro, L.W.: A bijection between ordered trees and 2-motzkin paths and its many consequences. Discrete Math. **256**(3), 655–670 (2002)
7. Rémy, J.L.: Un procédé itératif de dénombrement d'arbres binaires et son application à leur génération aléatoire. RAIRO - Theor. Inf. Appl. Informatique Théorique et Applications **19**(2), 179–195 (1985)
8. Tarau, P.: On a uniform representation of combinators, arithmetic, lambda terms and types. In: Albert, E. (ed.) PPDP 2015: Proceedings of the 17th International ACM SIGPLAN Symposium on Principles and Practice of Declarative Programming, pp. 244–255. ACM, New York, July 2015
9. Lescanne, P.: Quantitative aspects of linear and affine closed lambda terms. CoRR abs/1702.03085 (2017)
10. Bodini, O., Tarau, P.: On Uniquely Closable and Uniquely Typable Skeletons of Lambda Terms. CoRR abs/1709.04302, September 2017
11. Tarau, P.: On logic programming representations of lambda terms: de bruijn indices, compression, type inference, combinatorial generation, normalization. In: Pontelli, E., Son, T.C. (eds.) PADL 2015. LNCS, vol. 9131, pp. 115–131. Springer, Cham (2015). https://doi.org/10.1007/978-3-319-19686-2_9
12. Barendregt, H.P.: The Lambda Calculus Its Syntax and Semantics, vol. 103, Revised edn. North Holland, Amsterdam (1984)
13. Barendregt, H.P.: Lambda calculi with types. In: Handbook of Logic in Computer Science, vol. 2. Oxford University Press, New York (1991)
14. Lescanne, P.: On counting untyped lambda terms. Theoret. Comput. Sci. **474**, 80–97 (2013)
15. Grygiel, K., Lescanne, P.: Counting and generating lambda terms. J. Funct. Program. **23**(5), 594–628 (2013)
16. David, R., Raffalli, C., Theyssier, G., Grygiel, K., Kozik, J., Zaionc, M.: Some properties of random lambda terms. Logical Methods Comput. Sci. **9**(1) (2009)
17. Bodini, O., Gardy, D., Jacquot, A.: Asymptotics and random sampling for BCI and BCK lambda terms. Theoret. Comput. Sci. **502**, 227–238 (2013)
18. Genitrini, A., Kozik, J., Zaionc, M.: Intuitionistic vs. classical tautologies, quantitative comparison. In: Miculan, M., Scagnetto, I., Honsell, F. (eds.) TYPES 2007. LNCS, vol. 4941, pp. 100–109. Springer, Heidelberg (2008). https://doi.org/10.1007/978-3-540-68103-8_7

Answer Set Programming

Optimizing Answer Set Computation via Heuristic-Based Decomposition

Francesco Calimeri[1,2], Davide Fuscà[1], Simona Perri[1], and Jessica Zangari[1(✉)]

[1] Department of Mathematics and Computer Science,
University of Calabria, Rende, Italy
{calimeri,fusca,perri,zangari}@mat.unical.it
[2] DLVSystem Srl, Rende, Italy
calimeri@dlvsystem.com

Abstract. Answer Set Programming (ASP) is a purely declarative formalism developed in the field of logic programming and nonmonotonic reasoning. With ASP, computational problems are encoded by logic programs whose answer sets, corresponding to solutions, are computed by an ASP system. In general, several semantically equivalent programs might be defined for the same problem; however, performance of ASP systems while evaluating them might significantly vary. We propose an approach for automatically transforming an input logic program into an equivalent one that can be evaluated more efficiently. To this aim, one can make use of existing tree-decomposition techniques for rewriting selected rules into a set of multiple ones. The idea is to guide and adaptively apply them on the basis of proper new heuristics, in order to obtain a smart rewriting algorithm to be integrated into an ASP system. The method is rather general: it can be adapted to the system at hand and implement different preference policies. Furthermore, we define a set of new heuristics explicitly tailored at optimizing one of the main phases of the typical ASP computation, namely the grounding process; we make use of them in order to actually implement the approach into the ASP system *DLV*, and in particular into its grounding subsystem *I-DLV*, and carry out an extensive experimental activity aimed at assessing the impact of the proposal.

Keywords: Answer Set Programming · Artificial intelligence
ASP in practice

This work has been partially supported by the Italian Ministry for Economic Development (MISE) under project "PIUCultura – Paradigmi Innovativi per l'Utilizzo della Cultura" (n. F/020016/01-02/X27), and under project "Smarter Solutions in the Big Data World (S2BDW)" (n. F/050389/01-03/X32) funded within the call "HORIZON2020" PON I&C 2014-2020.

© Springer International Publishing AG 2018
F. Calimeri et al. (Eds.): PADL 2018, LNCS 10702, pp. 135–151, 2018.
https://doi.org/10.1007/978-3-319-73305-0_9

1   Introduction

Answer Set Programming (ASP) [7,20] is a declarative programming paradigm proposed in the area of non-monotonic reasoning and logic programming. With ASP, computational problems are encoded by logic programs whose answer sets, corresponding to solutions, are computed by an ASP system [27].

The evaluation of ASP programs is "traditionally" split into two phases: *grounding*, that generates a propositional theory semantically equivalent to the input program, and *solving*, that applies propositional techniques for computing the intended semantics [2,16,23,26]; nevertheless, in the latest years several approaches that deviate from this schema have been proposed [13–15,24].

Typically, the same computational problem can be encoded by means of many different ASP programs which are semantically equivalent; however, real ASP systems may perform very differently when evaluating each one of them. This behavior is due, in part, to specific aspects, that strictly depend on the ASP system employed, and, in part, to general "intrinsic" aspects, depending on the program at hand which could feature some characteristics that can make computation easier or harder. Thus, often, to have satisfying performance, expert knowledge is required in order to select the best encoding. This issue, in a certain sense, conflicts with the declarative nature of ASP that, ideally, should free the users from the burden of the computational aspects. For this reason, ASP systems tend to be endowed with proper pre-processing means aiming at making performance less encoding-dependent; intuitively, such means are of great importance for fostering and easing the usage of ASP in practice.

A proposal in this direction is *lpopt* [5], a pre-processing tool for ASP systems that rewrites rules in input programs by means of *tree-decomposition* algorithms. The rationale comes from the fact that, when programs contain rules featuring long bodies, ASP systems performance might benefit from a careful split of such rules into multiple, smaller ones. However, it is worth noting that, while in some cases such decomposition is convenient, in other cases keeping the original rule is preferable; hence, a black-box decomposition, like the one of *lpopt*, makes it difficult to predict whether it will lead to benefits or disadvantages.

In this work, we start from the *lpopt* idea and propose a method that aims at taking full advantage from decompositions, still avoiding performance drawbacks by trying to predict the effects of rewritings. Such method is rather general, as it is intended to be embedded into different ASP systems, and customized accordingly. It analyzes each input rule before the evaluation, and decides whether it could be convenient to decompose it into an equivalent set of smaller rules, or not. Furthermore, as many decompositions may be possible for each rule, further criteria can be defined in order to select a preferred one. We also propose an implementation explicitly tailored at optimizing the grounding process, and integrate it into $\mathcal{I}\text{-}DLV$ [10], the grounding subsystem of DLV [2]. To this end, we define new heuristic criteria relying on data and statistics on the grounding process; eventually, we perform an experimental activity in order to asses the effects of our technique on encoding optimization.

2   Answer Set Programming

In this section, we briefly recall ASP basic syntax and semantics. A significant amount of work has been carried out on extending the basic language of ASP, and the community recently agreed on a standard input language for ASP systems: ASP-Core-2 [8], the official language of the ASP Competition series [12,18]. For the sake of simplicity, we focus next on the basic aspects of the language; for a complete reference to the ASP-Core-2 standard, and further details about advanced ASP features, we refer the reader to [8] and the vast literature.

A *term* is either a *simple term* or a *functional term*. A *simple term* is either a constant or a variable. If $t_1 \ldots t_n$ are terms and f is a function symbol of arity n, then $f(t_1, \ldots, t_n)$ is a *functional term*. If $t_1, \ldots, t_k$ are terms and p is a *predicate symbol* of arity k, then $p(t_1, \ldots, t_k)$ is an *atom*. A *literal* l is of the form a or *not* a, where a is an atom; in the former case l is *positive*, otherwise *negative*. A *rule* r is of the form $\alpha_1 \mid \cdots \mid \alpha_k :\text{-} \beta_1, \ldots, \beta_n,$ *not* $\beta_{n+1}, \ldots,$ *not* $\beta_m.$ where $m \geq 0$, $k \geq 0$; $\alpha_1, \ldots, \alpha_k$ and $\beta_1, \ldots, \beta_m$ are atoms. We define $H(r) = \{\alpha_1, \ldots, \alpha_k\}$ (the *head* of r) and $B(r) = B^+(r) \cup B^-(r)$ (the *body* of r), where $B^+(r) = \{\beta_1, \ldots, \beta_n\}$ (the *positive body*) and $B^-(r) = \{not\ \beta_{n+1}, \ldots, not\ \beta_m\}$ (the *negative body*). If $H(r) = \emptyset$ then r is a *(strong) constraint*; if $B(r) = \emptyset$ and $|H(r)| = 1$ then r is a *fact*. A rule r is safe if each variable of r has an occurrence in $B^+(r)$[1]. For a rule r, we denote as $var(r)$ the set of variables occurring in r. An ASP program is a finite set P of safe rules. A program (a rule, a literal) is *ground* if it contains no variables. A predicate is defined by a rule r if it occurs in $H(r)$. A predicate defined only by facts is an *EDB* predicate, the remaining are *IDB* predicates. The set of all facts in P is denoted by $Facts(P)$; the set of instances of all *EDB* predicates in P is denoted by $EDB(P)$.

Given a program P, the *Herbrand universe* of P, denoted by U_P, consists of all ground terms that can be built combining constants and function symbols appearing in P. The *Herbrand base* of P, denoted by B_P, is the set of all ground atoms obtainable from the atoms of P by replacing variables with elements from U_P. A *substitution* for a rule $r \in P$ is a mapping from the set of variables of r to the set U_P of ground terms. A *ground instance* of a rule r is obtained applying a substitution to r. The *full instantiation Ground(P)* of P is defined as the set of all ground instances of its rules over U_P. An *interpretation* I for P is a subset of B_P. A positive literal a (resp., a negative literal *not* a) is true w.r.t. I if $a \in I$ (resp., $a \notin I$); it is false otherwise. Given a ground rule r, we say that r is satisfied w.r.t. I if some atom appearing in $H(r)$ is true w.r.t. I or some literal appearing in $B(r)$ is false w.r.t. I. Given a program P, we say that I is a *model* of P, iff all rules in *Ground(P)* are satisfied w.r.t. I. A model M is *minimal* if there is no model N for P such that $N \subset M$. The *Gelfond-Lifschitz reduct* [20] of P, w.r.t. an interpretation I, is the positive ground program P^I obtained from *Ground(P)* by: (*i*) deleting all rules having a negative literal false w.r.t. I; (*ii*) deleting all negative literals from the remaining rules. $I \subseteq B_P$ is an *answer set*

---

[1] We remark that this definition of safety is specific for the syntax considered herein. For a complete definition we refer the reader to [8].

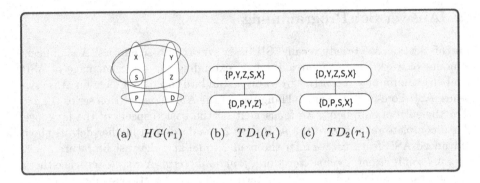

(a) $HG(r_1)$ (b) $TD_1(r_1)$ (c) $TD_2(r_1)$

Fig. 1. Decomposing a rule

for a program P iff I is a minimal model for P^I. The set of all answer sets for P is denoted by $AS(P)$.

3   A Heuristic-Guided Decomposition Algorithm

In this section we introduce a smart decomposition algorithm for the rules in an ASP program that makes use of *hypergraphs*, which are known to be useful for describing the structure of many computational problems. In general, decompositions are used to divide these structures into different parts so that the solution(s) of problems can be obtained by a polynomial divide-and-conquer algorithm that properly exploits this division [21,22]. Such ideas can guide the decomposition of a logic rule into multiple ones; indeed, an ASP rule can be represented as a *hypergraph* [28]. For instance, *lpopt* [5] uses *tree decompositions* for rewriting a program before it is fed to an ASP system. In particular, each rule r in the input program is analyzed and converted into a hypergraph $HG(r)$. Then a tree decomposition $TD(r)$ is computed and the original rule is transformed into a set of multiple ones $RD(r)$, according to the rewriting induced by $TD(r)$; in general, more than one decomposition is possible for each rule. The following running example, which we will refer to throughout the paper, illustrates this mechanism.

Example 1. Let us consider the rule:

  $r_1 : p(X, Y, Z, S) \text{ :- } s(S),\ a(X, Y, S-1),\ c(D, Y, Z),\ f(X, P, S-1),\ P >= D.$

from the encoding of the problem *Nomystery* from the 6th ASP Competition, where, for the sake of readability, predicates and variables have been renamed. Figure 1 depicts the conversion of r_1 into the hypergraph $HG(r_1)$, along with two possible decompositions: $TD_1(r_1)$ and $TD_2(r_1)$, that induce two different rewritings. According to $TD_1(r_1)$, r_1 can be rewritten into the set of rules $RD_1(r_1)$:

$r_2 : p(X,Y,Z,S) :\!- s(S), a(X,Y,S-1), f(X,P,S-1), fresh\_pred\_1(P,Y,Z).$
$r_3 : fresh\_pred\_1(P,Y,Z) :\!- c(D,Y,Z), P >= D, fresh\_pred\_2(P).$
$r_4 : fresh\_pred\_2(P) :\!- s(S), f(\_,P,S-1).$

On the other hand, according to $TD_2(r_1)$, r_1 can be rewritten into $RD_2(r_1)$:

$r_5 : p(X,Y,Z,S) :\!- a(X,Y,S-1), c(D,Y,Z), fresh\_pred\_1(D,S,X).$
$r_6 : fresh\_pred\_1(D,S,X) :\!- s(S), f(X,P,S-1), P >= D, fresh\_pred\_2(D).$
$r_7 : fresh\_pred\_2(D) :\!- c(D,\_,\_).$

Discussing tree decompositions and induced rewritings is out of the scope of this paper; we refer the reader to [5] and the existing literature. It is worth noting that different yet equivalent rewritings require, in general, significantly different evaluation times, when fed to real ASP systems. Thus, since one can choose among many different decompositions for each rule, proper means for making reasonable and effective choices are crucial. Furthermore, it might be the case that, whatever the choice, sticking to the original, unrewritten rule, is still preferable. A black-box approach, such as the one of *lpopt*, makes it difficult to effectively take advantage from the decomposition rewritings; this is clearly noticeable by looking at experiments, as discussed in Sect. 5.

The method herein introduced aims at addressing the above issues; it is designed to be integrated into an ASP system, and uses information available during the computation to predict, according to proper criteria, whether decomposing will pay or not; moreover, it chooses the most promising decomposition, among the several possible ones. In the following, we first describe the method in its general form, that can be easily adapted to different real systems; a complete actual implementation, specialized for the *DLV* system, is presented next.

The abstract algorithm SMARTDECOMPOSITION is shown in Fig. 2; we indicate as *tree decomposition* an actual tree decomposition of a hypergraph, while with *rule decomposition* we denote the conversion of a tree decomposition into a set of ASP rules. Given a (non-ground) input rule r, the algorithm first heuristically computes, by means of the ESTIMATE function, a value e_r that estimates how much the presence of r in the program impacts on the whole computation; then, the function GENERATERULEDECOMPOSITONS computes a set of possible rule decompositions RDS, from which CHOOSEBESTDECOMPOSITION selects the best $RD \in RDS$; hence, function ESTIMATEDECOMPOSITION computes the value e_{RD} that estimates the impact of having RD in place of r in the input program. Eventually, function DECOMPOSITIONISPREFERABLE is in charge of comparing e_r and e_{RD} and deciding if decomposing is convenient. We remark that functions ESTIMATE, CHOOSEBESTDECOMPOSITION, ESTIMATEDECOMPOSITION and DECOMPOSITIONISPREFERABLE are left unimplemented, as they are completely customizable; they must be implemented by defining proper criteria that take into account features and information within the specific evaluation procedure, and the actual ASP system the algorithm is being integrated into.

Figure 2 reports also the implementation of function GENERATERULEDECOMPOSITONS. Here, TOHYPERGRAPH converts a input rule r into a hypergraph HG, which is iteratively analysed in order to produce possible tree decompositions, by means of the function GENERATETREEDECOMPOSITIONS. Also these

```
function SMARTDECOMPOSITION(r : Rule) : RuleDecomposition
    var e_r : number, RDS : SetOfRuleDecompositions, e_RD : Number,
    RD: RuleDecomposition
    e_r ← ESTIMATE(r)
    RDS ← GENERATERULEDECOMPOSITIONS(r)
    if RDS ≠ ∅ then                              /* r is decomposable */
        RD ← CHOOSEBESTDECOMPOSITION(RDS,e_r)
        e_RD ← ESTIMATEDECOMPOSITION(RD)
        if DECOMPOSITIONISPREFERABLE(e_r,e_RD) then
            return RD
        end if
    end if
    return ∅
end function

function GENERATERULEDECOMPOSITONS(r : Rule) : SetOfRuleDecompo-
sitions
    var HG : Hypergraph, RDS : SetOfRuleDecompositions,
    RD : RuleDecomposition, TD : TreeDecomposition
    TDS : SetOfTreeDecompositions
    HG ← TOHYPERGRAPH(r)
    TDS ← GENERATETREEDECOMPOSITIONS(HG)
    for each TD ∈ TDS do
        RD ← TORULES(TD,r)
        RDS = RDS ∪ RD
    end for
    return RDS
end function
```

Fig. 2. The algorithm SMARTDECOMPOSITION and the GENERATERULEDECOMPOSI-TIONS function.

stages can be customized in an actual implementation, according to different criteria and the features of the system at hand; for space reasons, we refrain from going into details that are not relevant for the description of the approach. The function TORULES, given a tree decomposition TD and a rule r, converts TD into a rule decomposition RD for r. In particular, for each node in TD, it adds a new logic rule to RD, possibly along with some additional auxiliary rules needed for ensuring safety. The process is, again, customizable, and should be defined according to the function TOHYPERGRAPH.

The general definition of the algorithm provided so far is independent from any actual implementation, and its behaviour can significantly change depending on the customization choices, as discussed above. However, in order to give an intuition on how it works, we make use of our running example for illustrating a plausible execution.

Example 2. Given rule r_1 of Example 1, let us imagine that function GENER-ATERULEDECOMPOSITIONS computes the two tree decompositions $TD_1(r_1)$ and $TD_2(r_1)$ and then, by means of TORULES, the set of rule decompositions consisting of $RD_1(r_1)$ and $RD_2(r_1)$ is generated. Note that r_4 and r_7 are added for ensuring safety of rules r_3 and r_6, respectively. Next step consists of the choice between $RD_1(r_1)$ and $RD_2(r_1)$ for the best promising decomposition, according to the actual criteria of choice. Supposing that it is $RD_1(r_1)$, DECOMPOSITION-ISPREFERABLE compares the estimated impacts e_{r_1} and $e_{RD_1(r_1)}$, in order to decide if keeping r or substituting it with $RD_1(r_1)$.

4   Integrating the SmartDecomposition Algorithm into a Real System: The *DLV* Case

We illustrate next the adaptation of the algorithm to *DLV*, and in particular to its grounding subsystem *I-DLV* with the aim of optimizing the instantiation process. Even if a description of the *I-DLV* computation is out of the scope of this work (the interested reader is referred to [10]), we briefly recall the process of instantiating a rule, one of the crucial tasks in grounding, since SMARTDE-COMPOSITION directly interacts with it.

Grounding a rule essentially amounts to evaluate relational joins of the positive body literals, where predicate extensions can be seen as tables whose tuples consist of the ground instances. Many strategies are adopted to optimize the process: some operate in a pre-processing phase adjusting rules for a more efficient evaluation, such as join ordering strategies; others explicitly take place during the actual instantiation process, such as non-chronological backtracking; others operate across the two phases, such as indexing techniques for quick instances retrieval.

In the herein presented implementation, the SMARTDECOMPOSITION algorithm works in the pre-processing phase; we provide next some details on how we defined the functions that have been left unimplemented in the general description of Sect. 3 (ESTIMATE, CHOOSEBESTDECOMPOSITION, ESTIMATEDECOMPOSITION and DECOMPOSITIONISPREFERABLE), along with the proposed heuristics, and discuss further implementation issues.

4.1   The Estimate Function

The function ESTIMATE (Fig. 3) heuristically measures the cost of instantiating a rule r before it is actually grounded. To this aim, we propose a heuristics inspired by the ones introduced in the database field [29] and adopted in [25] to estimate the size of a join operation. In particular, it relies on statistics over body predicates, such as size of extensions and argument selectivities; we readapted it in order to estimate the cost of grounding a rule as the total number of operations needed in order to perform the task, rather than estimate the size of the join of its body literals. Let $a = p(t_1, \ldots, t_n)$ be an atom; we denote with $var(a)$ the set of variables occurring in a, while $T(a)$ represents the number of different tuples for a in the ground extension of p. Moreover, for each variable $X \in var(a)$, we denote by $V(X, a)$ the selectivity of X in a, i.e., the number of distinct values in the field corresponding to X over the ground extension of p. Given a rule r, let $\langle a_1, \ldots, a_m \rangle$ be the ordered list of atoms appearing in $B(r)$, for $m > 1$. Initially, the cost of grounding r, denoted by e_r, is set to $T(a_1)$, then the following formula is iteratively applied up to the last atom in the body in order to obtain the total estimation cost for r. More in detail, let us suppose that we estimated the cost of joining the atoms $\langle a_1, \ldots, a_j \rangle$ for $j \in \{1, \ldots, m\}$, and consequently we want to estimate the cost of joining the next atom a_{j+1}; if we denote by A_j the relation obtained by joining all j atoms in $\langle a_1, \ldots, a_j \rangle$, then:

$$e_{A_j \bowtie a_{j+1}} = \frac{T(a_{j+1})}{\prod\limits_{X \in idx(var(A_j) \cap var(a_{j+1}))} V(X, a_{j+1})} \cdot \prod\limits_{X \in (var(A_j) \cap var(a_{j+1}))} \frac{V(X, A_j)}{dom(X)} \quad (1)$$

where $dom(X)$ is the maximum selectivity of X computed among the atoms in $B(r)$ containing X as variable, and $idx(var(A_j) \cap var(a_{j+1}))$ is the set of the indexing arguments of a_{j+1}. We note that, at each step, once the atom a_{j+1} has been considered, $V(X, A_{j+1})$, representing the selectivity of X in the virtual relation obtained at step $j + 1$, has to be estimated in order to be used at next steps: if $X \in var(A_j)$, then $V(X, A_{j+1}) = V(X, A_j) \cdot (V(X, a_{j+1})/dom(X))$, otherwise $V(X, A_{j+1}) = V(X, a_{j+1})$. Intuitively, the formula tries to determine the cost of grounding r, by estimating the total number of operations to be performed. In particular, the first factor is intended to estimate how many instances for a_{j+1} have to be considered, while the second factor represents the reduction in the search space implied by a_{j+1}. To obtain a realistic estimate, the presence of indexing techniques, used in $\mathcal{I}\text{-}DLV$ to reduce the number of such operations [10], has been taken into account.

4.2   The EstimateDecomposition Function

The ESTIMATEDECOMPOSITION function is illustrated in Fig. 3: after some preprocessing steps, computes the cost of a given decomposition as the sum of the cost of each rule in it. Let r be a rule and $RD = \{r_1, \ldots, r_n\}$ be a rule decomposition for r. In order to estimate the cost of grounding RD, one must estimate the cost of grounding all rules in RD. For each $r_i \in RD$ the estimate is performed by means of Formula 1. Nevertheless, it is worth noting that each r_i, in addition to predicates originally appearing in r, denoted as *known predicates*, may contain some *fresh predicates*, generated during the decomposition. As for known predicates, thanks to the rule instantiation ordering followed by $\mathcal{I}\text{-}DLV$, actual data needed for computing the formula come directly from the instantiation of

```
function ESTIMATE(r : Rule) : Number
        /* Estimate the cost of grounding a rule according to Formula 1 */
end function
function ESTIMATEDECOMPOSITION(RD : SetOfRules) : Number
    var e_RD : number
    PREPROCESS(RD)
    e_RD ← 0
    for each r' ∈ RD do
        e_RD = e_RD + ESTIMATE(r')
    end for
    return e_RD
end function
```

Fig. 3. ESTIMATE and ESTIMATEDECOMPOSITION as implemented in $\mathcal{I}$-*DLV*

the previous rules. As for the fresh predicates, since they have been "locally" introduced and do not appear in any of the rules originally in the input program, such data are not available, and must be estimated. To this aim, the dependencies among the rules in RD are analyzed, and an ordering that guarantees a correct instantiation is determined. Intuitively, rules depending only on known predicates can be grounded first, while rules depending also on new predicates can be grounded only once the rules that define them have been instantiated. Assuming that for the set RD a correct instantiation order is represented by $\langle r_1, \ldots, r_n \rangle$, for each r' in this ordered list, if $H(r') = p'(t_1, \ldots, t_k)$ for $k \geq 1$, and if p' is a fresh predicate, we estimate the size of the ground extension of p', denoted $T(p')$, by means of a formula conceived for estimating the size of a join relation, based on criteria that are well-established in the database field and reported in [25]. The selectivity of each argument is estimated, accordingly, as $\sqrt[k]{T(p')}$. Therefore, the procedure PREPROCESS invoked in ESTIMATEDECOMPOSITION (see Fig. 3) amounts to preprocess the rules in RD according to a valid grounding order $\langle r_1, \ldots, r_n \rangle$ to obtain the extension sizes and the argument selectivities for involved fresh predicates, based on the above mentioned formula. Once estimates for fresh predicates are available, the actual estimate of grounding RD can be performed.

4.3 The ChooseBestDecomposition and Decomposition IsPreferable Functions

The function CHOOSEBESTDECOMPOSITION estimates the costs of all decompositions by means of ESTIMATEDECOMPOSITION, and returns the one with the smallest estimated cost; let us denote it by RD. The function DECOMPOSITIONISPREFERABLE is in charge of deciding whether RD can be supposed to be preferable with respect to the original rule r by relying on e_r and e_{RD}, that are the estimated costs associated to r and RD, respectively. Furthermore, it computes the ratio e_r/e_{RD}: if $e_r/e_{RD} \geq 1$, the decomposition is applied. Intuitively, when the ratio is less than 1 one might think that grounding r is preferable; nevertheless, it is worth remembering that the costs are estimated, and, in particular, as it will be better discussed in Sect. 4.2, the estimate of the cost of a decomposition requires to estimate also the extension of some additional predicates introduced by the rewriting, thus possibly making the estimate less accurate. This leads sometimes to cases in which the decomposition is preferable even when $e_r/e_{RD} < 1$. One can try to improve the estimations, in the first place; however, an error margin will always be present. For this reason, in order to reduce the impact of such issue, we decided to experimentally test the effects of the choices under several values of the ratio, and found that decomposition is preferable when $e_r/e_{RD} \geq 0.5$, that has also been set as a default threshold in our implementation; of course, the user can play with this at will. We plan to further improve the choice of the threshold by taking advantage from automatic and more advanced methods, such as machine learning guided machineries.

Example 3. Let us consider again the rule of our running Example 1 and the two corresponding rule decompositions $RD_1(r_1)$ and $RD_2(r_1)$. The cost of the three possible alternatives is estimated: (i) leave the rule as it is, (ii) choose $RD_1(r_1)$ or (iii) choose $RD_2(r_1)$. Because of the nature of the heuristics we implemented into our method as integrated in $\mathcal{I}$-*DLV*, such estimates tightly depends on the instance at hand, and hence the choices will possibly vary from instance to instance. Let us assume that the current instance contains the facts[2]:

$$s(1..5). \quad a(1..5, 1..5, 1..5). \quad c(1..5, 1..5, 1..5). \quad f(1..5, 1..5, 1..5).$$

the cost of grounding r_1 is estimated according to Formula (1); without reporting all intermediate calculations, e_{r_1} amounts to $390,625$. In order to compute $e_{RD_1(r_1)}$, according to what discussed in Sect. 4.2, we first need to determine a correct evaluation order of the rules in $RD_1(r_1)$; the only valid one is $\langle r_4, r_3, r_2 \rangle$ (intuitively, r_4 has only known predicates in its body, thus can be evaluated first; the body of r_3 contains, besides to known predicates, $fresh\_pred\_2$, whose estimates will be available just after the evaluation of r_4; eventually, r_2 depends also on $fresh\_pred\_1$, whose estimates will be available right after the evaluation of r_3). Once the estimates for the fresh predicates $fresh\_pred\_1$ and $fresh\_pred\_2$ are obtained, they are used for computing e_{r_2}, e_{r_3} and e_{r_4} with Formula (1), and then for obtaining $e_{RD_1(r_1)} = e_{r_2} + e_{r_3} + e_{r_4}$. Again, without reporting all intermediate calculations, $e_{RD_1(r_1)}$ amounts to $122,945$. Analogously, $e_{RD_2(r_1)}$ is computed as $53,075$. In this case, it is easy to see that the chosen decomposition is $RD_2(r_1)$. The ratio $e_{r_1}/e_{RD_2(r_1)}$ is computed as 7.36; as it is greater than 1, the decomposition is preferred over the original rule. Interestingly, with a different input instance, things might change. For instance, if the set of input facts for f is changed to $f(1..20, 1..20, 1..5)$., the decomposition $RD_1(r_1)$ is preferred.

---

[2] According to ASP-Core-2 syntax, the term $(1..k)$ stands for all values from 1 to k.

4.4   Fine-Tuning and Further Implementation Issues

In order to implement the SMARTDECOMPOSITION algorithm, one might rely on *lpopt* in order to obtain a rule decomposition for each rule in the program; in particular, this would lead to a straightforward implementation of TOHYPER-GRAPH and TORULES, the functions that convert a rule into a hypergraph and a tree decomposition into a rule decomposition, respectively. Nevertheless, in order to better take advantage from the features of $\mathcal{I}$-*DLV* and do not interfere with its existing optimizations, we designed ad-hoc versions for such functions.

For instance, $\mathcal{I}$-*DLV* supports the whole ASP-Core-2 language, which contains advanced constructs like aggregates, choice rules and queries; our implementation, even if resembling the one of *lpopt*, introduces custom extensions explicitly tailored to $\mathcal{I}$-*DLV* optimizations, and some updates in the way the aforementioned linguistic extensions are handled. In particular, before the invocation of SMARTDECOMPOSITION, a preliminary rewriting is applied to rules containing aggregates or choice constructs [8], in order to make them more transparent to the decomposition process, thus easing it. Furthermore, $\mathcal{I}$-*DLV*, differently from *lpopt*, explicitly handle queries, and employs the magic sets rewriting technique [4] to boost query answering; in our approach, SMARTDECOMPOSITION is applied after the magic rewriting has occurred, so that decompositions is applied also to resulting magic rules. In addition, given that $\mathcal{I}$-*DLV* performs other rewritings on the input rules for optimization purposes, the function TORULES is in charge of performing such already existing rewriting tasks also on the rules resulting from the decompositions.

Another relevant issue is related to the safety of the rules generated in a decomposition. Indeed, due to the abstract nature of SMARTDECOMPOSITION, we cannot assume that they are safe, since this depends on the schemas selected for converting a rule into a hypergraph, and a tree decomposition into a set of rules. Hence, the TORULES function must properly take this into account, as briefly noted in Sect. 3. In particular, our implementation, given a rule r and an associated tree decomposition TD, after a rule r' corresponding to a node in TD has been generated, checks its safety. If r' is unsafe, and UV is the set of unsafe variables in r', an atom a over a fresh predicate p, that contains the variables in UV as terms, is added to $B(r')$ and a new rule r'' is generated, having a as head; a set of literals L binding the variables in UV is extracted from $B(r)$ and added to $B(r'')$. Interestingly, the choice of the literals to be inserted in L is in general not unique, as different combinations of literals might bind the same set of variables; for instance, one might even directly add L to $B(r')$ without generating r''; however, this might introduce further variables in $B(r')$, and alter the original join operations in it. For this reason, in our implementation we decided to still add r'', and while choosing a possible binding, we try to keep the · number of literals taken from $B(r)$ small, also preferring to pick positive literals with small ground extensions. Interestingly, this allows to do better than what it would be obtained by using *lpopt* as a black box: in such a case, the choice of saviour literals could not rely on information that are available only from within the instantiation process.

The current implementation of function GENERATETREEDECOMPOSITIONS that, given a hypergraph HG returns a set of tree decompositions TDS, relies on the open-source C++ library htd [1][3], an efficient and flexible library for computing customized tree and hypertree decompositions; importantly, it allows to customize them via user-provided fitness functions, that we used in order to associate each computed decomposition with its cost estimation, and hence select the best one, accordingly. By default, $\mathcal{I}\text{-}DLV$ stops the generation of tree decompositions after 3 consecutive generations without improvements in the fitness values, and after 5 generations in total. These limits have been set by experimentally observing that no performance improvements arise with higher values; however, they can be customized by proper command-line options.

5   Experimental Evaluation

We report next the results of an experimental activity aimed at assessing the impact of SMARTDECOMPOSITION on the grounding performance of $\mathcal{I}\text{-}DLV$. As for benchmarks, we considered the whole 6th ASP Competition suite [17], the latest available at the time of writing[4]. Three versions of $\mathcal{I}\text{-}DLV$ have been compared: (i) $\mathcal{I}\text{-}DLV$ without any decomposition, (ii) lpopt (version 2.2) combined in pipeline with $\mathcal{I}\text{-}DLV$ (i.e., a black-box usage of lpopt), (iii) $\mathcal{I}\text{-}DLV^{\text{SD}}$, i.e. $\mathcal{I}\text{-}DLV$ empowered with the herein introduced version of SMARTDECOMPOSITION. For each problem, the average time over the 20 selected instances of the official competition runs is reported; in order to produce replicable results, the random seed used by lpopt for heuristics has been set to 0 for system (ii).

Results are reported in Table 1, where US indicates that corresponding configurations do not support syntax; in particular, we report number of grounded instances within the allotted time along with the average time spent. Some benchmarks names are reported in bold, indicating cases where there is a noticeable difference (either positive or negative) w.r.t. (i) for one of the two systems making use of decomposition (i.e., (ii) and (iii)). Results of the "blind usage" of lpopt $((ii))$ are conflicting: for instance, it enjoys a great gain w.r.t. the version of $\mathcal{I}\text{-}DLV$ without decomposition, in particular while dealing with the *Permutation Pattern Matching* problem, yet showing great losses in other cases. On the other hand, the "smart usage" of decomposition in $\mathcal{I}\text{-}DLV^{\text{SD}}$ allows to avoid negative effects of the black-box decomposition mechanism, still preserving the positive ones. It is worth noting that in a few isolated cases, namely *Labyrinth* and *Nomistery*, the black-box usage seems to be convenient over the heuristic-guided one; we investigated, and found that the reason is not related to the choices made according to the heuristics, but rather to a tight interaction with

---

[3] https://github.com/mabseher/htd.

[4] Experiments have been performed on a NUMA machine equipped with two 2,8GHz AMD Opteron 6320 and 128 GiB of main memory, running Linux Ubuntu 14.04.4 (kernel ver. 3.19.0-25). Binaries have been generated by the GNU C++ compiler 5.4.0. We allotted 15 GiB and 600s to each system per each single run, as memory and time limits.

Table 1. Grounding benchmarks: number of solved instances and average running times (in seconds), where US indicates that corresponding configurations do not support syntax.

Problem	I-DLV		LPOPT | I-DLV		I-DLV^{SD}	
	Solved	Time	Solved	Time	Solved	Time
Abstract dialectical frameworks	20	0.11	20	0.11	20	0.13
Combined configuration	20	13.53	20	13.52	20	13.33
Complex optimization	20	69.83	20	73.41	20	66.82
Connected still life	20	0.10	20	0.10	20	0.10
Consistent query answering	20	76.31	US		20	75.35
Crossing minimization	20	0.10	20	0.10	20	0.10
Graceful graphs	20	0.31	20	0.32	20	0.32
Graph coloring	20	0.10	20	0.10	20	0.10
Incremental scheduling	20	17.05	20	16.77	20	16.55
Knight tour with holes	20	2.36	20	6.53	20	2.34
Labyrinth	20	2.01	20	1.83	20	2.02
Maximal clique	20	4.39	20	20.70	20	4.31
MaxSAT	20	3.96	20	8.92	20	3.90
Minimal diagnosis	20	5.19	20	4.36	20	4.79
Nomistery	20	4.16	20	2.50	20	3.46
Partner units	20	0.43	20	0.44	20	0.44
Permutation pattern matching	20	135.04	20	4.35	20	4.31
Qualitative spatial reasoning	20	5.49	20	5.47	20	5.48
Reachability	20	142.64	US		20	134.91
Ricochet robots	20	0.37	20	0.40	20	0.39
Sokoban	20	1.23	20	1.25	20	1.25
Stable marriage	20	123.55	20	132.33	20	125.27
Steiner tree	20	29.83	20	29.90	20	29.73
Strategic companies	20	0.25	US		20	0.30
System synthesis	20	1.12	20	1.13	20	1.11
Valves location problem	20	2.58	20	2.61	20	2.66
Video streaming	20	0.10	20	0.10	20	0.10
Visit-all	20	1.22	20	0.45	20	0.44
Total solved instances	560/560		500/560		560/560	

some other internal rewriting-based optimizations that $\mathcal{I}$-DLV performs after the decomposition stage (for more details, we refer the reader to [10]). This also suggests that the heuristics could be further refined by even better tailoring them to the specific features of the grounding process they are integrated into.

Table 2. Solving benchmarks: number of solved instances and average running times (in seconds), where time outs and unsupported syntax are denoted by TO and US, respectively. In bold problems where the usage of decomposition techniques has some impact, either positive or negative.

Problem	I-DLV | CLASP		LPOPT | I-DLV | CLASP		I-DLV^{SD} | CLASP		I-DLV | WASP		LPOPT | I-DLV | WASP		I-DLV^{SD} | WASP	
	Solved	Time	Solved	Time	Solved	Time	Solved	Time	Solved	Time	Solved	Time
Abstract dialectical frameworks	20	6.80	20	7.35	20	6.73	11	32.58	11	20.85	11	32.66
Combined configuration	8	138.99	9	174.25	10	177.53	1	342.41	TO		TO	
Complex optimization	18	158.52	19	174.00	18	158.91	6	160.05	5	97.40	6	159.74
Connected still life	6	228.29	6	247.83	6	240.76	12	52.91	12	78.44	12	53.20
Consistent query answering	20	85.91	US		20	85.42	18	87.69	US		18	86.96
Crossing minimization	7	56.52	6	64.36	7	56.74	19	3.53	19	2.43	19	5.78
Graceful graphs	9	134.94	10	129.13	9	140.55	6	178.58	4	129.51	5	127.29
Graph coloring	15	162.29	15	166.51	15	162.01	8	120.76	9	261.49	8	113.37
Incremental scheduling	12	66.25	12	83.14	12	69.61	8	141.54	6	166.86	7	93.36
Knight tour with holes	11	56.85	10	27.12	11	59.06	10	35.51	8	67.01	10	35.28
Labyrinth	12	152.76	11	124.78	12	152.09	10	71.44	9	127.80	10	71.22
Maximal clique	TO		US		TO		9	367.55	9	367.06	9	361.82
MaxSAT	7	39.68	7	46.76	7	39.59	19	93.24	19	97.58	19	92.53
Minimal diagnosis	20	8.91	20	8.49	20	8.78	20	27.23	20	25.78	20	26.73
Nomistery	8	139.76	8	42.78	9	101.84	8	35.78	9	31.83	9	78.96
Partner units	14	20.34	14	20.34	14	20.24	5	134.54	9	140.24	9	140.92
Permutation pattern matching	11	161.75	16	124.80	20	15.68	20	181.89	8	199.78	20	23.26
Qualitative spatial reasoning	20	124.99	20	125.34	20	125.29	13	143.94	13	143.51	13	144.27
Reachability	20	145.85	US		20	145.75	6	142.13	US		6	141.04
Ricochet robots	9	66.51	12	118.13	11	158.58	7	217.92	8	90.08	9	135.68
Sokoban	8	73.76	9	82.82	8	76.71	8	88.05	9	62.83	8	79.22
Stable marriage	5	393.02	8	375.71	5	389.40	7	423.62	7	438.05	6	415.48
Steiner tree	2	69.99	2	70.02	2	69.68	1	122.75	1	122.63	1	122.69
Strategic companies	17	124.36	US		17	124.88	7	23.89	US		7	76.78
Valves location problem	16	42.71	16	25.90	16	45.33	15	40.05	15	38.29	15	39.60
Video streaming	13	62.40	10	77.52	13	62.22	9	8.64	TO		9	8.68
Visit-all	8	16.78	8	15.08	8	15.14	8	65.34	8	63.29	8	63.74
Total solved instances	316/560		268/560		330/560		271/560		218/560		274/560	

5.1 Impact of $\mathcal{I}\text{-}DLV^{SD}$ on ASP Solvers

We proved above how a smart decomposition strategy might significantly increase performance of a grounder like $\mathcal{I}\text{-}DLV$; unfortunately, simply improving the grounding times does not necessary imply improvements on the solving side, since these heavily depend on the form of the produced instantiation. While tailoring SMARTDECOMPOSITION also to the solving phase will definitely be subject of future works, we experimented with the proposed solution in order to evaluate the impact of $\mathcal{I}\text{-}DLV^{SD}$ on *wasp* [3], which is the solver module of *DLV*. In order to get a more clear picture, we took into account also the solver *clasp* [16]; in particular, we combined the same three versions of $\mathcal{I}\text{-}DLV$ tested above with both *clasp* and *wasp*, and launched the resulting configurations over the same set of benchmarks.

Average times and number of solved instances within the allotted time are reported in Table 2, where time outs and unsupported syntax are denoted by TO and US, respectively. First of all, we observe that there is no evident correlation between gain in grounding times and gain in solving times; in some cases, indeed, the improvements in grounding performance correspond to clear improvements for both *clasp* and *wasp*, while in other cases, both benefit from the decomposition rewriting even if there is no evidence of improvements on the grounding times. One can also note that the "blind usage" of *lpopt* leads, in general, to a loss of performance for both solvers: in spite the gain in some cases, the total number or solved instances within the suite is significantly lower. On the other hand, although the version of SMARTDECOMPOSITION has been explicitly tailored to the optimization of grounding times, both solvers show, in general, improved performance when coupled with $\mathcal{I}\text{-}DLV^{SD}$: they both solve a larger number of instances w.r.t. the configurations featuring $\mathcal{I}\text{-}DLV$. It can be observed that there are some corner cases in which the black-box approach eventually allows a solver to solve some instance more than both the version without decomposition and the one relying on $\mathcal{I}\text{-}DLV^{SD}$; however, the same does not hold for the other solver. This suggests that a deeper analysis is needed, and that one should explicitly tailor the heuristics guiding the smart decomposition to the given solver at hand; for instance, one can start from the results in [6], where emerged that the performance of modern solvers are influenced by the tree-width of the input program.

6 Conclusion

We introduced SMARTDECOMPOSITION, a novel technique for automatically optimizing rules of an ASP program by means of decompositions. The algorithm is designed to be adapted to different ASP implementations; furthermore it can be customized with heuristics of choice for discerning among possible decompositions for each input rule, and determining whether applying the selected decomposition appears to be actually a "smart" choice.

In addition, we embedded a version of SMARTDECOMPOSITION in the ASP system *DLV*, and in particular in its grounding module $\mathcal{I}\text{-}DLV$. We introduced heuristics criteria for selecting decompositions that consider not only the nonground structure of the program at hand, but also the instance it is coupled to. We experimentally tested our approach, and results are very promising: the proposed technique improves grounding performance, and highlights a positive impact, in general, also on the solving side. This is confirmed also by the results of the 7th ASP Competition [19]: here the winner was a system combining the version of $\mathcal{I}$-DLV implementing the preliminary decomposition rewriting described in [9] with an automatic solver selector [11], that inductively chooses the best solver depending on some inherent features of the instantiation produced.

As future work, we plan to take advantage from automatic and more advanced methods, such as machine learning mechanisms, in order to better tailor decomposition criteria and threshold values to the scenario at hand. Furthermore, we plan to design a version of SMARTDECOMPOSITION specifically geared towards solvers, in order to further automatically optimize the whole computational process.

References

1. Abseher, M., Musliu, N., Woltran, S.: htd – a free, open-source framework for (customized) tree decompositions and beyond. In: Salvagnin, D., Lombardi, M. (eds.) CPAIOR 2017. LNCS, vol. 10335, pp. 376–386. Springer, Cham (2017). https://doi.org/10.1007/978-3-319-59776-8_30
2. Alviano, M., et al.: The ASP system DLV2. In: Balduccini, M., Janhunen, T. (eds.) LPNMR 2017. LNCS (LNAI), vol. 10377, pp. 215–221. Springer, Cham (2017). https://doi.org/10.1007/978-3-319-61660-5_19
3. Alviano, M., Dodaro, C., Leone, N., Ricca, F.: Advances in WASP. In: Calimeri, F., Ianni, G., Truszczynski, M. (eds.) LPNMR 2015. LNCS (LNAI), vol. 9345, pp. 40–54. Springer, Cham (2015). https://doi.org/10.1007/978-3-319-23264-5_5
4. Alviano, M., Faber, W., Greco, G., Leone, N.: Magic sets for disjunctive datalog programs. Artif. Intell. **187**, 156–192 (2012)
5. Bichler, M., Morak, M., Woltran, S.: lpopt: a rule optimization tool for answer set programming. In: LOPSTR, pp. 114–130 (2016)
6. Bliem, B., Moldovan, M., Morak, M., Woltran, S.: The impact of treewidth on ASP grounding and solving. In: Sierra, C. (ed.) IJCAI, pp. 852–858. ijcai.org (2017). http://www.ijcai.org/Proceedings/2017/
7. Brewka, G., Eiter, T., Truszczynski, M.: Answer set programming at a glance. Commun. ACM **54**(12), 92–103 (2011)
8. Calimeri, F., Faber, W., Gebser, M., Ianni, G., Kaminski, R., Krennwallner, T., Leone, N., Ricca, F., Schaub, T.: Asp-core-2: input language format (2012). https://www.mat.unical.it/aspcomp2013/files/ASP-CORE-2.03b.pdf
9. Calimeri, F., Fuscà, D., Perri, S., Zangari, J.: The ASP instantiator I-DLV. In: PAoASP, Espoo, Finland (2017)
10. Calimeri, F., Fuscà, D., Perri, S., Zangari, J.: I-DLV: the new intelligent grounder of DLV. Intelligenza Artificiale **11**(1), 5–20 (2017)
11. Calimeri, F., Fuscà, D., Perri, S., Zangari, J.: $\mathcal{I}$-DLV +$\mathcal{MS}$: preliminary report on an automatic ASP solver selector. In: RCRA (2017, to appear)
12. Calimeri, F., Gebser, M., Maratea, M., Ricca, F.: Design and results of the fifth answer set programming competition. Artif. Intell. **231**, 151–181 (2016)

13. Dal Palù, A., Dovier, A., Pontelli, E., Rossi, G.: GASP: answer set programming with lazy grounding. Fundamenta Informaticae **96**(3), 297–322 (2009)
14. Dao-Tran, M., Eiter, T., Fink, M., Weidinger, G., Weinzierl, A.: OMiGA: an open minded grounding on-the-fly answer set solver. In: del Cerro, L.F., Herzig, A., Mengin, J. (eds.) JELIA 2012. LNCS (LNAI), vol. 7519, pp. 480–483. Springer, Heidelberg (2012). https://doi.org/10.1007/978-3-642-33353-8_38
15. Eiter, T., Kaminski, T., Weinzierl, A.: Lazy-grounding for answer set programs with external source access. In: IJCAI, pp. 1015–1022 (2017)
16. Gebser, M., Kaminski, R., Kaufmann, B., Romero, J., Schaub, T.: Progress in *clasp* series 3. In: Calimeri, F., Ianni, G., Truszczynski, M. (eds.) LPNMR 2015. LNCS (LNAI), vol. 9345, pp. 368–383. Springer, Cham (2015). https://doi.org/10.1007/978-3-319-23264-5_31
17. Gebser, M., Maratea, M., Ricca, F.: The design of the sixth answer set programming competition. In: Calimeri, F., Ianni, G., Truszczynski, M. (eds.) LPNMR 2015. LNCS (LNAI), vol. 9345, pp. 531–544. Springer, Cham (2015). https://doi.org/10.1007/978-3-319-23264-5_44
18. Gebser, M., Maratea, M., Ricca, F.: What's hot in the answer set programming competition. In: AAAI, pp. 4327–4329 (2016)
19. Gebser, M., Maratea, M., Ricca, F.: The design of the seventh answer set programming competition. In: Balduccini, M., Janhunen, T. (eds.) LPNMR 2017. LNCS (LNAI), vol. 10377, pp. 3–9. Springer, Cham (2017). https://doi.org/10.1007/978-3-319-61660-5_1
20. Gelfond, M., Lifschitz, V.: Classical negation in logic programs and disjunctive databases. New Gener. Comput. **9**(3/4), 365–385 (1991). https://doi.org/10.1007/BF03037169
21. Gottlob, G., Grohe, M., Musliu, N., Samer, M., Scarcello, F.: Hypertree decompositions: structure, algorithms, and applications. In: Kratsch, D. (ed.) WG 2005. LNCS, vol. 3787, pp. 1–15. Springer, Heidelberg (2005). https://doi.org/10.1007/11604686_1
22. Gottlob, G., Leone, N., Scarcello, F.: Hypertree decompositions: a survey. In: Sgall, J., Pultr, A., Kolman, P. (eds.) MFCS 2001. LNCS, vol. 2136, pp. 37–57. Springer, Heidelberg (2001). https://doi.org/10.1007/3-540-44683-4_5
23. Kaufmann, B., Leone, N., Perri, S., Schaub, T.: Grounding and solving in answer set programming. AI Mag. **37**(3), 25–32 (2016)
24. Lefèvre, C., Nicolas, P.: The first version of a new ASP solver: ASPeRiX. In: Erdem, E., Lin, F., Schaub, T. (eds.) LPNMR 2009. LNCS (LNAI), vol. 5753, pp. 522–527. Springer, Heidelberg (2009). https://doi.org/10.1007/978-3-642-04238-6_52
25. Leone, N., Perri, S., Scarcello, F.: Improving ASP instantiators by join-ordering methods. In: Eiter, T., Faber, W., Truszczyński, M. (eds.) LPNMR 2001. LNCS (LNAI), vol. 2173, pp. 280–294. Springer, Heidelberg (2001). https://doi.org/10.1007/3-540-45402-0_21
26. Leone, N., Pfeifer, G., Faber, W., Eiter, T., Gottlob, G., Perri, S., Scarcello, F.: The DLV system for knowledge representation and reasoning. ACM Trans. Comput. Log. (TOCL) **7**(3), 499–562 (2006)
27. Lifschitz, V.: Answer set planning. In: Gelfond, M., Leone, N., Pfeifer, G. (eds.) LPNMR 1999. LNCS (LNAI), vol. 1730, pp. 373–374. Springer, Heidelberg (1999). https://doi.org/10.1007/3-540-46767-X_28
28. Morak, M., Woltran, S.: Preprocessing of complex non-ground rules in answer set programming. In: LIPIcs-Leibniz International Proceedings in Informatics, vol. 17. Schloss Dagstuhl-Leibniz-Zentrum fuer Informatik (2012)
29. Ullman, J.D.: Principles of Database and Knowledge-Base Systems, vol. I. Computer Science Press, New York (1988)

*Lo*IDE: A Web-Based IDE for Logic Programming Preliminary Report

Stefano Germano$^{(\boxtimes)}$ [iD], Francesco Calimeri [iD], and Eliana Palermiti [iD]

Department of Mathematics and Computer Science,
University of Calabria, Via Bucci, Cubo 30B, 87036 Rende, Italy
{germano,calimeri}@mat.unical.it, eliana.palermiti@gmail.com

Abstract. Logic-based paradigms are nowadays widely used in many different fields, also thanks to the availability of robust tools and systems that allow the development of real-world and industrial applications. In this work, we present *Lo*IDE, an advanced and modular web-editor for logic-based languages that also integrates with state-of-the-art solvers.

Keywords: Logic programming · Development
Web-based applications

1 Introduction

In the latest years, declarative paradigms and approaches to solving problems have been crossing the border of academia and are now increasingly applied to real-world scenarios. This is especially the case for logic-based formalisms; indeed, after years of theoretical results, the availability of solid and reliable systems made viable the implementation of effective logic-based solutions, even in the industrial context. Along with the need for reliable solver technologies, the lack of suitable engineering tools for developing programs started to be properly addressed; as an example, we mention the work carried out by the Answer Set Programming (ASP, or AnsProlog) community [1,2], that explicitly tackled issues like writing, debugging and testing Answer Set programs as well as embedding them into external, traditionally-developed systems [5,10].

At the same time, scenarios of computing significantly changed as well, now heavily relying on network connections and tools, and the web-application paradigm become very popular, thus fostering cross-device and mobile computing: many existing desktop applications have been "ported" to the web, and many others have been created specifically according to this paradigm. Moreover, JavaScript, available on all types of devices ranging from servers to Internet of Things (IoT), became a real cross-platform language: on the one hand, it has been improved with many interesting features that made it an ideal language for developing full-fledged applications; on the other hand, cloud-computing technologies significantly eased development, deploying and use of such applications.

© Springer International Publishing AG 2018
F. Calimeri et al. (Eds.): PADL 2018, LNCS 10702, pp. 152–160, 2018.
https://doi.org/10.1007/978-3-319-73305-0_10

In this scenario, software development tools have been released as web-applications. As a result, code editors for many different programming languages are available to be used via web browsers, such as Codeanywhere, JSFiddle, Cloud9, repl.it, and more. Even developers of long-lasting and widespread environments, like Eclipse Foundation and Microsoft, released cloud-based environments (e.g., Eclipse Che and Visual Studio Team Services) that include also powerful IDEs. Editors for logic-based formalisms are no exception, from very simple playgrounds like the LogiQL REQPL to more complete editors like IDP Web-IDE [4], SWISH [15] and the PDDL Editor [12]. As for Logic Programming and ASP, Clingo in the Browser, dlvhex Online Demo and ASP for the Semantic Web - Tutorial have been proposed; however, these are quite "simplistic", and at an early stage of development; furthermore, each logic programming web-editor introduced so far is intended for a specific language, or even for a specific solver. This raises some issues about interoperability and limits the usage of these tools.

In this paper we present LoIDE, a web-based IDE for Logic Programming that explicitly addresses interoperability and flexibility, supporting multiple formalisms and solvers. The remainder of the paper is structured as described next.

In Sect. 2 we describe the LoIDE project and its main features, then we provide some implementation details on different components in Sect. 3. Eventually, we present a brief comparison with similar projects in Sect. 4 and discuss about the future developments of the LoIDE project.

2   The LoIDE Project

The main goal of the LoIDE project is a modular and extensible web-IDE for Logic Programming based on modern technologies. The LoIDE IDE will provide advanced features, specifically tailored for Logic Programming; it has been conceived in order to be extended over time, and support as many logic-based languages and solvers as possible. A further goal is a web-service with a common set of APIs for different logic-based languages; at the time of writing, this is still at an early stage of development.

LoIDE is released as open-source software (OSS) and it's publicly available at https://goo.gl/sDGMhA. Moreover, it has been released as Free Software[1], with the explicit aim of providing the scientific community with a free tool to be studied, used, distributed and even improved. A prototypical running demo is available at https://goo.gl/s4g6zA.

The LoIDE IDE provides all basic editing features that can be of use for Logic Programming. We started from basic features available in Ace, a JavaScript embeddable code editor that constituted the base for LoIDE (see Sect. 3.3). Among the most relevant, we mention here:

---

[1] Under MIT License. https://goo.gl/nrXtN4.

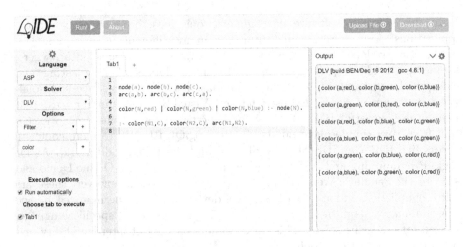

Fig. 1. An ASP program addressing a toy instance of the 3-colorability problem, and the corresponding run performed by the DLV system via *LoIDE*.

indentation: automatically indent and outdent the code;
document size: handles huge documents;
key bindings: customizable key bindings (including *vim* and *Emacs* modes);
search and replace: search and replace text via regular expressions;
brace matching: highlight matching parentheses;
mouse gestures: drag and drop text;
advanced cursors management: multiple cursors and selections;
clipboard management: cut, copy, and paste functionalities;
themes: over 20 themes available (standard .tmtheme files can be imported).

We extended such basic functionalities in order to properly meet the specific requirements of Logic Programs development.

Syntax highlighting. Ace supports syntax highlighting, already covering 110 languages; unfortunately, the logic-based languages we were interested in are not included. Relying on the specifications for cross-browser syntax highlighting, we introduced a basic support for ASP programs, and plan to include other languages as soon as the support for their specific solvers will be added to *LoIDE*.

Editor layout and appearance. The user can customize layout and appearance of the "Input" and the "Output" fields of the IDE. The user can change theme and fonts of each part of the interface, independently. Moreover, size and position of the two fields are customizable as well. It's worth noting that all options are automatically saved in the Web Storage, in order to make the experience persistent across different browser sessions.

Output highlighting. One of the most annoying aspects of developing and testing logic programs in practice is the need for checking output in test cases: given that output is often constituted of a (possibly very long) list of instances of many predicates, it can be quite tricky. Most solvers allow to filter predicates, but this does not solve the problem and it is not a very flexible solution. *LoIDE* features an ad-hoc output highlighting: when the user selects an element of the output (for instance, a predicate name), all the elements with the same "name" will be automatically highlighted. The user can dynamically play with such highlighting and, as a consequence, the analysis of the results might be dramatically simplified[2].

Keyboard shortcuts. LoIDE supports many keyboard shortcuts. We properly extended the typical code-editors shortcuts provided by *Ace*[3] for (a) Line operations, (b) Selection, (c) Multi-cursors, (d) Go-to, (e) Find/Replace, (f) Undo/Redo, (g) Indentation, (h) Comments and (i) Word/Character variations; and added specific shortcuts to Save/Load programs and Run them.

Moreover, we implemented other custom features around the *Ace*-based stem.

Multiple file support. When dealing with real-world problems in practice, logic programs are often split into several files (for instance, separating problem specification from problem instances). *LoIDE* explicitly supports multiple files management: the user can create and manage many different tabs, and also selectively decide which one has to be composed into the actual program to run.

Options. LoIDE settings can be customized, along with the behaviour of the underlying systems of use. The user can select the logic language of choice, and also the solver to be used to run the programs. Moreover, specific options can be selected for each solver, with predefined typical settings available for the most common. There are also more general options; for instance, the user can ask to automatically run the program at the end of each statement, so that the output dynamically changes as the user is crafting the program: this increases the interaction with the system, and it might significantly ease the development of non-trivial programs, being of great help in educational settings (sucn as in the context of a Logic Programming class).

Import and Export files. Contents of the editor, all options and outputs can be downloaded to the device of use as *JSON* files; they can be later restored, possibly over a different device (Drag-and-Drop can be used, if the device supports it). This is crucial for practically provide the user with a working environment which is virtually immaterial and free from specific physical workstations.

3   Implementation

We provide next some insights on the design and implementation of *LoIDE*.

3.1   General Architecture

Figure 2 drafts the system architecture, that relies on a typical client-server framework. The back-end (or *server-side* component) consists of the main *LoIDE* Web-Server, developed using *Node.js*®, which exposes *APIs* used by the client.

---

[2] More features for improving comprehension of the results will be added, such as different forms of visualization.

[3] https://github.com/ajaxorg/ace/wiki/Default-Keyboard-Shortcuts.

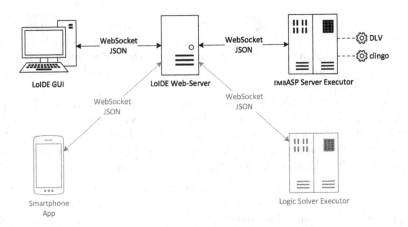

Fig. 2. Architecture of the *LoIDE* project

The front-end (or *client-side* component) consists of the Graphical User Interface (GUI), developed using modern web technologies such as *HTML5*, *CSS3* and *JavaScript*. The execution of the logic solvers is not performed directly from within the main *LoIDE* web-server; rather, external components are in charge of this: for instance, it might be the EMBASP *Server Executor*. However, as shown in Fig. 2, other executors can be easily attached to the main *LoIDE* web-server in order to provide support to different logic-based formalisms. This choice is due to the aim of keeping the system modular and extensible; indeed, such modularity ease the management of additions, upgrades, and security issues.

LoIDE APIs. As already mentioned, one of the goals of the *LoIDE* project is a set of (Web) APIs for easily and efficiently controlling different solvers over different logic programming languages. All components communicate using the *WebSocket* communication protocol and the *JSON* data-interchange format; the choice was straightforward, as these have well-defined "standards" and are widely used in almost all the modern web-applications. Specifications and implementation of APIs are at an early stage; currently, a call type is available, that given the description of the `language`, the `solver`, the list of `options` and the `program`, executes the solver over the program, and returns either the `output` of the solver or any `error` messages. We think of this as a very important topic: it will be part of a specific future work. See *LoIDE* API documentation[4] for further details.

We remark, again, that the proposed architecture and the use of standard technologies over all components, new modules can be easily added or modified while maintaining the scalability of the whole architecture, as shown in the lower part of Fig. 2.

---

[4] *LoIDE* APIs. https://goo.gl/6XJeDN.

3.2 Back-End – The *LoIDE* Web-Server

The *LoIDE* Web-Server has been developed using Node.js®. In order to effectively use *WebSockets*, we relied on the socket.io package to enable real-time, bidirectional event-based communications between client and server; the package provided us with means for enabling several useful features, such as Reliability, Auto-reconnection and Disconnection detection.

3.3 Front-End – The *LoIDE* GUI

As the front-end relies on modern standard web technologies (HTML5, CSS3, JavaScript), *LoIDE* is compatible with virtually any device currently available. Popular frameworks and libraries have been employed with the aim of improving user experience and making the IDE robust and powerful.

ace. *Ace* is a JavaScript embeddable code editor. It matches features and performance of native editors such as Sublime, Vim and TextMate, and can be easily embedded in any web page or JavaScript application.

Bootstrap. Bootstrap is the most popular front-end component library framework for developing responsive, mobile-first projects on the web.

jQuery and its UI Layout plugin. jQuery is a small and fast JavaScript library rich of features. The jQuery UI Layout plugin allows the creation of advanced UI layouts with sizable, collapsible, nested panels and tons of options.

bimap. BiMap is a powerful, flexible and efficient JavaScript bidirectional map implementation.

keymaster.js. Keymaster is a simple micro-library for defining and dispatching keyboard shortcuts in web applications.

The web-based GUI is divided into 4 different parts (Fig. 1). The *navigation bar*, at the top, contains dedicated *Run*, *Upload* and *Download* buttons. The *code editor*, in the middle, contains the editing tabs holding the program(s) to execute. The *output panel*, on the right side, dynamically shows the output of the computations and the link to the editor's layout options. The *IDE options panel*, on the left side, contains all the options described in Sect. 2; this panel can be automatically toggled in order to save space for the main editor.

The layout is built using the Responsive Web Design (RWD) approach, i.e., it automatically adapts to the viewing environment and offers the possibility to be viewed on different devices with virtually the same User Experience.

3.4 The EMBASP *Server Executor*

In order to decouple the web-requests management from logic-programming solvers execution, we developed EMBASP *Server Executor* as a completely different component; it is even implemented in a different programming language. EMBASP *Server Executor* is a Java server application that is able to execute

ASP programs with different solvers; we remark that the focus on ASP is just for the prototype, and other formalisms will be supported soon. It has the usual structure of a Java web-app with the following modules: (i) Control, (ii) Model, (iii) Service, and (iv) Resources. For space reasons, we do not discuss them in details, as the names are self-explanatory. EMBASP *Server Executor* runs on top of Apache Tomcat® and exposes a set of APIs for invoking the solvers. In order to execute the desired solver, it makes use of EMBASP[5] [7], a framework for the integration (embedding) of Logic Programming in external systems for generic applications; it helps developers with designing and implementing complex reasoning tasks by means of different solvers on different platforms.

Similarly to *LoIDE*, EMBASP *Server Executor* is provided as open-source software (OSS), is publicly available at https://goo.gl/2WUeb4, and is released as Free Software[6].

4   Related Works

The work herein presented is naturally comparable to other Logic Programming IDEs and other web-based editors. Several stand-alone, "native" editors and IDEs have been proposed for Logic Programming over different platforms; we refer the reader to the ample literature on the topic [3, 6, 9, 13, 14, 16]; moreover, many web-based editors, that are the closely related with the project presented in this paper, have been recently introduced [4, 11, 12, 15].

All tools and environments share the same core of basic features, many of them are quite stable, some are already well-known. *LoIDE*, similarly to most web-based editors, has currently fewer features w.r.t. the "native" ones; however, even if quite young, it is already stable and effectively provides access to logic programming without the need for installing and configuring local applications, and from almost any platform connected to the Internet. Furthermore, it could even run locally on any device featuring the Node.js runtime, with a few additional configuration steps. Some tools (as SWISH, for instance) rely on platforms that provide functionalities via specific APIs over HTTP; it is worth noting that this is not the case of *LoIDE*. Indeed, it started from Answer Set Programming, for which no such platforms were available, and makes use of the EMBASP *Server Executor*, implemented on purpose, that makes the project also more general and extensible.

All mentioned editors have peculiar, sometimes very interesting features; however, each one is tailored to a specific language and tightly coupled with some specific solver(s) in the back-end. On the other hand, the aim of *LoIDE* is to have a robust platform that seamlessly integrates different languages and different solvers. We do believe that this approach is more general, and could foster the use of logic programming in many contexts, especially in practical context and in education, also fruitfully promoting exchanges among the various communities in the logic programming area.

---

[5] EMBASP. https://goo.gl/mE5kAo.
[6] Under MIT License. https://goo.gl/VfPknG.

5   Conclusion and Future Work

In this paper, we presented the *Lo*IDE project, an advanced and modular web-editor for logic-based languages that is also capable of integrating with state-of-the-art solvers. Even if equipped with relevant features that make it effectively usable in practice, the project is still at an early stage of development; hence, we have already identified many future works and improvements. For space reason, we can not mention them here: more details can be found in [8]. We mention here that we are working to take advantage from the modular and extensible nature of *Lo*IDE in order to support more *executors* (web-services), logic-based *languages* and *solvers* (engines); this will help to increase the audience, and with this respect we plan to add interactive tutorials for allowing users to became more familiar with declarative programming. We expect that a larger user base will foster a discussion in the communities about the features a cloud-based IDE for Logic Programming languages should have, and what the specifications of standard APIs should be to allow data interchange among different applications.

References

1. Baral, C.: Knowledge Representation, Reasoning, and Declarative Problem Solving. Cambridge University Press, New York (2003)
2. Brewka, G., Eiter, T., Truszczynski, M.: Answer set programming at a glance. Commun. ACM **54**(12), 92–103 (2011)
3. Busoniu, P., Oetsch, J., Pührer, J., Skocovsky, P., Tompits, H.: Sealion: an eclipse-based IDE for answer-set programming with advanced debugging support. TPLP **13**(4–5), 657–673 (2013)
4. Dasseville, I., Janssens, G.: A web-based IDE for IDP. CoRR abs/1511.00920 (2015)
5. Erdem, E., Gelfond, M., Leone, N.: Applications of answer set programming. AI Mag. **37**(3), 53–68 (2016)
6. Febbraro, O., Reale, K., Ricca, F.: ASPIDE: integrated development environment for answer set programming. In: Delgrande, J.P., Faber, W. (eds.) LPNMR 2011. LNCS (LNAI), vol. 6645, pp. 317–330. Springer, Heidelberg (2011). https://doi.org/10.1007/978-3-642-20895-9_37
7. Fuscà, D., Germano, S., Zangari, J., Anastasio, M., Calimeri, F., Perri, S.: A framework for easing the development of applications embedding answer set programming. In: PPDP 2016, pp. 38–49. ACM (2016)
8. Germano, S., Calimeri, F., Palermiti, E.: Loide: a web-based IDE for logic programming - preliminary technical report. CoRR abs/1709.05341 (2017)
9. Koziarkiewicz, M.: iGROM - an integrated development environment for answer set programs (2007). http://igrom.sourceforge.net. Accessed Aug 2017
10. Leone, N., Ricca, F.: Answer set programming: a tour from the basics to advanced development tools and industrial applications. In: Faber, W., Paschke, A. (eds.) Reasoning Web 2015. LNCS, vol. 9203, pp. 308–326. Springer, Cham (2015). https://doi.org/10.1007/978-3-319-21768-0_10
11. Marcopoulos, E., Reotutar, C., Zhang, Y.: An online development environment for answer set programming. CoRR abs/1707.01865 (2017)
12. Muise, C.: Planning. Domains. In: ICAPS System Demonstration (2016)

13. Strobel, V., Kirsch, A.: Planning in the wild: modeling tools for PDDL. In: Lutz, C., Thielscher, M. (eds.) KI 2014. LNCS (LNAI), vol. 8736, pp. 273–284. Springer, Cham (2014). https://doi.org/10.1007/978-3-319-11206-0_27
14. Sureshkumar, A., Vos, M.D., Brain, M., Fitch, J.: APE: an AnsProlog* environment. In: SEA 2007, Proceedings, pp. 101–115 (2007)
15. Wielemaker, J., Lager, T., Riguzzi, F.: SWISH: SWI-Prolog for sharing. CoRR abs/1511.00915 (2015)
16. Wielemaker, J., Schrijvers, T., Triska, M., Lager, T.: SWI-Prolog. Theory Pract. Logic Program. **12**(1–2), 67–96 (2012)

A REST-Based Development Framework for ASP: Tools and Application

Gelsomina Catalano[2], Giovanni Laboccetta[2], Kristian Reale[2], Francesco Ricca[1(✉)], and Pierfrancesco Veltri[2]

[1] DeMaCs, University of Calabria, Rende, Italy
ricca@mat.unical.it
[2] DLVSystem Srl, Rende, Italy
{catalano,laboccetta,reale,veltri}@dlvsystem.com

Abstract. Answer Set Programming (ASP) is a declarative programming paradigm that has been successfully used in a number of industry-level applications also thanks to the availability of development tools. *REpresentation State Transfer (REST) Web Services* recently became a common and widely-used tool for enterprise applications. A service-oriented infrastructure for ASP would further catalyze the adoption of ASP-based solutions in real-world contexts. This paper introduces a REST-based framework for ASP, and reports on an application of the framework in the field of surveillance for photovoltaic plants.

Keywords: Answer Set Programming · Service-oriented applications
Green energy

1 Introduction

Answer Set Programming (ASP) [3] is a declarative paradigm for knowledge representation and reasoning. Nowadays, ASP is successfully used to solve many real-world problems from several areas ranging from Artificial Intelligence, to Knowledge Management and Database (for a survey see [5]). Since ASP is not a full general-purpose language, ASP programs are always encapsulated in systems components developed via imperative and object-oriented programming languages. This has brought into light the need of reliable APIs and tools for integrating ASP technologies in well-assessed software-development processes and platforms [13]. Recently, the well-known ASP system DLV [11] has been profitably employed in a number of industry-level applications [12], and a key advantage of DLV for applications development is its endowment with powerful development APIs and tools [6,7].

The paper has been partially supported by the MISE under project "PIU-Cultura – Paradigmi Innovativi per l'Utilizzo della Cultura" (n. F/020016/01-02/X27), and under project "Smarter Solutions in the Big Data World (S2BDW)" (n. F/050389/01-03/X32) - "HORIZON2020" PON I&C 2014-2020.

© Springer International Publishing AG 2018
F. Calimeri et al. (Eds.): PADL 2018, LNCS 10702, pp. 161–169, 2018.
https://doi.org/10.1007/978-3-319-73305-0_11

Today more than ever applications are becoming more and more intelligent and pervasive. In general, intelligent services are expensive from a computational point of view, whereas mid-range devices are equipped with limited computational resources. Hence, there is a strong need of "remote intelligence providers" which take in charge of executing heavy reasoning tasks, allowing to devise lightweight apps that are runnable by common devices. In this context web services[1] became a common and widely-used technology. Indeed, intelligent web services are provided by a number of enterprise platforms like for example IBM Watson[2] and Microsoft Azure[3]. Also in the field of logic programming, preliminary efforts in this direction [4,14] lead to a client-server infrastructure for tuProlog and SWI-Prolog, respectively. However, we are not aware of similar efforts for delivering ASP-based reasoning services, despite such an infrastructure would promote the development of ASP-based solutions.

In this paper, we report on the implementation of a service-oriented interface devised with the aim of simplifying the creation of intelligent web services using ASP. Our interface allows the exposition of services that can be invoked via HTTP using a REpresentational State Transfer (REST) interface [8]. In particular, ASP programs can be managed and executed by making REST invocations to a server and by passing as parameter the program P to be executed in the JSON[4] format; the server runs DLV over P and returns the obtained results back to the client. The interface has been integrated in ASPIDE [7], one of the most comprehensive Integrated Development Environments for ASP, to further reduce the work that has to be done by developers in devising intelligent web services with ASP. In order to show practical implications of this work, we present here a case of study in the area of intelligent energy management. In particular, we implemented a tool of surveillance, that relies on DLV, for monitoring and diagnosing anomalies in photovoltaic plants. Our REST interface was the key ingredient for deploying an intelligent service in an existing service-oriented system, and ASPIDE helped reducing the implementation efforts. Thus, ASP-based services enhanced the system's ability to reason over and act upon it inputs by allowing the development of an intelligent service relying on an expressive declarative language and a powerful reasoning engine.

2   The *DLVService* REST Application

In this section we present *DLVService*, a RESTful Web Service implemented in Java which provides service-oriented features for managing and executing ASP programs. RESTful Web Services are implemented using a REpresentational State Transfer (REST) interface in which every request made from a service requester (GET, POST, PUT, DELETE, etc.), to a resource's URI, will cause the service provider to react generating a response, containing data, that may be

---

[1] https://www.w3.org/TR/ws-arch/#id2260892.

[2] https://www.ibm.com/watson/.

[3] https://azure.microsoft.com/.

[4] http://www.json.org.

in XML, HTML, JSON or some other defined format. Intuitively, a client which wants to use *DLVService* has to make REST invocations passing, as parameter encoded in the JSON format, the program to be executed; the server will call the DLV system in order to obtain execution results in the JSON format.

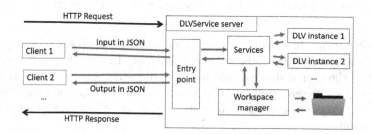

Fig. 1. The *DLVService* architecture

Figure 1 shows the architecture of *DLVService*: "Entry point" is the server listener which handles REST invocations made by clients, and "Services" makes available all the services exposed by *DLVService*. When a client makes an execution request to *DLVService*, an instance of DLV is launched by the server to compute results; note that a client can request several solver executions at the same time and, in this case, different instances of DLV will be launched in parallel. Moreover, *DLVService*, using the "Workspace manager" module (Fig. 1) allows one to have a *remote workspace management*; in this case, a user that is registered on the server will have a remote workspace where she can create program files and organize them in folders and subfolders. New users can be registered by the server administrator using a procedure which is similar to the one used to add users to Concurrent Versions Systems (CVS). In order to invoke *DLVService*, a registered user needs to make REST invocations using OAuth 2.0, a secure protocol ensuring a secure authentication. The workspace maintains all the defined execution configurations (e.g. which files were executed, which execution options were used, etc.), and all the results obtained from different execution tasks; note that an execution result stores a reference to the execution configuration used to obtain it.

Exposed Services and Complex Input/Output Objects. In order to use the features of the *DLVService*, several remote calls has to be done such as uploading new programs to the server, making several remote solver executions and retrieving results. A single remote service call is performed (assuming the server runs locally) by making an HTTP POST invocation with the URL:

```
http://localhost:8080/ASPWebService/DLVService?action=SERVICE_NAME
```

where SERVICE_NAME has to be replaced by the name of one of the services provided by *DLVService*; e.g. if a client wants to call service *executeProgram*, the last part of the URL will be *action=executeProgram*.

The most important services exposed by *DLVService* are described below in separated paragraphs.

registerProgram. It uploads an ASP program into a specific remote file.

getProgram. Given an array of remote file paths, it checks whether the files exist remotely and retrieves a *Program* object which contains the list of remote files.

executeProgram. It executes a given program. The program content will be saved into a specific file of the remote workspace. Execution results are both returned to the user and saved into a results file which can be accessed by the user even in a different moment; this feature is useful, e.g., for long reasoning tasks because the user can access in each moment the results file in order to see partials results.

createExecutionSettingsWithSolver. It creates a new *ExecutionSettings* object by specifying following parameters: an object name, the *Program* to be executed, the *Solver* to be run and the *Options* to be used.

executeConfiguration. For a given *ExecutionSettings* object, this service executes the relative configuration and retrieves the results.

Input parameters and output results of a service are complex objects encoded in the JSON format and the most important ones are described below:

Program. The program to execute containing a remote file paths list referring to program files.

ExecutionSettings. Execution settings composed by the program to be executed, the remote solver containing solver name/path/options, and a *datetime* field that can be used to retrieve the last created *ExecutionSettings*.

Results. Object containing the results of DLV after an execution invocation.

Run. Object built after a DLV execution task; it contains the run state (*finished*, *error*, etc.), two *datetime* objects identifying when the execution started and ended, the results of the execution and the *ExecutionSettings* which was used to perform the execution.

Solver. This object specifies a solver to use for execution. Default solvers are: DLV, DLV+ODBC, DLV^{DB} and $DLV^{\exists}$ [10].

Options. Object containing options to use on executing DLV.

A complete user manual for invoking all the exposed services, is available at https://www.mat.unical.it/ricca/aspide/dlvservice.html.

3   An Industry-Level Case of Study: Surveillance for Photovoltaic Systems

In this section, we present a case of study developed within the project "Project PON03PE_00001_1 Business Analytics to Know (BA2KNOW)" in collaboration with the energy company Omnia Energia[5]. We realised an ASP-based service solving a problem arising in the area of intelligent energy management. In particular, we developed a module for surveilling and monitoring a photovoltaic grid. Our module engages in a system where each module was developed according to the REST approach. Using the REST service was therefore of fundamental importance to develop the application described later. In the following we assume that the reader is familiar with ASP, we refer the reader to [2] for a nice tutorial on the language of DLV and to [1,9] for a comprehensive descriptions of ASP as a modeling language.

The goal of this application is monitoring and diagnosing anomalies in the photovoltaic grid: in case of incidents both customers and the company itself are notified with programmed warnings. Anomalies are detected by comparing actual data measured on the grid with the expected values for these data as provided by other modules of the system (the description of these is out of the scope of this paper). The expected values can be obtained in the system either by running a mathematical model of the grid or by getting the results out of a previously-trained neural network, which also takes as input weather data and other measurements. Data which is coming from one or more predictive models are fed as input to our module, together with actual device measurements (such as instant and peak power). Our module is then able to compare the actual values with the expected ones, and to issue programmable alerts to users (where users are intended as both company customers and the company itself).

By using logical rules, it is possible to reason on input data, allowing, for instance, to identify devices whose behavior differs from estimated values. Comparisons can be tuned over different time windows, such as days, weeks, months or years. One can also reason in terms of how many time slots came outside of thresholds with respect to predictive models, and also about consecutive time slots in which anomalies were detected; also one can combine the different predictive models at will (i.e. whether one particular predictive model must be considered, or whether triggering alerts when thresholds are exceeded with respect to at least one predictive model). The module allows to quickly intervene in case of anomalies, thus keeping a steady power production to the best extent.

Input data is modeled in ASP with predicates *production* and *prediction*. The first predicate encodes current device readings: fact `production(Id_device, Peak_power,Day,Month,Year,Hour,Instant_power)` tells the ASP solver about readings of the *Id_device* which gave *Peak_power* and *Instant_power* at the given time and date. The fact `prediction(Model,Id_device,Peak_power,Day, Month,Year,Hour,Instant_power)` expresses that a given predictive model was expecting a value of *Peak_power* and a value of *Instant_power* for device *Id_device* at the given time and date, where the attribute model can be, e.g., one of {*physics, neural_net_1, neural_net_2, ..., neural_net_n*}. The system also waits for input thresholds that must cause alert messages when they are exceeded (above or under). For instance, the fact *percentage_threshold(30)* fixes a limit value of 30%.

---

[5] http://www.omniaenergia.it/.

In the following, just for example, we report a rule which generates an alert when the percentage threshold of the daily production deviation per device is exceeded:

```
alert_daily_production(over,Id_device,Model,Week,Day,Month,Year,Value):-
    inweek(Week,Day,Month,Year),
    daily_production_deviation(over,Id_device,Model,Day,Month,Year,Value),
    percentage_threshold(S),Value > S.
```

This alert reports the device where the deviation occurred, specifying that it was an over-production, also reporting the value of the percentage deviation (*Value* attribute) and time data (*Week, Day, Month, Year*). The predicate *daily_production_deviation* stores information about the deviation.

Similar rules allow to control other aggregate productions (weekly, monthly, yearly) and to produce any corresponding alerts. Likewise, similar rules are introduced in order to catch total production deviations.

In order to point out possible anomalies, our module calculates how many days in a week the production differs from estimated values above or under the given threshold, with respect to at least one predictive model; or how many days in a month, how many days in a year, how many weeks in a month, how many weeks in a year, how many months in a year. If these values exceed the set thresholds, alarms are generated to warn about any equipment that has an abnormal output trend over a certain period of time.

The system also performs the same calculations on the data above but refers to consecutive time slots. This is interesting because, for example, if a device exceeds the thresholds in production for more than a given number of days (or months, weeks or years) consecutively, it suggests a different interpretation of the anomaly with respect to the case when the deviation occurs in non-consecutive days. In this case, the count is not immediate, but requires intermediate calculations. In particular, via a transitive closure, a set of rules first determines which consecutive days, consecutive weeks, and consecutive months of production, trigger an alert. Then, groups of days, weeks or consecutive months are identified, and finally another rule calculates the maximum length of consecutive slot groups.

4   Setting up Services with ASPIDE

The ASPIDE [7] development environment for ASP was extended with a plug-in that allows the user to configure and run the *DLVService*. The user can use ASPIDE as usual by creating and editing program files, setting up run configurations and viewing results in a tabular way; the difference consists of the fact that (i) the program files will be immediately updated remotely, (ii) the execution is done by invoking the *DLVService* via JSON parameters, and (iii) the results, returned in JSON by the server, will be handled by ASPIDE and shown in a tabular way. Basically, the remote service is handled transparently by ASPIDE, precisely like the program and the execution were carried out locally. This interface

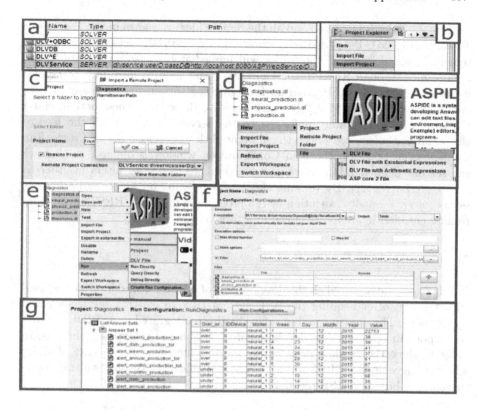

Fig. 2. Diagnostics use case in ASPIDE

makes the process of implementing a new service more user friendly. For exploiting *DLVService* in ASPIDE, a connection string format has been introduced for specifying the URL of *DLVService*, a username and a password. A new executable of type *SERVER* (Fig. 2a) has to be added to the *preferences window* of ASPIDE; the connection string has to be structured as follow:

```
dlvservice:username:pass@http://localhost:8080/ASPWebService/DLVService
```

In the following, we describe how we can exploit the *DLVService* in ASPIDE to implement the tool of *surveillance for photovoltaic systems*. We know that there is a remote folder on the server side associated to the user *userD* which contains folder *Diagnostics* referring to our use case ASP program which was previously uploaded to the server. To exploit that program we have to import, in ASPIDE, that remote folder as a *Remote Project*: we make a right-click to the *Workspace Explorer* and click on *Import Project* (Fig. 2b); in such a way, the import project window is open (Fig. 2c). We then select *Remote Project* checkbox and indicate the remote project connection defined to the *preference window*. By clicking on *View Remote Folders* button, a window will show all the folders located on the remote workspace, which are associated to the user *userD*. By clicking on *Diagnostics* and confirming (Fig. 2c), a virtual representation of the remote folder is imported and all the remote files are shown in the *Workspace Explorer* (Fig. 2d). Users can open those files in ASPIDE; actions like editing, renaming and deleting of those files will immediately cause an update to the remote files through REST invocations. We want now to introduce *thresholds* input as facts to the ASP program for launching the diagnostic reasoning: we create a new *DLV File* (Fig. 2d) where we write those facts; these actions cause the file to be immediately uploaded to the server. To launch all the files of the *Remote Project*, we select them, right-click and select *Run->Create Run Configuration* (Fig. 2e): the Run Configuration window is opened, so that we can set our defined *DLVService* as solver and we can write filters in order to detect *alerts* (Fig. 2f). By running the *Run Configuration*, since *DLVService* is set as solver, a remote execution of the program is made via REST invocation; results, encoded in JSON, is shown in a tabular way (Fig. 2g).

5   Conclusion

In this paper, we reported on the development of a REST-based interface devised with the aim of embedding the ASP system DLV in existing service-oriented applications. The implemented interface has been integrated in ASPIDE in order to support and promote the development of ASP-based enterprise solutions. In order to show the framework at work, we presented here a real case of study where we developed a REST service-oriented application for photovoltaic plants surveillance based on ASP technologies.

References

1. Baral, C.: Knowledge Representation, Reasoning and Declarative Problem Solving. Cambridge University Press, Cambridge (2003)
2. Bihlmeyer, R., Faber, W., Ielpa, G., Lio, V., Pfeifer, G.: DLV - user manual (2002). http://www.dlvsystem.com/html/DLV_User_Manual.html
3. Brewka, G., Eiter, T., Truszczynski, M.: Answer set programming at a glance. Commun. ACM **54**(12), 92–103 (2011)
4. Calegari, R., Denti, E., Mariani, S., Omicini, A.: Towards logic programming as a service: experiments in tuProlog. In: WOA, pp. 79–84 (2016)
5. Erdem, E., Gelfond, M., Leone, N.: Applications of answer set programming. AI Magaz. **37**(3), 53–68 (2016)
6. Febbraro, O., Grasso, G., Leone, N., Ricca, F.: JASP: a framework for integrating answer set programming with Java. In: Proceedings of KR 2012. AAAI Press (2012)
7. Febbraro, O., Reale, K., Ricca, F.: ASPIDE: integrated development environment for answer set programming. In: Delgrande, J.P., Faber, W. (eds.) LPNMR 2011. LNCS (LNAI), vol. 6645, pp. 317–330. Springer, Heidelberg (2011). https://doi.org/10.1007/978-3-642-20895-9_37
8. Fielding, R.T., Taylor, R.N.: Architectural styles and the design of network-based software architectures. University of California, Irvine Doctoral dissertation (2000)
9. Gebser, M., Kaminski, R., Kaufmann, B., Schaub, T.: Answer Set Solving in Practice. Synthesis Lectures on Artificial Intelligence and Machine Learning. Morgan & Claypool Publishers, San Rafael (2012)

10. Leone, N., Manna, M., Terracina, G., Veltri, P.: Efficiently computable datalog programs. In: Proceedings of KR 2012, pp. 13–23 (2012)
11. Leone, N., Pfeifer, G., Faber, W., Eiter, T., Gottlob, G., Perri, S., Scarcello, F.: The DLV system for knowledge representation and reasoning. ACM Trans. Comput. Logic **7**(3), 499–562 (2006)
12. Leone, N., Ricca, F.: Answer set programming: a tour from the basics to advanced development tools and industrial applications. In: Faber, W., Paschke, A. (eds.) Reasoning Web 2015. LNCS, vol. 9203, pp. 308–326. Springer, Cham (2015). https://doi.org/10.1007/978-3-319-21768-0_10
13. Lierler, Y., Maratea, M., Ricca, F.: Systems, engineering environments, and competitions. AI Magaz. **37**(3), 45–52 (2016)
14. Wielemaker, J., Lager, T., Riguzzi, F.: SWISH: SWI-prolog for sharing. arXiv preprint arXiv:1511.00915 (2015)

Navigating Online Semantic Resources
for Entity Set Expansion

Weronika T. Adrian[1,2](✉) ⓘ and Marco Manna[1] ⓘ

[1] Department of Mathematics and Computer Science,
University of Calabria, 87036 Rende, Italy
{w.adrian,manna}@mat.unical.it
[2] AGH University of Science and Technology, Kraków, Poland

Abstract. Semantic resources (WordNet, Wikidata, BabelNet, ...) offer invaluable knowledge that can be exploited by humans and machines to solve a variety of tasks. Among these, we address here the one called entity set expansion: extend a given a set of words –called seeds– with new ones being of the same "sort". Differently from classical approaches, we determine "optimal" common categories of the given seeds by analyzing the semantic relations among the objects these seeds refer to. In particular, we define the notion of an entity network to integrate information from different semantic resources, and show how to use such networks to disambiguate word senses. Finally, we propose a proof-of-concept implementation in answer set programming with external predicates to query online semantic resources and perform optimization tasks.

Keywords: Answer set programming · External predicates
Entity set expansion · Information extraction
Natural language processing · Information integration
Word sense disambiguation

1 Introduction

Nowadays, a lot of information on the Web is stored in various *semantic resources* —databases, created manually, automatically or semi-automatically— that codify different aspects of human knowledge with some degree of formalization. Some of them, often called "encyclopedic", provide information about the real world objects; others, referred to as "terminological", deal with abstract concepts and relations. Integrating information from several resources allows to combine different points of view on the problem at hand and helps to solve complex tasks, such as understanding, comparing or classifying entities.

The paper has been partially supported by the Italian Ministry for Economic Development (MISE) under project "PIUCultura – Paradigmi Innovativi per l'Utilizzo della Cultura" (n. F/020016/01-02/X27), and under project "Smarter Solutions in the Big Data World (S2BDW)" (n. F/050389/01-03/X32) funded within the call "HORIZON2020" PON I&C 2014-2020.

F. Calimeri et al. (Eds.): PADL 2018, LNCS 10702, pp. 170–185, 2018.
https://doi.org/10.1007/978-3-319-73305-0_12

The problem we study in this paper goes under the name of *entity set expansion* (ESE). Informally, given a set of words called *seeds*, the goal is to extend the original set with new words of the same "sort". For example, starting from *Rome* and *Budapest*, one could expand these seeds with *Amsterdam, Athens, Berlin, ...,* *Warsaw,* and *Zagreb*, which are also capital cities of European Union member states. But is this the most appropriate way? In fact, an alternative expansion could be made by *Amsterdam, Berlin, Dublin, ..., Paris*, and *Prague*, which are also Europe's capitals situated on rivers. Moreover, *Rome* is not only a 'capital', but also a 'drama television series', a 'female deity', and many other things, while *Budapest* is also a 'film series' and a 'rock band', apart from being a 'capital' too. Hence, which is the "best" common sort putting together the original words? Are they 'capitals' or 'films'? As complicated as it is, this problem has practical applications in both "personal" information management (think, for example, about the Google Sets, now discontinued and with the techniques protected with a patent [28]) and "enterprise" solutions (automatic lexicon generation [15,22,23,27] in Information Extraction systems used in recruitment etc.).

Several methods for ESE have been proposed in the literature. A classical approach is to employ *bootstrapping* algorithms [6,15,22,27] that iteratively expand the initial set by repeating in turns two steps: "pattern generation" and "instance extraction". The former consists in learning the "context" in which seed words appear in a corpus, and the latter aims to find more words that appear in such context. The intuition is to identify entities "similar" to the ones given as seeds. But the notion of "similarity" motivates another approach in which the seeds are used to train a classifier, the so-called *class tagger* [5,10,12] that would recognize more entities "like them" [24]. Recently, to calculate the similarities of words, a method of *word embeddings* [4,9,11] has been proposed. Finally, a simple yet effective in some settings approach is to identify *enumerations* in text and collect the entities from them [29]. As one can see, ESE poses several challenges that give rise to specific subproblems: to *understand* the seeds, to *characterize* them in a way that will define their category, and to propose a systematic way to *extend* this category with new instances.

However, there are some problems with existing approaches. First, most of them do not disambiguate word senses when analyzing the seeds. Consequently, if the same word appears in different "contexts" depending on the meaning, the lack of discrimination of them may lead to a wrong classification (e.g., there will be a different set of related words or usage patterns for the word *Prater* depending on if we refer to a park or a person[1]). Moreover, not taking into consideration the actual meaning of a word may work well for generating general lexicons, but fail with domain-specific dictionaries, when the context of words do not agree with statistics [10]. Secondly, the intended categories are usually as simple as a 'person', an 'animal', or a 'city', which is often insufficient to fully characterize the seeds. Finally, the methods are usually not "transparent" i.e., one cannot get the explanation of why certain instances are added to the set.

---

[1] See http://babelnet.org/search?word=prater&lang=EN.

To overcome the above limitations, we propose to use knowledge available on the Web, specifically, stored in selected semantic resources that represent semantics of objects, their categorization and relations with other objects. We use these resources to *understand and disambiguate* word senses and to discover *commonalities* among objects represented with them – that would serve to formulate their common category. Once the common category is defined, we utilize the Web-harvested knowledge to *extend the set*, and verify the new instances. To this end, we design a novel framework that exploits existing semantic resources and implement our strategy using Answer Set Programming (ASP) [2] enriched with external predicates [3]. Application of Datalog/ASP proved to be successful in related domains and problems such as *data extraction* and *integration* [14].

The contribution of the paper can be summarized as follows:

1. *Knowledge representation.* We introduce the notion of *entity network*, a general knowledge representation model able to integrate information from several *semantic resources* (see Sect. 2).
2. *Word-sense disambiguation.* Given a set of seeds and an entity network, we define the notion of *optimal common ancestors* for them, which are the "best" common *classes* from the entity network (see Sect. 3).
3. *ASP-based Design and Implementation.* We propose logic-based implementation that uses Answer Set Programming to (*i*) construct an entity network from a set of seeds and to (*ii*) compute the optimal common ancestors for a set of seeds and their associated entity network (see Sects. 2 and 3).
4. *Entity set expansion.* We proposed a new algorithm for ESE that uses both structured and unstructured knowledge from the Web (see Sects. 4 and 5).

2   Integrating Semantic Resources

In order to understand the meaning of words and a common category of objects, we will use the online *semantic resources*. We aim to integrate information available in them to combine the strengths and minimize weaknesses of the resources. To reason over the integrated knowledge, we will represent it with a single model of an *entity network*. In this section, we introduce selected semantic resources, define the entity networks, and propose an ASP-based encoding that dynamically creates such networks given a set of seeds.

2.1   Semantic Resources

Currently, more and more machine-readable knowledge is available on the Web in a form of *semantic resources*. These knowledge bases formalize and organize human knowledge about the world in different scope and manners, focus on various dimensions and areas of knowledge. For the problem we address, we decided to use a combination of selected resources presented next.

WordNet [16] is a computational lexicon of English[2] that organizes concepts into sets of synonyms, called *synsets*. The synsets are interlinked via lexical

---

[2] There exist satellite projects for other languages, not integrated with the core system.

and semantic relations (a different set of relations is defined for different parts of speech). As WordNet is manually curated, the resulting network is reliable and thus this knowledge base became a widely acknowledged reference source in Natural Language Processing community and beyond.

Wikidata (http://wikidata.org) is a free, open and collaboratively edited knowledge base, that can be read and edited by humans and machines. Wikidata is a document-oriented database, focused on *items*. Each item represents a topic and is identified by a unique number. The items are described with a set of *statements*: key-value pairs, consisting of a property and an object, both equipped with identifiers.

BabelNet [18] is a multilingual terminological resource that integrates information from Wikipedia, Wordnet and other Web resources. It provides both encyclopedic knowledge about multiple instances and dense network of relations among the entries. What is important, BabelNet provides links to other resources, by means of which it indicates which entries in other knowledge bases correspond to the given entry (synset) in BabelNet.

WebIsADatabase [25] is a publicly available database containing more than 400 million hypernymy relations extracted from the CommonCrawl web corpus. The tuples of the database are created by harvesting the corpus and applying lexico-syntactic patterns, such as: NP_t *is a* NP_h, NP_h *such as* NP_t etc., where NP_t indicates the hyponym and NP_h the hypernym. The dataset can be queried both for classes of a given instance, and for instances of a given class.[3]

2.2   Entity Networks

In order to integrate knowledge from several semantic resources, we propose a model that can uniformly represent information acquired from them. The basic notions we will use are *(semantic) entities* and an *(entity) network*. An entity is a pair $\varepsilon = \langle id(\varepsilon), names(\varepsilon) \rangle$, where $id(\varepsilon)$ is the identifier of ε, and $names(\varepsilon)$ is a set of (human readable) terms describing ε.

From a syntactic viewpoint, $id(\varepsilon)$ is a set of strings of the form *src* : *code* where *src* identifies the semantic resource where ε is classified, and *code* is the local identifier within source *src* and $names(\varepsilon)$ is a set of strings that is a sum of sets of names associated to the entity in the considered resources. For example,

$$\varepsilon = \langle \{\texttt{wn:08864547, wd:Q40, bn:00007266n}\}, \{\texttt{Austria, Republic of Austria,} \ldots\} \rangle$$

is an entity representing the object in real world, the Republic of Austria, referred to in WordNet (abbreviation wn with identifier 08864547), Wikidata (abbreviated wd with item identifier Q40), and BabelNet (synset identifier bn:00007266n).

From a semantic point of view, entities may refer to three different kinds of objects. Namely, they can either point to (i) individuals, called hereafter *instances*, such as in the previous example, where the entity denotes a particular country, or (ii) concepts that generalize a *class* of objects e.g., $\varepsilon = \langle \{\ \texttt{wn:08562388},$

---

[3] See online demo at: http://webisadb.webdatacommons.org/webisadb/.

`wd:Q6256, bn:00023235n` }, {`country`} ⟩ or to (iii) *(semantic) relations* that hold between two objects e.g., $\varepsilon = \langle\{$`wd:P31`$\}, \{$`instance of, is a, ...`$\}\rangle$ or $\varepsilon = \langle\{$ `wd:P131`$\}, \{$`is located in, ...`$\}\rangle$ etc. For convenience, we group the entities representing instances and classes into one group, so-called *(knowledge) units*, and the relations form a separate group.

An *(entity) network* is a four-tuple $\mathcal{N} = \langle Uni, Rel, Con, type\rangle$ where: (*i*) *Uni* is a set of knowledge units, both classes and instances; (*ii*) *Rel* is a set of semantic relations; (*iii*) $Con \subseteq Uni \times Uni$ is a set of ordered pairs denoting that two units are connected via some (one or more) semantic relations; and (*iv*) $type : Con \rightarrow (2^{Rel} \setminus \emptyset)$ is a function that assigns to each connection a set of semantic relations. A network $\mathcal{N}$ is consistent if for each pair $\varepsilon_1, \varepsilon_2$ of different entities of $\mathcal{N}$, $id(\varepsilon_1) \cap id(\varepsilon_2) = \emptyset$.

Example 1. Consider a network $\mathcal{N} = \langle Uni, Rel, Con, type\rangle$ shown in Fig. 1. For clarity, identifiers are left implicit, and each entity is described by one name. In particular, $Uni = \{\varepsilon_1, \ldots, \varepsilon_5\}$, where only ε_5 is a class, $Rel = \{\varepsilon_6, \ldots, \varepsilon_{10}\}, Con$ are the arcs connecting units and, for each pair (u, v) of connected units, $type(u, v)$ contains the relations graphically associated to arc (u, v).

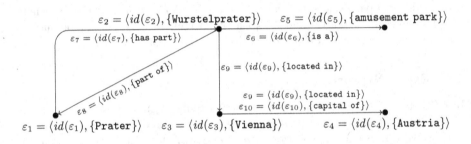

Fig. 1. An entity network example

From a knowledge representation viewpoint, two semantic relations are commonly referred to as "is-a": the membership relation "instance-of" and the subtype relation "subclass-of". In particular, BabelNet follows this standard by displaying only "is-a" when referring both to membership and to subtype relations. On the contrary, Wikidata keeps separate pages (and identifiers) for them. Finally, WordNet does not give any explicit identifier to these relations, but it considers the "instance" relation as a specific form of hyponym.[4] In our approach, both relations are treated uniformly as in BabelNet. To this end, we define the set *Isa* containing the following relations: $\langle\{$`wd : P279`$\}, \{$`subclass of, is a, ...`$\}\rangle$ and $\langle\{$`wd : P31`$\}, \{$`instance of, is a, ...`$\}\rangle$, grouping together the discussed entities and using identifiers from Wikidata. Given a network $\mathcal{N}$ as defined above, it is convenient to refer to the set $Con|_{Isa} = \{(u, v) \in Con \mid Isa \cap type(u, v) \neq \emptyset\}$ to select the "is-a" connections only.

---

[4] See http://wordnet.princeton.edu/wordnet/man/wngloss.7WN.html.

2.3 Entity Network Construction via ASP with External Predicates

An entity network can be constructed from a set of words or a set of (knowledge) units. When starting from words, the first step is to create a set of units that represent possible meanings of the words (this step is omitted in the second variant). This "first level" of nodes in a network is then *expanded* such that for each object (a node in the network) appropriate queries to selected resources are posed, and the results are added to the network. We say that a network expands in two "directions": (i) *vertically* – along the hypernymy relations i.e., by querying for classes and superclasses of the object of interest, and (ii) *horizontally* – along the rest of relations with other objects.

To realize the construction and expansion of a network, we propose an implementation in Answer Set Programming enriched with *external predicates*, by means of which semantic resources can be queried. Hereafter, we assume the reader is familiar with ASP. The external predicates refer to functions, implemented separately, that encapsulate requests to semantic resources and interpret their responses. The use of external predicates makes the solution modular and extensible: addition of a new resource requires only an addition of a new rule and a new (typically very simple) function, compatible with the resource's API. Technically, the "network builder" program consists of logical rules of the form $h \leftarrow l_1, \ldots, l_n$, where h is an atom in the head of rule, and $l_1, \ldots, l_n$ are positive literals in the body of rule. The literals may be either atoms of the form: $p(t_0, ..., t_n)$ where p is a predicate name and $t_0, ..., t_n$ are terms, or external predicates encoded as $\&p$ $(t_0, ..., t_n ; u_0, ..., u_m)$ where: $\&p$ is an external predicate (the name must start with a $\&$ symbol), $t_0, ..., t_n$ are input terms, $u_0, ..., u_m$ are output terms, and a semicolon symbol (";") separates input from output terms. In fact, all the rules that call external predicates are of the general form: $newConnection(InputU, OutputU [, optionArguments]^*) \; :- \; unitID(InputU), \&externalPredicate(InputU; OutputU) [, optionRestrictions]^*$.

This general idea can be used to integrate information from any set of suitable resources. However, an analysis of available resources revealed some peculiarities that we have used in our expansion strategy specifically tailored for the ESE problem. In particular, we selected BabelNet, WordNet and Wikidata and we "parametrized" the implementation to allow for the resources' strengths and limitations. For instance, because BabelNet integrates information from Wikipedia and WordNet, it has the biggest coverage of objects and most informative descriptions of them, including more informative names of the classes they belong to. On the other hand, when going up into the class hierarchy, BabelNet can sometimes get into a cycle, while WordNet ensures a carefully built taxonomy that forms a directed acyclic graph (considering nouns and hypernymy relations among them). Thus, we query both BabelNet and WordNet for hypernyms of concepts, but we restrict BabelNet queries only to some level (using a *bNetDepth* predicate, e.g. `bNetDepth(3).`). Finally, for the (semantic) relations between objects, Wikidata proved to be the most comprehensive source: relations in Wikidata have their own identifiers and sets of properties such as transitivity etc. To sum up:

1. We use BabelNet as a primary resource for word senses due to its wide coverage of instances and integration of knowledge from multiple sources.
2. We utilize BabelNet's links to other resources to keep the network consistent.
3. For vertical expansion, we query BabelNet only up to some limit, fixed with a parameter and WordNet without limits, up to the most general class 'entity'.
4. Horizontal expansion bases on Wikidata statements and relations identifiers.

Let us now consider a set W of seed words. The construction of a network starts with a mapping μ which associates a fact to each word $w \in W$ as follows: $\mu(W) = \{\texttt{seed}(w) \mid w \in W\}$. The following rule starts from the seed words and queries BabelNet for possible meanings of them using an external predicate &extBNetSense to infer a relation senseOf:

```
senseOf(Word, SenseID) :- seed(Word), &extBNetSense(Word; SenseID).
```

The external predicates call functions of the same names that are implemented in accordance with semantic resources' programming interface (API) or dedicated libraries. For instance, the function extBNetSense is implemented in Python according to the BabelNet API guide[5]. It takes as an input a string representing a word (Word) and returns strings that denote the BabelNet identifiers of synsets representing this word's possible senses (each string is an instantiation of the variable SenseID present in the head of rule). The implementation is a set of instructions that prepare and pose an appropriate request to BabelNet and interpret the response.

The identifiers of seeds' senses serve to create the first nodes in the network. With the following rules, we create them and expand their BabelNet taxonomy:

```
bNetID(SenseID,1) :- senseOf(Word, SenseID).
bNetID(PID,Level) :- bNetISA(ID, PID, Level).
bNetISA(ID, PID, PLevel) :- bNetID(ID,Level), &extBNetISA(ID; PID),
                    bNetDepth(BNetMax), Level < BNetMax, PLevel = Level + 1.
```

The second and third rules form a loop. In particular, bNetID/1 depends on bNetISA/2 and vice versa. To limit the application of these rules and query BabelNet only for a desired number of times, we assign "levels" to nodes in the network and put them as the second argument of the predicate bNetID. In the third rule, the level of the starting unit is checked (parameter *Level* is compared to the value *BNetMax*), and the level of its hypernym is set to the level one step higher. This limits the number of applications of the rule.

Having BabelNet identifiers not only allows to navigate within this resource, but also to reach equivalent entities in other resources. With the following rules, we obtain corresponding concepts in WordNet and expand their taxonomy within it (without limits i.e., until reaching the most general concept 'entity'):

```
bNetWNetEq(BID, WNID) :- bNetID(BID,Lv), &extBNetWNetEq(BID; WNID), Lv>1.
wNetID(ID)   :- bNetWNetEq(_, ID).
wNetID(PID) :- wNetISA(ID, PID).
wNetISA(ID, PID) :- wNetID(ID), &extWNetISA(ID;PID).
```

---

[5] See http://babelnet.org/guide.

As for the other semantic relations, we use Wikidata as a primary source. For each property, we get information about the name and identifier of the relation (*ID* and *Name*) and the target item Y. We reach Wikidata objects and establish new connections representing the statements with the following rules:

```
bNetWDataEq(BID, WDID) :- bNetID(BID,Lv), &extBNetWDataEq(BID; WDID).
wDataID(ID) :- bNetWDataEq(_, ID).
wDataRel(X, Y, ID, Name) :- wDataID(X), &extWDataRel(X; Y, ID, Name).
```

3   Word Sense Disambiguation

Due to the words' polysemy, an entity network constructed for a set of words W may contain multiple units for each single word $w \in W$ that represent the word's different meanings. To determine the "correct" meaning of words in the given context, we need to establish a *mapping* from this set of words to the knowledge units of the network. In this section, we introduce a notion of an *optimal common ancestor (OCA)* in a directed acyclic graph. This notion captures an intuition that if we analyze the taxonomy of the objects that represent different word senses, then finding the "closest" common supertype of all the words will point the correct senses of words. We also describe a declarative encoding in answer set programming that uses the *guess-check-optimize* paradigm to determine the set of optimal common ancestors given a set of words and their entity network.

3.1   Classical Approaches

Following the definition stated in [17], given a text T that can be viewed as a sequence of words $(w_1, w_2, \ldots, w_n)$, *word sense disambiguation* (WSD) is a task of assigning the appropriate sense(s) to all or some of the words in T, that is to identify a mapping A from words to senses, such that $A(i) \subseteq Senses_D(w_i)$, where $Senses_D(w_i)$ is the set of senses encoded in a dictionary D for word w_i and $A(i)$ is that subset of the senses of w_i which are appropriate in the context T. Note that our setting is a little bit different: we do not consider words in a sequence, but in a set (of seed words), and instead of one dictionary, we assume a combination of semantic resources. However, the goal remains the same: out of possible meanings, select the one that is "the best" in the given context.

Out of multiple approaches to WSD: supervised and unsupervised, knowledge-rich (dictionary-based) or knowledge-poor (corpus-based), our method is closest to the so-called *structural approaches* based on existing terminological resources. Given a measure of semantic similarity defined as *score* : $Sense_D \times Sense_D \rightarrow [0,1]$ where $Senses_D$ is the full set of senses listed in a reference lexicon, a general disambiguation framework based on the similarity measure has been defined. Namely, a target word w_i in a text $T = (w_1, \ldots, w_n)$ is disambiguated by choosing the sense S of w_i which maximizes the following sum:

$$\hat{S} = \underset{S \in Senses_D(w_i)}{\operatorname{argmax}} \sum_{w_j \in T : w_j \neq w_i} \underset{S' \in Senses_D(w_j)}{\max} score(S, S')$$

Given a sense S of our target word w_i, the formula sums the contribution of the most appropriate sense of each context word $w_j \neq w_i$ and the sense with the highest sum is chosen. Some well-known similarity measures include: the one of Rada et al. [20] which basically counts the shortest distance in WordNet between pairs of word senses, Sussna [26], based on the observation that concepts deep in a taxonomy appear to be more closely related to each another than those in the upper part of the taxonomy, Leacock and Chodorow [13] that scales the distance by the overall depth of the taxonomy, or Resnik [21], that uses the notion of *information content* shared by words in context (the more specific the concept that subsumes words, the more semantically related they are assumed to be).

The existing metrics are tailored mainly towards assessing similarity between classes, and use pairwise comparison within a unified network of WordNet. In our approach, we use the intuition of "counting edges" to assess the appropriateness of particular classes, but we have had to redefine the method to suit our setting and goals (determining the best senses represented by instances in a network).

3.2   Optimal Common Ancestors

Our approach follows the intuition that the "correct" meaning of the word may be selected out of its possible senses with the help of other seed words. More precisely, if we pick a sense per word, find a common supertype for all the picked senses, assign a score to this ancestor, that will reflect its "closeness" to the words, then we will be able to determine the best combination of senses, and thus – the best sense for each word in W.

Let us now formalize the notions. Consider a directed acyclic graph $G = (N, A)$, and a nonempty set $S \subseteq N$ of nodes called *seeds*. A node $a \in N$ is a *common ancestor* of S with respect to G if, for each seed $s \in S$, either $s = a$, or there is a path in G from s to a. If so, a is often called a common ancestor of (S, G), for short. Moreover, we say that a common ancestor a is a *candidate* to be an OCA if $\forall s \in S$ there is no other common ancestor on the path from s to a. As an example, consider the directed graph $G = (\{1, 2, 3, 4\}, \{(1, 2), (1, 3), (2, 4), (3, 4)\})$, which is clearly acyclic. One can verify that nodes 2 and 4 are common ancestors of $(\{1, 2\}, G)$ since there is a path from nodes 1 and 2 to node 4, and there is also a path from nodes 1 and 2 to node 4. Moreover, 2 is a candidate OCA of $(\{1, 2\}, G)$. Conversely, 3 is not a common ancestor of $(\{1, 2\}, G)$ since node 3 is not reachable from node 2. But 3 is a common ancestor of $(\{1, 3\}, G)$ since 3 is also a seed and there is an edge from node 1 to node 3.

Consider now a common ancestor a of some pair (S, G), with $G = (N, A)$. The *distance* of a from S in G, denoted by $dist(a, S, G)$, is the nonnegative integer k s.t. the following conditions are satisfied: (i) there is $V \subseteq A$ s.t. both $|V| = k$ and a is a common ancestor of $(S, (N, V))$; and (ii) there is no $V' \subseteq A$ such that both $|V'| < |V|$ and a is a common ancestor of $(S, (N, V'))$. Note that $dist(a, \{a\}, G) = 0$ trivially holds. Basically, the distance counts the minimum number of arcs sufficient for connecting each seed to the given ancestor. According to the previous example, $dist(4, \{1, 2\}, G) = 2$ since $V = \{(1, 2), (2, 4)\}$ is the smallest set of arcs sufficient to connect both seeds to node 4.

Definition 1. *A candidate common ancestor a of a pair (S, G) is optimal if, for each common ancestor a' of (S, G), it holds that $dist(a, S, G) \leqslant dist(a', S, G)$. Hereinafter, optca$(S, G)$ denotes the set of all OCAs of (S, G).*

Given an OCA a, we call *witness*(a) the set $\{V \subseteq A \mid dist(a, S, G) = |V|\}$. Since G is acyclic, each $V \in witness(a)$ represents a tree connecting each node of S to a. In the previous example, $optca(\{1, 2\}, G) = \{2\}$ since $dist(2, \{1, 2\}, G) = 1$ due to the unique witness $V = \{(1, 2)\}$.

3.3 Problem Definition and ASP-Based Sense Detector

We now define the main problem to detect appropriate senses for a set of words. Hereinafter, fix a set W of words and an entity network $\mathcal{N} = \langle Uni, Rel, Con, type \rangle$. The directed acyclic graph of W and $\mathcal{N}$ is defined as $G(W, \mathcal{N}) = (N, A)$, where $N = W \cup Uni$ and $A = Con|_{Isa} \cup \{(w, u) \mid w \in W \wedge u \in Uni \wedge w \in names(u)\}$. For notational convenience, let G denote $G(W, \mathcal{N})$. Roughly, this graph represents the taxonomy of all the meaning of W's words. The word sense disambiguation problem via optimal common ancestor (WSD-OCA) is defined next:

Definition 2. *From any pair $(W, \mathcal{N})$ as above, problem WSD-OCA asks for the maximal set of total functions $\sigma : W \to Uni$ for which there exists some $a \in optca(W, G)$ such that, for each $w \in W$, the pair $(w, \sigma(w)) \in witness(a)$.*

To solve the problem with ASP, we define a mapping μ that encodes the input pair (W, G) as set of facts, and design a program P and a weak constraint ω such that, a_{opt} is an optimal common ancestor of (W, G) if, and only if, a_{opt} is encoded as appropriate atom in some answer set of $\mu(W, G) \cup P \cup \omega$.

For the input, we have $\mu(W, G) = \{\text{edge}(u, v) \mid (u, v) \in A\} \cup \{\text{seed}(w) \mid w \in W\}$. Regarding P, we gradually introduce and explain its rules. To reduce the search space, we identify a suitable set $C \subseteq Uni$ of candidate common ancestors:

```
unit(U) :- edge(_,U).
hasAncestor(W,U) :- seed(W), edge(W,U).
hasAncestor(W,V) :- hasAncestor(W,U), edge(U,V).
partialAncestor(U) :- seed(W), unit(U), not hasAncestor(W,U).
ancestor(U) :- unit(U), not partialAncestor(U).
superAncestor(V) :- ancestor(U), edge(U,V).
candidateOptimalAncestor(U) :- ancestor(U), not superAncestor(U).
```

The first rule determines the set $\{\text{unit}(u) \mid u \in Uni\}$. The subsequent two rules determine, for each $w \in W$, which are the ancestors of w. The forth rule defines units that are not common ancestors. Rule five identifies the common ancestors. Rule six detects parents of common ancestors, which of course cannot be optimal. Rule seven defines the candidate optimal common ancestors.

All the atoms derived so far are obtained deterministically, and they are part of every answer set of $\mu(W, G) \cup P \cup \omega$. Conversely, to identify the optimal common ancestors of (W, G), we need to consider separately each candidate optimal common ancestor:

```
keepAncestor(X) | discardAncestor(X) :- candidateOptimalAncestor(X).
:- not #count{X:keepAncestor(X)} = 1.
```

The first rule guesses some candidate ancestors. The second rule (a strong constraint) imposes that each answer set may contain only one candidate ancestor.

Once a candidate ancestor is kept, we need to guess a suitable witness. To this end, to reduce again the search space, we consider only arcs forming paths to the guessed ancestor:

```
activeEdge(U,V) :- edge(U,V), keepAncestor(V).
activeEdge(U,V) :- edge(U,V), activeEdge(V,T).
keep(U,V) | discard(U,V) :- activeEdge(U,V).
senseOf(W,U) :- seed(W), keep(W,U).
reach(W,U) :- senseOf(W,U).
reach(W,V) :- reach(W,U), keep(U,V).
:- seed(W), keepAncestor(U), not reach(W,U).
```

The first two rules mark as *active* the arcs reaching the kept ancestor. Disjunctive rule three guesses a witness. Rule four determines the sense associated to each word. Rules five and six determine which units are reachable from the seeds, according to the guessed witness. Rule seven (a strong constraint) guarantees that the guessed ancestor is reachable from each seed.

For each guessed ancestor a, we compute the distance $dist(a, W, G)$. For safety, we add to P auxiliary set of atoms distanceRange$(1..\kappa)$, where $\kappa = |A|$:

```
distance(N) :- distanceRange(N), N = #count{X,Y:keep(X,Y)}.
:∼ distance(N). [1:N]
```

Finally, the last rule defines the weak constraint ω, which guarantees that the witness (and thus the ancestor a) is not ignored, only if it has minimal size.

The answer sets of the program $\mu(G) \cup P$ enhanced with ω are representative of all the optimal common ancestors for (W, G). Moreover, the correct word senses are encoded in the answer set of the program and can be easily retrieved.

4   Least Common Subsumers

This is a short section complementing the previous one. After disambiguating word senses, we obtain a mapping from W to a set of kowledge units that represent the actual objects of interest.[6] Once the optimal combination of senses is fixed, we proceed to the phase of characterizing the objects. Inspired by the notion of *least common subsumers* [1], introduced in the context of Description Logics (DLs), we describe how to provide a "concept description" for a set of instances of some entity network. (The detailed translation from the network to DL is beyond the scope of this paper. In what follows, we present the main intuition of this rather straightforward interpretation.) In general, to characterize

---

[6] If there are more possible combinations of senses, a user can add more seeds and repeat the process, or just select the intended meaning.

the seeds, we create a new network $\mathcal{N}_1$ from $\sigma(W)$, expand it, and analyze: vertical expansion to determine the (set of) common ancestor(s) and horizontal – the common relations.

To determine the common supertype(s) of objects in $\sigma(W)$, we analyze the vertical expansion of the network created for them and determine the set of optimal common ancestors. Interestingly, while for sense disambiguation, we tend to go to WordNet hierarchy as soon as possible, due to the reliability and structure of WordNet taxonomy, when we look for actual common ancestors for already known senses, we explore BabelNet deeper — the reason for it is that the classes of BabelNet are more descriptive and human-readable (we realize this distinction by adjusting the *babelnetDepth* parameter in the network expansion, see Sect. 2.3). The set of optimal common ancestors serves to create the first part of the category description. Namely, for the $optca(\sigma(W), G(\mu(W), \mathcal{N}_1)) = c_1, \ldots, c_k$, the corresponding partial description would be $C_1 \sqcap \ldots \sqcap C_k$ (for clarity, we select one of the entity names for a corresponding concept name).

Once we get the common ancestors, we analyze the other relations. For each relation, say r, that is shared by all the starting nodes, we obtain a set U_r of units that are the *image* of the relation w.r.t. the seed units. If the set U_r is a singleton, say $U_r = \{u^*\}$, it means that the seed units are connected via the relation r to the same unit u^*. We stop exploring the relation and obtain a partial description of the common relation, namely $\exists r.\{u^*\}$. If, however, the image of the relation is a set of distinct objects, say $\{u_{r_1}, \ldots, u_{r_k}\}$, we obtain a concept description $\exists r.U_r$, where $U_r = \{u_{r_1}, \ldots, u_{r_k}\}$. We can now discard this relation or analyze it further by determining the common category of units in U_r. In this case, we treat the set of units U_r as the new seed set, for which we repeat the process of finding a common ancestor and analyzing common relations. To ensure termination, we fix the parameter denoting the depth of the analysis.

The output of this step is a concept description (in DL notation) of the form $(C_1 \sqcap \ldots \sqcap C_k) \sqcap \exists r_1.U_{r_1} \sqcap \ldots \sqcap \exists r_l.U_{r_l}$, where $C_1, \ldots, C_k$ are optimal common ancestors, $r_1, \ldots, r_l$ are common (shared) relations of seeds, and $U_1, \ldots, U_l$ are the images of the relations (either concept descriptions or sets of instances). A DL sufficient for our method is $\mathcal{ALCO}$.[7]

5 Entity Set Expansion

In this section, we explain how we use the notions introduced in Sects. 2, 3 and 4 to realize the ESE task. In particular, we address problems of: disambiguating word senses, characterizing seeds to formulate the target category, expanding the set by discovering new candidate instances, and evaluate new instances.

5.1 Existing Approaches to ESE

Several approaches to tackle the problem of entity set expansion have been proposed. In particular, the idea of *bootstrapping algorithms* [22] consists in

---

[7] See DL navigator at: http://www.cs.man.ac.uk/~ezolin/dl/.

starting from a set of seeds, discovering *patterns* in which they appear in a given corpus, then using those patterns find more examples and repeating the process until an end condition is met. The patterns are usually lexico-syntactics. However, more complex ways of characterizing the words within a category have also been proposed. In particular, in recent years the *word embeddings* are the most studied approach [4]. As far as the corpus is concerned, the great potential of the Web has been recognized and used to extend the set of seeds [7,19,24]. As for the process itself, improvements have been proposed for each step: representing words [9], discovering patterns [5,12], evaluating them [8] and minimizing so-called *semantic drift* [6].

5.2   ESE Using Entity Networks

In the proposed approach, we use the notions and sub-problems introduced in the previous sections, and combine them in the following framework: First, we *construct an entity network $\mathcal{N}_0$ from a set of seed words W*: In this step, for the set of seed words given as input, we create a knowledge representation that integrates information from different *semantic resources*. Then, we *construct a graph $G(W, \mathcal{N}_0)$ from W and $\mathcal{N}_0$*: This step prepares the structure for the operation of resolving the polysemy of words (if it appears). Having the graph representing the taxonomies of possible meanings of seeds, we *disambiguate word senses to obtain a set of mappings $\sigma_1, \ldots, \sigma_k$ from words to "knowledge units"*: In this step, we determine the "correct" (intended) meaning of words (see Sect. 3). *If there are several optimal mappings ($k \geq 1$), we ask the user to add more seeds (and go to step 1) or to select one option*: A user can clarify the intentions by adding more seeds or by selecting one meaning. Once the intended meaning is clarified, we *construct a network $\mathcal{N}_1$ from $\sigma(W)$*. This step is similar to step 1. From the network $\mathcal{N}_1$, we *create a semantic description of $\sigma(W)$ (the common category to expand)*: The output is a formula that semantically describes all the seed objects. Then we *look for more instances that belong to the intended category*. To discover new object of the target category, we query WebIsADatabase for instances of the common ancestors of the seeds. We set a threshold to filter out noisy results (those having too few witness pages). We *verify the new instances by checking their compliance with the semantic description from step 6*. The retrieved set of instances is *evaluated* against the concept description constructed earlier. In particular, we check if the new instances are hyponyms of one of the desired common ancestors, and if they share the relations discovered for the seeds.

The results of the evaluation may be three-fold: (i) the instance can be found in reference semantic resources, in particular BabelNet, and in the entity network constructed for it all the properties agree (so it belongs to the target category), (ii) the network can be created, but not all the properties agree (it does not belong to the category), (iii) the network cannot be created for the candidate instance. Recall that WebIsADatabase contains more of less popular instances than major semantic resources. So, these candidates are presented to the user as not validated, but proposed.

5.3   Real-World Use Cases

Let us now consider two examples that will illustrate different challenges.

Amusement parks in Europe. Let us say that we want to organize a family trip, and we are looking for something like *Efteling* or *Gardaland* – two places we visited and liked. Let us put these two words as seeds. A network created for them, limited to the hypernymy relations, consists of 14 nodes and 13 edges. Moreover, for each words, exactly one sense has been found. *Efteling* has been recognized as a 'theme park', and *Gardaland* – an "amusement park'. An optimal common ancestor for these two classes is the 'amusement park' (represented by an entity $\langle\{$`wn:8494231n, bn:00003695n, wd:Q194195`$\}, \{$`amusement park, funfair, , ...`$\}\rangle$) that is a superclass of the 'theme park'. A shared relation, $\langle\{$`wd:P17` $\}, \{$`country`$\}\rangle$ has the image set that contains two units: *Italy* for *Gardaland*, and *Netherlands* for *Efteling*. We further expand a network for *Italy* and *Netherlands*, and we obtain that both are classified as a 'European country'. As *Italy* and *Netherlands* are popular entities with numerous relations, we can discover a lot of common relations such as: 'continent' –*Europe*, 'located in time zone' –*Central European Time* etc. The modularity of our approach lets us stop whenever we are satisfied with the seed description, e.g., taking into account only the common superclass, we obtain the target category: *AmusementPark* ⊓ ∃*country.EuropeanCountry* After querying WebIsADatabase and evaluating new instances, we obtain the following list of entities: *Portaventura, Euro disney, Tivoli gardens, Europa park, Legoland, Terra mitica, Parc Asterix, Disneyland Paris* and *Puy du fou.*

Cities or movies? Let us recall the example of *Rome* and *Budapest* – words that have a lot of meanings. With 27 possible senses for *Rome* and 6 for *Budapest*, we obtain a representative entity network whose underlying graph (limited to hypernymy relations) consists of 248 nodes and 430 edges(!). For this quite a big structure, the sense detector computes the optimal sense combinations very efficiently. In fact, we obtain 8 "best" combinations of senses, associated with their 11 optimal common ancestors. The disambiguated meanings include: capital cities, bands, films and more. We can select the intended sense, or add a new seed to clarify our intentions. Let us add the word *Vienna* (19 senses) to the seed set. The resulting graph has 294 nodes and 558 edges. Here, the situation is even more complicated, because for each seed, there are two examples of a musical album or single. So, even though some senses are discarded, we obtain 9 best combinations grouped under 7 optimal common ancestors. If we now add another seed, say *Zagreb* (2 senses), we get a slightly bigger graph, but we obtain a single best combination of senses denoting the capital cities with optimal common ancestors: {'national capital','provincial capital'}. Further analysis reveals that the seeds share the relation: 'country' and again, as in the first example, we expand the network for the countries related to the our seeds and obtain that all of them are in Europe. Moreover, they are all connected with the relation $\langle\{$`wd:P421` $\}, \{$`located in time zone`$\}\rangle$ to the same instance, namely *UTC+01:00.* The expanded list yields among others the following new instances: *Amsterdam, Berlin, Bratislava, Paris, Prague, Vienna* and *Warsaw.*

6   Conclusion

The problem of entity set expansion is not a new topic. Over the last two decades, there has been work on gradually improving the classification methods and expansion algorithms. More recently, the improvements concentrate on details such as: the quality of the seeds and their influence on the process, metrics for patterns and seeds evaluation, etc. The approaches described in literature come with some small examples, but a systematic comparison with the real tools is difficult, because they are not available on-line. To the best of our knowledge, there is no complete system for entity set expansion available for comparison.

With our approach, we address the old problem in a modern semantic way. Instead of relying strictly on lexical level, we utilize the online *semantic resources*, that were not available before, to build a better representation, based on semantic relations. Our approach allows to leverage existing resources, and we believe that with the theoretical foundations and efficient ASP-based implementation of prototypes, that we already have, we can build, with further engineering effort, an integrated, configurable system.

There are several directions for future work. First, the semantic relations can be analyzed in more details, using DBPedia or Wikidata. Using their properties such as *transitivity, symmetry* etc. would allow for better network expansion and reaching more accurate concept descriptions. Moreover, new instances discovered in the expansion step, instead of being simply accepted or rejected, could be scored based on the degree to which they agree with the intended category. Finally, the proof-of-concept implementation, tested with idlv grounder[8] and wasp solver[9] could be evaluated also with other tools, and eventually optimized.

References

1. Baader, F., Sertkaya, B., Turhan, A.Y.: Computing the least common subsumer w.r.t. a background terminology. J. Appl. Logic **5**(3), 392–420 (2007)
2. Brewka, G., Eiter, T., Truszczynski, M.: Answer set programming at a glance. Commun. ACM **54**(12), 92–103 (2011)
3. Calimeri, F., Fuscà, D., Perri, S., Zangari, J.: I-DLV: the new intelligent grounder of DLV. Intelligenza Artificiale **11**(1), 5–20 (2017)
4. Camacho-Collados, J., Pilehvar, M.T., Navigli, R.: A unified multilingual semantic representation of concepts. In: Proceedings of ACL 2015, pp. 741–751 (2015)
5. Carlson, A., Betteridge, J., Wang, R.C., Hruschka Jr., E.R., Mitchell, T.M.: Coupled semi-supervised learning for information extraction. In: Proceedings of WSDM 2010, pp. 101–110 (2010)
6. Curran, J.R., Murphy, T., Scholz, B.: Minimising semantic drift with mutual exclusion bootstrapping. In: Proceedings of PACLING 2007, pp. 172–180 (2007)
7. Etzioni, O., Cafarella, M., Downey, D., Popescu, A.M., Shaked, T., Soderland, S., Weld, D.S., Yates, A.: Unsupervised named-entity extraction from the web: an experimental study. Artif. Intell. **165**(1), 91–134 (2005)

---

[8] See https://github.com/DeMaCS-UNICAL/I-DLV.
[9] See https://github.com/alviano/wasp.

8. Gupta, S., Manning, C.: Improved pattern learning for bootstrapped entity extraction. In: Proceedings of CoNLL 2014, pp. 98–108 (2014)
9. Gupta, S., Manning, C.D.: Distributed representations of words to guide bootstrapped entity classifiers. In: Proceedings of HLT-NAACL 2015, pp. 1215–1220 (2015)
10. Huang, R., Riloff, E.: Inducing domain-specific semantic class taggers from (almost) nothing. In: Proceedings of ACL 2010, pp. 275–285 (2010)
11. Iacobacci, I., Pilehvar, M.T., Navigli, R.: Sensembed: learning sense embeddings for word and relational similarity. In: Proceedings of ACL 2015, pp. 95–105 (2015)
12. Kozareva, Z., Riloff, E., Hovy, E.: Semantic class learning from the web with hyponym pattern linkage graphs. In: Proceedings of ACL 2008, pp. 1048–1056 (2008)
13. Leacock, C., Chodorow, M.: Combining local context and wordnet similarity for word sense identification. WordNet Electron. Lex. Database 49(2), 265–283 (1998)
14. Lehmann, J., et al.: DEQA: deep web extraction for question answering. In: Cudré-Mauroux, P., et al. (eds.) ISWC 2012. LNCS, vol. 7650, pp. 131–147. Springer, Heidelberg (2012). https://doi.org/10.1007/978-3-642-35173-0_9
15. Mcintosh, T., Curran, J.R.: Weighted mutual exclusion bootstrapping for domain independent lexicon and template acquisition. In: Proceedings of ALTA 2010, pp. 97–105 (2008)
16. Miller, G.A.: Wordnet: a lexical database for English. Commun. ACM 38(11), 39–41 (1995)
17. Navigli, R.: Word sense disambiguation: a survey. ACM Comput. Surv. 41(2), 10 (2009)
18. Navigli, R., Ponzetto, S.P.: Babelnet: the automatic construction, evaluation and application of a wide-coverage multilingual semantic network. Artif. Intell. 193, 217–250 (2012)
19. Pantel, P., Crestan, E., Borkovsky, A., Popescu, A.M., Vyas, V.: Web-scale distributional similarity and entity set expansion. In: Proceedings of EMNLP 2009, pp. 938–947 (2009)
20. Rada, R., Mili, H., Bicknell, E., Blettner, M.: Development and application of a metric on semantic nets. IEEE Trans. Syst. Man Cybern. 19(1), 17–30 (1989)
21. Resnik, P.: Using information content to evaluate semantic similarity in a taxonomy. arXiv preprint cmp-lg/9511007 (1995)
22. Riloff, E., Jones, R.: Learning dictionaries for information extraction by multi-level bootstrapping. In: Proceedings of AAAI 1999 and IAAI 1999, pp. 474–479 (1999)
23. Roark, B., Charniak, E.: Noun-phrase co-occurrence statistics for semiautomatic semantic lexicon construction. In: Proceedings of ACL 1998, pp. 1110–1116 (1998)
24. Sarmento, L., Jijkoun, V., de Rijke, M., Oliveira, E.: "More like these": growing entity classes from seeds. In: Proceedings of CIKM 2007, pp. 959–962 (2007)
25. Seitner, J., Bizer, C., Eckert, K., Faralli, S., Meusel, R., Paulheim, H., Ponzetto, S.P.: A large database of hypernymy relations extracted from the web. In: Proceedings of LREC 2016 (2016)
26. Sussna, M.: Word sense disambiguation for free-text indexing using a massive semantic network. In: Proceedings of CIKM 1993, pp. 67–74. ACM (1993)
27. Thelen, M., Riloff, E.: A bootstrapping method for learning semantic lexicons using extraction pattern contexts. In: Proceedings of EMNLP 2002, pp. 214–221 (2002)
28. Tong, S., Dean, J.: System and methods for automatically creating lists, 25 March 2008, US Patent 7,350,187
29. Wang, R.C., Cohen, W.W.: Language-independent set expansion of named entities using the web. In: Proceedings of ICDM 2007, pp. 342–350. IEEE (2007)

Automatic Web Services Composition for Phylotastic

Thanh H. Nguyen, Tran Cao Son$^{(\boxtimes)}$, and Enrico Pontelli

New Mexico State University, Las Cruces, NM 88003, USA
{tnguyen,tson,epontell}@cs.nmsu.edu

Abstract. This paper describes an automatic web service composition framework for *Phylotastic,* a platform for extracting and reusing phylogenetic trees. The paper begins with a short review of Phylotastic, followed by a description of the overall architecture of the framework and its core components, such as the ontology API, the planning module, the workflow configuration module, and the execution & monitoring module. The paper provides examples of execution of Phylotastic using a scientific use case and discuss the future features of the final system.

1 Introduction

Web service composition has been long considered as a fundamental contribution of the Semantic Web. Over the last decades, several frameworks for automatic web service composition have been proposed (e.g., [1,11,16,17,19,20]). Nevertheless, none of such approaches seems to be able to fully realize the potential of web service composition [11]. In fact, none of the frameworks for web service composition mentioned in the surveys [1,11,16,17,19,20] seems to function nowadays or be publicly available. As another example, the EU-funded Interoperability Solutions (ISA2) Programme developed the platform joinup,[1] which offers several services for sharing knowledge between e-Government professionals. To the best of our knowledge, this platform does not yet offer a way to combine available services to create and execute new ones.

A main difficulty in developing and maintaining an automatic web service composition framework is the lack of web services with enabling semantics. In other words, most available web services are provided without a semantic description. This prevents a system from automatically searching and discovering web services (e.g., based on the needs of a specific application), as well as it challenges automated composition, due to the lack of semantic information necessary to reason about web services (e.g., properly match inputs and outputs). One of the key issues that contributes to this problem is the lack of a domain-specific ontology that can be used in describing web services. Let us consider, as an example, the collection of web services from Google. It contains hundreds of services. To use a service (e.g., adding an appointment in the Google calendar), a user needs

---

[1] https://joinup.ec.europa.eu/homepage.

© Springer International Publishing AG 2018
F. Calimeri et al. (Eds.): PADL 2018, LNCS 10702, pp. 186–202, 2018.
https://doi.org/10.1007/978-3-319-73305-0_13

to identify the necessary parameters (e.g., date, time, etc.) and then invoke the service with such parameters. The main problem with this approach is that the description of how to use a service is (at best) in a text file or implicitly given in the service call.

In this paper, we revisit the idea of automatic web service composition, within the more manageable confinement of a specific application domain drawn from evolutionary biology. We focus on the development of an automatic web service composition platform for a specific application, called *Phylotastic*. In this application, several web services with some form of semantic annotation are available. The semantic descriptions are built using a formal ontology, describing the entities and artifacts of interest within the domain of evolutionary biology. Logic programming technology is used to provide a declarative and elaboration tolerant platform for reasoning about semantic web services. The proposed framework demonstrates that effective automated web service composition can be achieved within a specific applications domain, meeting the needs of scientists. It also differentiates from a system aimed at generating controllers, such as those developed by the AI community (e.g., [5]), as such controllers are not executed automatically—the integration of such type approaches to handle the planning aspects of Phylotastic is interesting and will be the focus of future work.

2   Background

2.1   Phylotastic

A phylogeny (phylogenetic tree) is a depiction of the evolutionary history of a set of organisms. Typically, this is a branching diagram showing relationships between species, but phylogenies can be drawn for individual genes, for populations, or for other entities. Phylogenetic trees are built using morphological traits (such as body shape, placement of bristles or shapes of cell walls), biochemical, behavioral, or molecular features of species or other groups. In building a tree, species are organized into nested groups based on shared derived traits (traits different from those of the group's ancestor) and the sequences of genes or proteins can be compared among species and used to build phylogenetic trees. Closely related species typically have few sequence differences, while less related species tend to have more. Currently, phylogenetic trees can be either explicitly constructed (e.g., from a collection of descriptions of species), or extracted from repositories of phylogenies, such as `OpenTree` and `TreeBASE`.[2] In a phylogeny, the topology is the branching structure of the tree. It is of biological significance, because it indicates patterns of relatedness among `taxa`, meaning that trees with the same topology provide the same biological interpretation. Branches show the path of transmission from one generation to the next. Branch lengths indicate genetic change, i.e., the longer the branch, the more genetic change (or divergence) has occurred. A variety of methods have been devised to estimate a phylogeny from the traits of the taxa (e.g., [7]).

---

[2] http://tree.opentreeoflife.org https://treebase.org .

Phylogenetic trees are useful in all areas of biology, both to organize knowledge by guiding classification (taxonomy), and for process-based models that allow scientists to make robust inferences from comparisons of evolved entities (genes, species, etc.). The transformative potential of assembling a *Tree of Life (ToL)*, a phylogeny covering 10^7 or more species [15], was articulated in an NSF workshop report [4]. The first draft of a grand phylogenetic synthesis, a single synthetic tree with 2.5×10^6 species (tree.opentreeoflife.org)—recently emerged from the Open Tree of Life (OpenTree) project.

Though useful, neither this tree, nor any other single tree, will be the sole authority on phylogenetic knowledge. When we refer to "the ToL" or "ToL knowledge" here, we do not mean any single tree, but the dispersed set of available trees that represent the current state of ToL knowledge. While experts continue expanding the ToL, addressing gaps and conflicts, the focus of the *Phylotastic* project [23] is on **dissemination**—putting ToL knowledge in the hands of researchers, educators, and the public. To achieve the goals of the Phylotastic project, the investigators proposed to build an open web-based system, that enables flexible on-the-fly delivery of phylogenetic knowledge. The premise of disseminating knowledge is that it will be re-used. How do trees get re-used? On a per-tree basis, re-use is rare; most trees are inferred *de novo* for a specific study, stored on someone's hard drive, and not used again [24]. Yet, large species trees are re-used in ways that other trees are not. In a sample of 40 phylogeny articles, we found only 6 cases in which scientists obtained a desired tree by extraction from a larger species tree [24]. This mode of re-use currently presents technical barriers requiring considerable expertise and effort to overcome. The vast majority of users simply cannot handle a tree with more than a thousand species, even if they knew how to find and obtain the right tree—a challenge, as only 4% of trees are archived [15]. Tree files generally lack machine-processable metadata on sources and methods, crucial for quality evaluation; common tree formats do not support such metadata. The largest and most valuable species trees often provide a topology without branch lengths, yet users often need branch lengths in downstream analysis steps: to close this gap, proficient users may create crude branch lengths with specialized software. Even matching a list of species names with a source tree is problematic, given the proliferation of aberrant names.

Thus, whereas subtree extraction is conceptually simple, real-world uses are surrounded by complications, currently requiring a combination of expert skills, hands-on attention, and specialized software. The typical workflow begins with upstream steps that establish the user's focus on a particular set of species, and proceeds with: (1) discovery and acquisition of an appropriate ToL source tree; (2) negotiating an optimal alignment with the set of query names; (3) subtree extraction and optional grafting; and (4) scaling the extracted subtree. The Phylotastic project proposed a flexible system for on-the-fly delivery of custom trees that would support many kinds of tree re-use, and be open for both users and data providers. Phylotastic proposes to develop an open architecture, composed of a collection of *web services* relevant to reuse of phylogenetic knowledge, that can be assembled in user-defined workflows through a portal (Fig. 1).

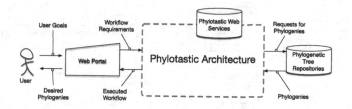

Fig. 1. Overall Phylotastic structure

2.2   The Web Service Composition Problem

The literature on automated composition of web services is extensive and beyond the scope of this paper. Intuitively, the need for composition of web services originates from the necessity to achieve a predetermined complex goal that cannot be realized by a standalone service. A composition of web services allows the execution of several web services, according to a determined pattern, to achieve the desired goals; individual services belonging to the composition communicate by exchanging results of their executions.

The open challenge of the web service composition problem is, given a collection of services and given a desired objective, to determine which services and which workflows based on such services will achieve the desired objective. A variety of techniques to respond to this challenge have been proposed in the literature (e.g., see [1,11,16,17,19,20] for some surveys). In Phylotastic, we adopt the view, advocated by several researchers, of mapping the web service composition problem to a *planning problem* [3,13,14,16]. In this perspective, available web services are viewed as *actions* (or *operations*) that can be performed by an agent, and the problem of determining the overall workflow can be reduced to a planning problem. In general, a planning problem can be described as a five-tuple (S, S_0, G, A, I'), where S is set of all possible states of the world, $S_0 \subseteq S$ denotes the initial state(s) of the world, $G \subseteq S$ denotes the goal states of the world the planning system attempts to reach, A is the set of actions the planner can perform to change one state of the world to another state, and the transition relation $I' \subseteq S \times A \times S$ defines the precondition and effects for the execution of each action. In term of web services, S_0 and G are the initial state and the goal state specified in the requirement of web service requesters (i.e., the available input and the desired output of the workflow). The set of actions A is a set of available services; I' describes the effect of the execution of each service.

3   Web Service Composition Framework for Phylotastic

Figure 2 shows an overview of our web service composition framework for Phylotastic. It consists of a web service registry, an ontology, a planning engine, a web service execution monitoring system, and a workflow description tool. The flow of execution of the architecture starts with the workflow description tool—a graphical user interface that allows the user to provide information about the

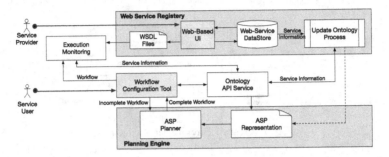

Fig. 2. The Phylotastic architecture

desired requirements of the phylogenetic trees extraction process. The information collected from the user interface are mapped into components of the planning problem instance that will drive the web service composition process. The planning problem instance representing the web service composition problem is obtained by integrating the user goals with the description of web services obtained from the service registry and the ontology. The planning engine is responsible for deriving an executable workflow, which will be enacted and monitored by a web service execution system. The final outcome of the service composition and execution is presented to the user using the same workflow description tool.

3.1   Ontology and Ontology API

The services registered with the Phylotastic registry are semantically described through a dedicated Phylotastic ontology. The ontology is composed of two parts: an ontology that describes the artifacts manipulated by the services (e.g., alignment matrices, phylogenetic trees, species names) and an ontology that describes the actual operations performed by the services. A dedicated API provides programmatic access to the ontology, necessary to provide the planner with information about the type of services that can be composed.

The description of the artifacts is based on an existing phylogenetic ontology, called *Character Data Analysis Ontology (CDAO)* [18]. *CDAO* provides a formal ontology for describing phylogenies and their associated character state matrices. CDAO is implemented in OWL. It provides a general framework for talking about the relationships between taxa, characters, states, their matrices, and associated phylogenies. The ontology is organized around four central concepts: OTUs, characters, character states, phylogenetic trees, and transitions. A phylogenetic analysis starts with the identification of a collection of *Operational Taxonomic Units* (OTUs), representing the entities being described (e.g., species, genes). Each OTU is described, in the analysis, by a collection of properties, typically referred to as *characters*. The values that characters can assume are called *character states*. In phylogenetic analysis, it is common to collect the characters and associated states in a matrix, the *character state matrix*, where the rows correspond to the OTUs and the columns correspond to the characters.

Phylogenetic trees and net-works are used to represent paths of descent-with-modification, capturing the evolutionary process under-lying the considered OTUs. Since evolution moves forward in time, the branches of a tree are typically directed. The terminal nodes are anchored in the present, as they rep-resent observations or mea-surements made on existing organisms. The internal nodes represent common ancestors, with the deepest node as the root node of the tree. Differ-ent types of representations of evolutionary knowledge are

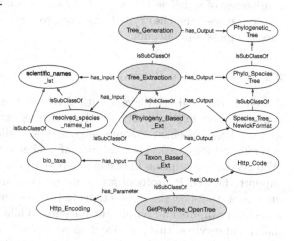

Fig. 3. Fragment of the Phylotastic ontology

available—differentiated based on structure of the representation (e.g., resolved trees, unresolved trees, rooted trees), the nature of the encoded knowledge (e.g., phylogenies vs. taxonomies) and the methods used to derive them.

The second component of the ontology provides a description of the oper-ations and transformations that are implemented by the services registered with the Phylotastic architecture. The description of the services follows a log-ical structure that is partly inherited from established bioinformatics service ontologies (e.g., myGrid [10]). The particular emphasis is on the classifica-tion of services that deal with the manipulation of species (e.g., names, pic-tures, phyloreferences)—e.g., deriving and resolving scientific names, retrieving relevant images, retrieving popular species—and representations of evolution-ary knowledge (e.g., taxonomies, phylogenies)—e.g., extracting phylogenies for selected species from authoritative evolutionary knowledge. The classes of ser-vices include also auxiliary services, such as manipulations of lists and shim services (data format transformations). The connection between the two compo-nents of the ontology (services and artifacts) is realized through object proper-ties, such has **has_input**, **has_output**, **has_parameter** and **has_data_format**. Figure 3 shows a small fragment of the Phylotastic ontology.

The Phylotastic architecture provides a web service to access and manipu-late the ontology, referred to as the *Ontology API Service*. This service allows searching and retrieving concepts and resources from the Phylotastic ontology. The use of a programmatic approach to using the ontology has several advan-tages, in terms of convenience and standardization of use. In particular, the *Ontology API Service* ensures that the ontology data is synchronized between clients components which are dependent on the ontology—updates and extensions of the ontology are immediately visible to all clients components, ensuring consistency of use. The *Ontology API Service* is a REST service implemented in Python; it uses the `cherrypy` framework to serve requests, and it uses JSON to encode inputs and outputs.

3.2   Web Service Registry

A web service registry plays a critical role at the design time of a web service composed system [6]. Ideally, a web service registry contains information about web services—specified in some language—and allows for the services to be discovered and executed. The majority of available web service registries use the Web Service Description Language (WSDL) 1.0 as the description language and support the SOAP protocol for service execution. To invoke a service, a user only needs to follow the instructions (a text document), provide the service with a necessary inputs and obtain the outputs. While convenient for users to invoke individual services, this practice does not provide a means for automatic service composition, as the instruction for service execution is often not understandable by machines. In addition, the trend has been to replace SOAP with the HTTP RESTful Protocol, which requires WSDL 2.0. All of these necessitate a web service registry for the present application. We implemented a *Web Service Registry (WSR)* as a web-based application for services registering, storing, discovering, and executing. WSR includes a database that stores the services meta-data, descriptions of available web services and their end point URLs, using WSDL 2.0. Each service is defined in four parts:

1. The first part defines the elements of a WSDL description. Each element is defined by its name, type, and constraints on it. For example, the `status_code` element whose type is `integer` and cannot be `null` is specified by: `<xs:element name="status_code" nillable="false" type="xs:integer"/>`.
2. The second part defines an operation's structure of a web service by specifying its name, inputs, and outputs.
3. The third part defines the functionality of the operation, i.e., its method, location, and encoding format of its inputs and outputs.
4. The last part defines the Web service's functionality which is its Web service end point, HTTP address, and the binding data.

3.3   Workflow Configuration Module

The result of the web service composition process (next subsection) is a plan that can be executed by the execution monitoring module. In the current implementation, we use a data structure, called *workflow*, to represent plans. Intuitively, a workflow is a directed graph whose nodes represent the services at different levels of granularity and whose links represent the data flow between the services as well as the constraints on the execution of the workflow. The *Workflow Configuration Module*, a web-based application built using HTML5 and Javascript technology, is a graphical user interface that allows users to configure and refine workflows. It interacts with the users and other modules of the system to allow users to specify different types of requirements about their workflows:

- *Input*: the input of the workflow can be anything that could be used as inputs to the registered web services. Often, the input of a workflow is a collection of data component classes and their data formats described in Subsect. 3.2. For this reason, the module allows users to specify the input via pop-up menus and dialogs.
- *Output*: the output of the workflow can be anything that could be produced via outputs of the registered web services (Subsect. 3.2). Again, users can specify outputs via pop-up menus and dialogs.
- *Preferred service*: the module allows users to attach known web-services (or classes of web services) to nodes of the workflow. For example, associating the class `Get_Phylogenetic_Tree_Open_Tree` to a node indicates that the user wants to use a service of such type (i.e., extract a phylogenetic tree from the OpenTree repository) to produce a `phylo_species_tree`, instead of using a service of type `Get_Phylogenetic_Tree_TreeBase`, which could also produce `phylo_species_tree` given a `bio_taxa` (by extracting it from the TreeBase repository instead).

In addition to allow users to specify the workflow requirements, the module also provides users with the following capabilities:

- *Workflow configuration*: A workflow can be saved, updated and reused.
- *Feasibility checking*: A workflow is an "underspecified" plan that, ideally, can be expanded to a plan whose execution yields the desired results. To provide this capability, the workflow module sends the workflow to the planning engine and requests a possible completion. When no possible completion exists, the workflow configuration module informs the user that the current workflow is not executable.
- *Workflow execution*: The module provides a button for activating the execution of the workflow (See Subsect. 3.5).

3.4   Planning Engine

The planning engine is responsible for creating an executable workflow from the (often incomplete) workflow from the user, received from the workflow configuration module. It does so by employing *Answer Set Planning (ASP)* [12]. The reason for the use of ASP is twofold. First, ASP is well-known for its ability for reasoning about specificity, a task important in identifying the inputs/outputs of services within an ontology where information associated with more specific classes override those in less specific ones. Second, planning with preferences and different types of constrains will be an important issue in this framework. These features can be integrated in ASP [21,22]. We start with a brief review the notion of answer sets of logic programs [9] for completeness of the paper.

3.4.1   Answer Set Programs and Answer Sets

An ASP program is built on a signature consisting of a set of constants $\mathcal{C}$, a set of variables $\mathcal{X}$ and a set of predicate symbols $\mathcal{P}$. The definitions of terms and atomic formulae (atoms) are the traditional ones. An answer set program is a set of rules of the form: $a_0: -a_1, ..., a_m,$ not $a_{m+1}, ...,$ not a_n, where $0 \leq$ m $\leq$ n, each a_i is an atom, and not represents *negation-as-failure (naf)*. A naf-literal has the form not a, where a is an atom. Given a rule of this form, the left and right hand sides are called the *head* and *body*, respectively. A rule may have either an empty head or empty body, but not both. Rules with an empty head are called *constraints*—the empty head is implicitly assumed to represent False; rules with an empty body are known as *facts*. The language allows the use of variables, and they are simply viewed as placeholders for any element of $\mathcal{C}$; thus a rule with variables (non-ground) is simply a syntactic sugar for the set of rules obtained by consistently replacing each variable with any element of $\mathcal{C}$ (ground rules).

A set of ground atoms X satisfies the body of a ground rule if $\{a_{m+1}, ..., a_n\} \cap X = \emptyset$ and $\{a_1, ..., a_m\} \subseteq X$. A *constraint* is *satisfied* by X if its body is not satisfied by X. X is a model of a rule if either it does not satisfy the body or $a_0 \in X$. X is a model of a program if it satisfies all of its rules.

If a ground program Π does not contain any naf-literals, then the semantics of Π is given by its unique subset-minimal model. Given a ground program Π and a set of ground atoms X, the *reduct* of Π w.r.t X (denoted by Π^X) is the program obtained from Π by: (*i*) deleting all the rules that have a naf-literal not a in the body and $a \in X$, and (*ii*) removing all remaining naf-literals.

A set of ground atoms X is an *answer set* of a program Π if X is the subset-minimal model of Π^X. Several syntactic extensions have been introduced to facilitate the development of program. For example, *choice atoms* have the form $l\{b_1, ..., b_k\}u$, where each b_j is an atom, and l and u are integers such that $l \leq u$. A set of atoms X satisfies a choice atom $l\{b_1, ..., b_k\}u$ if $l \leq |X \cap \{b_1, ..., b_k\}| \leq u$. Non-ground versions of choice atoms allow the use of syntax analogous to that of intensional sets, e.g., $l\{p(X) : q(X)\}u$.

3.4.2   Computing Executable Workflows via Answer Set Planning: The Planning Engine

The computation of an executable workflow using answer set planning begins with the encoding of the Phylotastic Ontology, the web service descriptions, and the information about incomplete workflow as ASP programs. The planning engine will compute answer sets of these programs using an answer set solver. In this work, we use the solver CLINGO [8]. The detailed encoding of each component is described next.

Representing Ontologies in ASP. The entities of the Phylotastic Ontology and the Web Services Ontology (classes, instances and properties) are represented in ASP using the unary predicate class and the binary predicate subClass. Equality is encoded by the binary predicate equalClasses.

The predicates `cl(X)`, `subcl(X,Y)`, and `equalClasses(X,Y)` say that X is a class, X is a subclass of Y, and X equals Y, respectively. For instance, the set of facts

```
{cl(gene_tree). cl(species_tree).cl(resource_tree).
subcl(gene_tree, resource_tree). subcl(species_tree, resource_tree).}
```

encode three classes `gene_tree`, `species_tree`, and `resource_tree`, and `gene_tree` and `species_tree` are sub-classes of `resource_tree`. To reason about subclass relationship, the encoding contains the rule `subcl(X,Y) :- subcl(Z,Y), subcl(X,Z)`.

Individuals (instances) of classes are represented by the predicate `t_of`. For instance, the information `http_Url` is of type `resource_HttpUrl`; this is encoded by the fact: `t_of(http_Url,resource_HttpUrl)`. The encoding also contains a rule for reasoning about membership of an individual `t_of(X,C):- t_of(X,D),subcl(D,C)`.

With this information, additional memberships of individuals can be derived, e.g., for `http_Utl` we have that `t_of(http_Url,resource_WebUrl)`. In the current system, the ontologies are translated into ASP programs via a module that interacts with the Ontology API, creates the OWL-representation, and exports it to an ASP program. For later reference, we call the ASP program encoding the ontologies as the *ASP Representation*.

Representing Web Services in ASP. Each web service is represented in ASP using the following predicates:

- `op(O)`: O is an operation.
- `op_cl(S)`: S is a class of service.
- `has_input(S, N, I)`: service class S has an input I with name N.
- `has_output(S, N, O)`: service class S has an output O with name N.
- `has_parameter(S, P)`: service class S has a parameter P.
- `has_inp_df(S, O, C, DF)`: concrete operation O of service class S has a input component C with data format DF.
- `has_out_df(S, O, C, DF)`: concrete operation O of service class S has a output component C with data format DF.

The membership of an operation, input, output, and parameter to a class of the ontology is encoded by a `t_of` statement. For example, class `taxon_based_ext` has input parameter that contains a component `bio_taxa` (a list of biological *taxa*) and its output contains component species tree in Newick format and a HTTP status code. The ASP encoding of this information is as follows:

```
op_cl(tree_extraction_operation). op_cl(taxon_based_ext).
cl(bio_taxa). cl(species_tree). cl(http_code).
subcl(taxon_based_ext,tree_extraction_operation).
has_input(taxon_based_ext,set_of_names_1,bio_taxa).
has_output(taxon_based_ext,phylo_tree_1,species_tree).
has_output(taxon_based_ext,http_code_1,http_code).
has_output(taxon_based_ext,phylo_tree_1,resource_tree).
subcl(species_tree,resource_tree).
```

In addition, concrete service operation `getPhyloTree_V1` is an instance of class `taxon_based_ext` and the data formats of components `bio_taxa`, `species_tree` and `http_code` in this concrete operation are `list_of_strings`, `newickTree` and `integer` respectively. The ASP encoding of this information is as follows:

```
op(getPhyloTree_V1).
t_of(getPhyloTree_V1,taxon_based_ext).
has_inp_df(taxon_based_ext,getPhyloTree_V1,bio_taxa,list_of_strings).
has_out_df(taxon_based_ext,getPhyloTree_V1,species_tree,newickTree).
has_out_df(taxon_based_ext,getPhyloTree_V1,http_code,integer).
```

Given an input from the workflow configuration module, the system identifies the set of web services related to the input, translates it to ASP for use in computing the executable workflows. This process is invoked whenever the workflow design module calls the planning engine with an incomplete workflow and requests an executable workflow. A web service is related to another web service if some of the former service's outputs are related to an input of the latter. Two classes are related to each other if one is a subclass of the other.

ASP Planner—Overview. The most important part of platform is the ASP Planner; this is responsible to generate the workflow of web services, i.e., perform web services composition. Due to the fact that *(i)* a class of web services describes several concrete web services whose inputs/outputs may have different input/output formats; for example, the class of name extraction services contains services that take as input a URL, a text file, or a PDF file, and produce a list of names; *(ii)* the specification provided by a user in the workflow module can be used at two possible levels: **abstract** level and **concrete** level. At the abstract level, the planner deals with *classes* of services; at the concrete level, the planner deals with actual executable services. This leads to two levels in the composition process—first composing classes of services, and successively concretizing each class by selecting specific web services from each class. The separation is important to facilitate presentation of the workflow to the user and possible incremental refinements.

Planning at the Abstract Level—Basic Part. The ASP encoding of the ontologies and web services are used as facts for the web service composition process. They will be used in conjunction with a set of ASP rules that computes a workflow from the given inputs. This module assumes the user has specified:

- *Input:* specifying what is available at the start; this information will be encoded by facts of the form `initially(x,y)` which denotes that x is a resource class with data format y.
- *Output:* the desirable outcome; this information will be encoded by facts of the form `final(x,y)` (x: class, y: data format); and
- The web service, possible inputs/outputs associated with each node in the workflow.

In keeping with the answer set planning terminologies, we assume a constant n indicating the maximal length of the executable workflow and a set of constants time(0),...,time(n) denoting time steps. In all the rules, T or T1 denotes a time step. Furthermore, we use available(x,t) to indicate that x is available at the time moment t. The rule

```
ext(a, 0) :- initially(a,df).
```

states that the resource a exists at the time moment 0.

To encode that an operation A can be executed at the time T, we use the following rules:

```
{executable(A,T)} :- op_cl(A).
:- executable(A,T), has_input(A,N,I), not match(A, I, T).
p_m(A,I,T,O,T₁) :- op_cl(A), has_input(A,N,I), T₁≤T,
                     ext(O,T₁),subcl(O,I).
1 {map(A,I,T,O,T₁) : p_m(A,I,T,O,T₁)}1.
match(A,I,T ) :- map(A,I,T,_,_).
```

The first rule uses the choice rule to state that an operation can either be executed or not at the time T. The second rule, a constraint, prevents an operation to be executed if some of its inputs are not matched with some available outputs. The third rule defines when an input could be available. The fourth and fifth rule select a unique available output for use as input of another service, which is reflected by the atom $map/5$, and define the predicate match for use with the second rule. To generate a possible sequence of operations and record the effects of the operations, the following rules are used:

```
1 { occ(A,T): op_cl(A) } 1.
:- occ(A,T), not executable(A,T).
ext(O,T+1) :- occ(A,T), has_output(A,N,O).
```

The first rule generates an occurrence of an operation. The second one makes sure that an operation can only be executed if its inputs are available. The third rule allows for the computation of the availability of resources in the next time moment, by direct effects of an operation. Since artifacts produced by a service are available in all subsequent steps, we do not need an inertial rule.

Planning at Abstract Level—Extended Part. We next describe the extended part of the ASP Planner that is used for dealing with other aspects of web services. Specifically, to consider the desires of the users from the workflow design. We describe how this type of information is encoded.

- There will be some input of type c, e.g., initially(i,df). t_of(i,c).
- There will be some output o of type c at the end: final(o,df). t_of(o,c).
- A certain class of services c will have to be used in the workflow used(c).
- A certain service of class c and the other one of class d will have to be involved in the workflow. In which service of class d has to be executed **after** service of class c is executed: used(c). used(d). before(c,d). (see also Fig. 4).

To take into consideration the above information, we add to the ASP planner the following rules:

```
ext(I, 0) :- initially(I).
goal(O, C) :- ext(O, n),final(O), t_of(O,C).
:- final(O), t_of(O,C), not goal(O,C).
is_used(C):- op(A), t_of(A, C), occ(A, T).
:- used(C), not is_used(C).
satisfy(C,D):-op(A),t_of(A,C),occ(A,T),op(B),t_of(B,D),occ(B,T1),T<T1.
:- before(C,D), not satisfy(C,D).
```

The first rule specifies the resources available at the time step 0. The second rule defines that a goal O of type C exists. The third rule, a constraint, enforces the constraint that the user wishes to have an individual O of type C as the output. Similarly, the fourth and fifth rule make sure that a certain service of type c is used during the workflow execution if `used(C)` is specified; and the last two rules guarantee that a service of type C must be used before a service of type D if `before(C,D)` is specified.

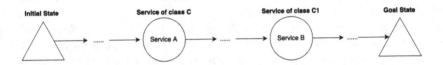

Fig. 4. Workflow with constraints

Planning at Concrete Level—Data Format Conversion. As we have mentioned earlier, a class of services might be associated with specific classes of inputs/outputs at the abstract level, but specific web services can require the inputs in specific data format. For example, the class of name extraction services contains distinct services that may take as input a URL, a text file, or a PDF, and produce a list of names. For this reason, data conversion between abstract levels is necessary when abstract services are instantiated with concrete ones. For example, different services of the `gene_based_extraction` class output `GeneTree` in different formats; `GeneTree` is an input for the services in the class `name_extraction_tree`. Each service in this class accepts `GeneTree` in different formats. Data conversion operations are also available as web services. This means that we can employ the same methodology used in planning at abstract level to complete the data format conversion process. Due to space limitation, we will only briefly describe the components of this module.

- *Output of the planning engine at abstract level.* This will contain atoms of the following forms: *(i)* `occ(a,t)` (a service of class a occurs at step t); *(ii)* `map(a,i,t,o,t1)` (the input named i of the service named a takes the output o at step t_1 as input).

- *Encoding of the data conversion format services*: this part is similar to the encoding of abstract web services.
- *ASP code for selecting conversion services when needed*: this part is similar to the planning code showed above.

3.5   Execution Monitoring

As discussed earlier, the outcome of the planning module is a complete workflow, composed of a sequence of web services, whose execution is expected to lead to the result requested by the user. Each web service in the workflow is described by its WSDL profile. In order to execute the workflow, the Phylotastic architecture provides a *workflow execution module*; such module makes use of the information in the WSDL profiles and the structure of the workflow (e.g., connections between inputs and outputs of the services) to execute the services. The goal of this module is not only to enact the workflow producing an execution, but also to monitor the execution to identify possible failures and take appropriate recovery actions. In the current implementation, the recovery process is based on repeating the configuration phase with an added constraint that excludes the failed service. The *execution module* has multiple components. The first component is a *a WSDL 2.0 parser*—its goal is to parse the WSDL information into data structure models such as web services object model, operations object model, parameters components and elements. This parser uses the libraries from the **Apache Wooden** (https://ws.apache.org/woden).

The second component is the *execution program* that can execute a concrete web service operation based on their description in the WSDL profiles. This software consumes several parameters: the *WSDL URI*; the *name of the operation*, and the *list of input components data*. More precisely, the execution module performs the following steps:

○ Given the URI pointing to the service WSDL profile, the execution modules calls the WSDL parser to interpret the profile;
○ The detailed profile of selected service operation (the second parameter mentioned earlier, *name of the operation*) is extracted from WSDL data. This profile includes service endpoint, input and output parameters, content encoding, protocol, etc.
○ The execution module issues HTTP/SOAP requests based on the service endpoints and the operation information derived during the previous step (getting from step 2). The body of the HTTP/SOAP request includes the inputs to the service (the third parameter mentioned earlier, *list of input components data*), arranged according to the description of the structure of input parameters obtained in the previous step.
○ After receiving the response from the service host, the execution module parses the response based on the structure of output parameters of this operation, and analyzes the response to determine how to continue.

The third component is *a combination program* that automatically performs repeated calls to the *execution program*, in order to execute the entire workflow.

The calls follow the structure of the workflow, properly matching inputs and outputs of the different services executed.

The last component is a *recovery process* that will be activated when there exists a failure or error in the processing of a single *execution program* that is corresponding with the status of web service (unavailable, failure, timeout exception, etc.). As mentioned earlier, in current implementation, *recovery process* performs the following steps:

o Detect the web service that is fails or unavailable.
o Back to configuration phase, add an rule constraint into ASP *planning engine* to ignore involving *failed service* in plan. For example,

```
:- executable(failed_service,T).
```

o Re-run *planning engine* with new above constraint to generate new workflow without *failded serivce*,
o Re-run *workflow execution module* again with the new workflow.

4   Use Case

We illustrate the working of our system using an use case of the Phylotastic project. In this use case, the user want to generate a phylogenetic reconciliation tree from a set of gene names. Let us assume that this is the only information that the user provided via the *Workflow Configuration Module*. This information is passed to the planning engine. The planning at abstract level produces a plan whose output is displayed in Fig. 5 (top part), where the triangles identify the input and output states and the name of the service class that should be executed at each step. For example, a `gene_based_extraction` service should be executed, at step 1, a `names_extraction_tree` service needs to be executed

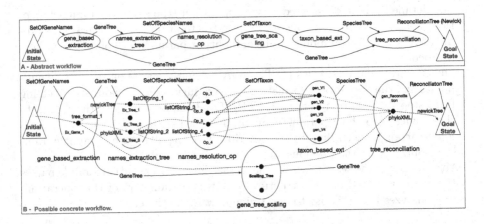

Fig. 5. Abstract and concrete workflow levels (Color figure online)

at step 2, etc. Observe that the input for step 2 is a `GeneTree`, step 6 is a `GeneTree` and a `SpeciesTree`, etc. The bottom part of Fig. 5 shows how the concrete level instantiation looks like. Each black circle represents a concrete web service. Each service is associated with their input/output format (e.g., for `Ex_Tree_1` is (`newickTree`, `list_of_strings`) and `Ex_Tree_3` is (`phyloXML`, `list_of_strings`), etc. The red line (resp. the blue line), together with the line through the node using a `Scaling_Tree` service, represents a possible execution of the abstract plan.

5   Discussion and Future Work

In this paper, we presented a framework for automatic web service composition developed for the Phylotastic project. We described the overall architecture of the system and its components, with special emphasis on the Planning Engine and the Execution Monitoring Module. In the process, we show how answer set planning can be employed in web service composition. We also describe a detailed execution of the system using a use-case.

The proposed system is currently begin evaluated by biology researchers participating to the Phylotastic project. Presently, we are focusing on two activities.

First, we need to complete a new version of the *Workflow Configuration Module*, which allows the user not only to view the concrete workflow generated by the planning engine, but also to manually modify it—e.g., by replacing one operation node with a different one. This will lead to a replanning process, where the workflow is regenerated to accommodate the new requirement introduced by the user, while preserving as much as possible of the previously generated workflow. The replanning process will raise interesting challenges, such as defining what does it entail to *"preserve as much as possible the existing workflow."* We are exploring how this problem can be resolved using techniques borrowed from research in planning with preferences [2, 22].

In addition, we need to evaluate the scalability and efficiency of the planning engine; among other things, we would like to develop algorithms that exploit the fact that most web service composition does not really need to use the complete ontology.

References

1. Bartalos, P., Bielikov, M.: Automatic dynamic web service composition: a survey and problem formalization. Comput. Inform. **30**, 793–827 (2011)
2. Brafman, R., Chernyavsky, Y.: Planning with preferences and constraints. In: ICAPS. AAAI Press (2005)
3. Carman, M., Serafini, L., Traverso, P.: Web service composition as planning. In: Proceedings of ICAPS 2003 Workshop on Planning for Web Services (2004)
4. Cracraft, J., et al.: Assembling the tree of life: harnessing life's history to benefit science and society. Technical report U.C., Berkeley (2002)
5. De Giacomo, G., Gerevini, A.E., Patrizi, F., Saetti, A., Sardiña, S.: Agent planning programs. Artif. Intell. **231**, 64–106 (2016)

6. Dustdar, S., Treiber, M.: A view based analysis on web service registries. Distrib. Parallel Databases **18**, 147–171 (2005)
7. Felsenstein, J.: Inferring Phylogenies. Oxford University Press, Oxford (2003)
8. Gebser, M., Kaufmann, B., Neumann, A., Schaub, T.: *clasp*: a conflict-driven answer set solver. In: Baral, C., Brewka, G., Schlipf, J. (eds.) LPNMR 2007. LNCS (LNAI), vol. 4483, pp. 260–265. Springer, Heidelberg (2007). https://doi.org/10.1007/978-3-540-72200-7_23
9. Gelfond, M., Lifschitz, V.: Classical negation in logic programs and disjunctive databases. New Gener. Comput. **9**, 365–387 (1991)
10. Hull, D.: Data integration in myGrid with Taverna. In: Workshop on the Interoperability of Biological Information Resources (2006)
11. Lemos, A.L., Daniel, F., Benatallah, B.: Web service composition: a survey of techniques and tools. ACM Comput. Surv. **48**, 33 (2015)
12. Lifschitz, V.: Answer set programming and plan generation. Artif. Intell. **138**(1–2), 39–54 (2002)
13. McIlraith, S., Son, T., Zeng, H.: Mobilizing the semantic web with DAML-enabled web services. In: SemWeb, pp. 46–53 (2001)
14. McIlraith, S., Son, T.C.: Adapting golog for composition of semantic web services. In: KR 2002, pp. 482–493 (2002)
15. Mora, C., Tittensor, D., Adl, S., Simpson, A., Worm, B.: How many species are there on earth and in the ocean? PLoS Biol. **9**(8), e1001127 (2011)
16. Peer, J.: Web service composition as ai planning - a survey. Technical report, University of St. Gallen (2005)
17. Portchelvi, V., Venkatesan, V.P., Shanmugasundaram, G.: Achieving web services composition - a survey. Softw. Eng. **2**(5), 195–202 (2012)
18. Prosdocimi, F., et al.: Initial implementation of a comparative data analysis ontology. Evol. Bioinf. **5**, 47–66 (2009)
19. Rao, J., Su, X.: A survey of automated web service composition methods. In: Cardoso, J., Sheth, A. (eds.) SWSWPC 2004. LNCS, vol. 3387, pp. 43–54. Springer, Heidelberg (2005). https://doi.org/10.1007/978-3-540-30581-1_5
20. Sheng, Q.Z., Qiao, X., Vasilakos, A.V., Szabo, C., Bourne, S., Xu, X.: Web services composition: a decade's overview. Inf. Sci. **280**, 218–238 (2014)
21. Son, T.C., Baral, C., Tran, N., McIlraith, S.: Domain-dependent knowledge in answer set planning. ACM Trans. Comput. Logic **7**(4), 613–657 (2006)
22. Son, T.C., Pontelli, E.: Planning with preferences using logic programming. Theory Pract. Logic Program. **6**, 559–607 (2006)
23. Stoltzfus, A., et al.: Phylotastic! Making tree-of-life knowledge accessible, reusable and convenient. BMC Bioinform. **14**, 158 (2013)
24. Stoltzfus, A., et al.: Sharing and re-use of phylogenetic trees (and associated data) to facilitate synthesis. BMC Res. Notes **5**, 574 (2012)

Author Index

Printed in the United States
By Bookmasters